The
Director
and the Stage

from Naturalism
to Grotowski

The purpose of this book is to chart the rise of the theatre director in the late 19th century and follow his emergence as one of the most important figures behind the staging of any play today. Beginning with the triple impulses of Naturalism, Symbolism and the Grotesque, the bulk of the book concentrates on the most famous directors of this century, Stanislavsky, Reinhardt, Craig, Meyerhold, Piscator, Brecht, Artaud and Grotowski. Eschewing the purely theoretical, Braun is concerned to delineate the kind of theatre practice inherited by each of the major figures and to show how he proceeded to change it.

Originally published in much shorter form as a companion to the Open University Modern Drama course, this book fulfils a long felt need in setting out the changing conditions in which playwriting and the theatre have developed over the last hundred years. Edward Braun is Reader in Modern Drama at Bristol University, the author of **The Theatre of Meyerhold** and compiler of **Meyerhold on Theatre**.

The photo on the front cover shows Helene Weigel as Mother Courage in the Berliner Ensemble production of the play by Bertolt Brecht directed by the author. Photo by Ruth Berlau reproduced by courtesy of Barbara Brecht-Schall, the Brecht Archive and Johannes Hoffmann.

The
Director
and the Stage

From Naturalism
to Grotowski

EDWARD BRAUN

Methuen · London

For Felix and Joe

First published in Great Britain in 1982 in simultaneous hardback and paperback editions by Methuen London Ltd, 11 New Fetter Lane, London EC4P 4EE

Reprinted 1983, 1986

ISBN 0 413 46290 0 (Hardback)
0 413 46300 1 (Paperback)

Printed and bound in Great Britain by
Butler & Tanner Ltd, Frome and London.

Contents

List of Illustrations

SOURCES OF ILLUSTRATIONS

1, 8, 12 University of Bristol Theatre Collection; 2 Gösta Bergman, *Den Moderna Teatern Genombrott 1890–1925* (Albert Bonniers Förlag, 1966); 3 Collection Lugné-Poe; 4 Michel Arrivé, *Lire Jarry* (Editions Complexe, 1976); 5, 6, 10 Moscow Art Theatre Museum; 7 Hugo Held, Berlin; 9, 11 Author's collection; 13 Willi Saeger, Berlin; 14 Bertolt-Brecht-Archiv; 15 Lipnitzki-Viollet; 16 Piotr Baracz, Warsaw.

Introduction

Ever since Aeschylus supervised the presentation of his tragedies at the Athenian festivals of the fifth century BC it is safe to assume that someone has had overall responsibility for the rehearsal of any play that has reached the stage. Sometimes, as in the case of Shakespeare or Racine, it would have been the dramatist; sometimes, an actor-playwright such as Molière; later it would have been the leading actor or some more humble functionary like the stage manager or the prompter. In the eighteenth century, when the star actor achieved unprecedented heights, little attention was paid to anything but his performance. However, there were some who became concerned with the overall impression of the performance; by the 1830's Charles Kemble, Charles Macready and Eliza Vestris in England and Conrad Ekhof, Friedrich Schroeder and Goethe in Germany had all demonstrated the value of lengthy rehearsals and close attention to the details of costume and setting. As the urge for spectacle took hold of the nineteenth century, actor-managers such as Charles Kean and Samuel Phelps mounted remarkable displays of scenic art, but there was hardly the coordination of expressive means based on an interpretation of the play-text that seems to me the fundamental requirement of theatre production as we have come to understand it. That crucial advance was achieved first at Meiningen, which will be the subject of my first chapter.

All the directors who follow are virtually self-selecting, though a comprehensive account would certainly include more: Copeau, Yeats, Tairov, Granville Barker, Tyrone Guthrie, to name only a few whose omission I regret. But the only comprehensive account of modern stagecraft (in Swedish by Gösta Bergman) runs to close on six-hundred pages and even then does not extend beyond 1925. So what follows is not intended as a complete survey; rather, it is an attempt to describe in some detail the key events that mark the emergence of the modern stage director in Europe, setting them in their context and examining the theories that they exemplify. I have not set out to recount the entire career of every director, but have concentrated on the areas of his work that seem best to convey his significance. Thus, there is little on the later work of Antoine, Lugné-Poe, Stanislavsky, Reinhardt and Piscator. With Brecht I have concentrated on the emergence of his ideas in the pre-Hitler period. With Meyerhold I have restricted myself to two five-year periods, conscious of omitting his masterpiece, *The Government Inspector*, but reluctant to describe it in less detail than I did in my earlier books on him, which I hope the interested reader will find easily accessible. As it is, Meyerhold extends over two chapters, which I think is justified by the extreme contrast they offer, and is not merely the outcome of my personal bias as his translator and biographer.

I end with a chapter on Grotowski by Jennifer Kumiega, whose first-hand knowledge of his work seemed to me preferable to anything I could extract from the few accounts of his work available in print. To come closer to the present day with accounts of Littlewood, Brook, Planchon, Stein, Strehler, Garcia, Mnouchkine, Lyubimov, Efros, and others equally demanding of inclusion would require a separate book. When it is written, I think it will acknowledge the inspiration drawn from those included here; for my fascination in writing has been to discover in accounts of productions going back a hundred years artistic truths that inform theatre practice to this day. For this reason, though I have written primarily with the student in mind, I hope that theatre practitioners may find some stimulus in the pages that follow.

In recent years the study of theatre performance has benefited from numerous published works, a selection of which I append in a bibliography; but there are a number I have found particularly stimulating and enlightening, and which require specific acknowledgement: Max Grube, *The Story of the Meininger*; André Antoine, *Memories of the Théâtre Libre*; Francis Pruner, *Les Luttes d'Antoine*; Samuel Waxman, *Antoine and the Théâtre Libre*; Jacques Robichez, *Le Symbolisme au Théâtre*; John Henderson, *The First Avant-Garde (1887-1894)*; John Stokes, *Resistible Theatres*; Roger Shattuck, *The Banquet Years*; Noel Arnaud, *Alfred Jarry d'Ubu Roi au Docteur Faustroll*; Marianna Stroeva, *Rezhisserskie iskania Stanislavskogo 1898-1917*; Denis Bablet, *The Theatre of Edward Gordon Craig*; Edward Craig, *Gordon Craig: The Story of his Life*; Heinrich Braulich, *Max Reinhardt*; Hugo Fetting (ed.), *Max Reinhardt: Schriften*; Gottfried Reinhardt, *The Genius: A Memoir of Max Reinhardt*; Konstantin Rudnitsky, *Rezhissyor Meyerhold*; Erwin Piscator, *The Political Theatre* (ed. and trans. Hugh Rorrison); four books by John Willett: *Erwin Piscator*, *The New Sobriety: Art and Politics in the Weimar Republic*, *Brecht on Theatre*, *The Theatre of Bertolt Brecht*; Antonin Artaud, *Collected Works* (ed. and trans. Victor Corti); Alain Virmaux, *Antonin Artaud et le théâtre*; Jerzy Grotowski, *Towards a Poor Theatre*; in *The Drama Review*, Martin Esslin on Max Reinhardt, and the casebooks on Brecht's Munich years and on Artaud's *The Cenci*; in the greatly missed *Theatre Quarterly*, John Osborne on the Meininger, Laurence Senellick on the Craig-Stanislavsky

Hamlet, and Hugh Rorrison on *Hoppla, Wir Leben*. The sections on Meyerhold are drawn mainly from Chapters 2, 3, 6 and 7 of my own *The Theatre of Meyerhold*.

I am most grateful to the Open University for permission to use material from my earlier and shorter work, *The Director and the Stage*, published by them as a companion to their Drama Course in 1977. Finally, I should like to thank my students and colleagues in the Drama Department at the University of Bristol for their questions, criticism and stimulus, my wife and sons for their forbearance over a lengthy period, my typist, Janet Clarke, and my friend and editor, Nick Hern.

E.B.
Bristol, November 1981

1. The Meiningen Theatre

In 1866 there occurred a sequence of political events that was to have far-reaching consequences for the modern theatre. In the brief war between Prussia and Austria Duke Bernhard of Saxe-Meiningen, a small and obscure principality in Thuringia, sought to preserve his independence by allying himself with Austria; following the Prussian victory he found the *Residenzstadt* of Meiningen occupied by Bismarck's troops, and was forced to abdicate in favour of his son, Duke Georg II. At forty, Georg had been allowed little experience of government by his father and for some years had served in the Prussian Royal Guards. At his accession he was ready enough to acknowledge the sovereignty of Prussia over the nascent German Empire, and to devote himself to internal reforms, and to patronage and practice of the arts in the Duchy of Meiningen.[1]

With time on his hands during his father's reign, Georg had been free to develop his considerable talent as a graphic artist, and was greatly influenced by the current German school of historical realism, exemplified by the paintings of Kaulbach, Piloty, Menzel and Makart. At university he also studied history and archaeology, and developed a great interest in the theatre, which took him as far afield as London in the 1850's to see the celebrated Shakespeare 'Revivals' staged by Charles Kean at the Princess's Theatre. As the principal exponent of historical reconstruction, Kean represented the culmination of an English tradition inherited directly from Macready and originating with John Philip Kemble in the late eighteenth century. Although he never toured abroad, Kean's influence on the German theatre was considerable, and there is no doubt that initially at least Duke Georg was greatly indebted to what he had seen in London.[2] More immediately, there was the example of Friedrich Haase's staging for the Duke of Saxe-Coburg in 1867 of *The Merchant of Venice*, modelled closely on Kean's London production of 1858. Shortly after his accession, Georg took his newly-appointed artistic director, Friedrich Bodenstedt, to see Haase's production, and subsequently its designers, Max and Gotthold Brückner, were employed at Meiningen.

The historical development of Germany, and in particular the catastrophic Thirty Years War (1618-1648), had impeded the emergence of a national German drama until the second half of the eighteenth century. But these same historical factors furnished a source of strength that remains to this day: beginning with Gotha in 1775, resident court theatres sprang up all over Germany, nourished by local pride and the rivalries of the numerous petty dukes and princes. Thus, by the time national unity was imposed by Bismarck in 1866, there was scarcely a town of any size that lacked a theatre and permanent companies performing drama, opera and ballet, to say nothing of a full-scale orchestra. Thus, a permanent theatre for drama and opera was opened in Meiningen* in 1831, and for the next forty years functioned successfully, unknown to all but the 8,000 inhabitants and completely overshadowed by such companies as Weimar, Dresden, Vienna and Munich.

Shortly after his accession Duke Georg signalled the seriousness of his artistic ambitions by dissolving the Court Opera in order to concentrate all his resources on the Court Orchestra (directed by Hans von Bülow) and Court Theatre. Bodenstedt, his new *Intendant* (artistic director), a poet and translator of English Renaissance drama, found the Duke's favour thanks to his advocacy of Shakespeare performed uncut and unadulter-ated. However, he was equally an adherent of Goethe, who as *Intendant* at the Court Theatre of Weimar had promoted the classical virtues of restraint and balance in production, and had valued correct diction more highly than stage effects. By 1870 the Duke found it impossible to work with Bodenstedt, and for the next five years he functioned as his own *Intendant*.

Duke Georg was assisted in the artistic direction of the company by Ellen Franz and Ludwig Chronegk. The former was an actress recruited from Mannheim in 1867, who retired from the stage in 1873 when she became the Duke's wife. Henceforth she shared in the selection and adaptation of texts and was responsible for schooling the company in interpretation and delivery. However, being herself trained in the strictly formal style developed by Goethe at Weimar, she never succeeded in encouraging the naturalness of speech that the Meiningen style de-manded, and in this respect the company was often found wanting by critics. For instance, when they came to London in 1881, *The Saturday Review* found their acting in *Julius Caesar* 'distinctly stagey and their elocution monotonous', suggesting 'a lesson mechanically repeated after a master'; *The Athenaeum* considered their 'declamatory and scholastic style' more suited to Goethe than Shakespeare; Clement Scott in *The Daily Telegraph* compared their 'over-emphasis and over-gesticulation' unfavourably with 'the new and more moderate method' preferred on the English stage.[3] Similarly, when the French director Antoine saw them in

* Situated on the River Werra, now in the South West of the German Democratic Republic.

Brussels in 1888 he was much impressed with the crowd work, but reported that the actors were 'adequate and nothing more' and their training 'generally of the most rudimentary sort'.[4] Finally, Stanislavsky, who did not miss a single performance when the company paid their second visit to Moscow in 1890, found that 'the Meiningen Players brought but little that was new into the old stagey methods of acting', and that much depended on the organising genius of the stage director, Ludwig Chronegk.[5]

There is no doubt that Chronegk was the crucial member of the Meiningen production team. He had joined the company as a comic actor in 1866 and soon impressed everyone with his good humour and keen intelligence. However, he had little literary education, so it came as a great surprise when shortly after the Duke's wedding to Ellen Franz he was appointed as stage-director. But so successful was he, that in 1875 he took over from the Duke as *Intendant* and continued to hold both posts until his death in 1891.

The artistic relationship of the Duke and Chronegk was an unusual but harmonious one: whilst the overall interpretation and visualisation of the play was the Duke's, Chronegk had the job of running the company, conducting rehearsals, and translating Georg's impressionistic instructions and illustrations into the language of stage action. A similar relationship existed between the Duke and his designers: he would carry out research and produce detailed drawings, which they would realise in plastic terms. During the lengthy rehearsal period of a play at Meiningen the Duke was invariably present to ensure that his conception was faithfully interpreted, but once on tour, Chronegk was in sole charge. In fact, between 1874 and 1890 affairs of state allowed the Duke to see only three performances away from Meiningen. It was Chronegk's idea originally to display the company's achievements in Berlin in 1874, and between then and the final tour to Russia in 1890 they gave over 2,500 guest performances in eighty-one appearances throughout Europe. Far more than the ducal purse, it was the revenue from these tours that financed the productions of some forty plays, most of them with large casts and demanding lavish period costumes and settings.

The company numbered about seventy, but was frequently boosted to as many as two hundred by the employment of local extras. Chronegk's disciplined conduct of the company's rehearsals became legendary. Stanislavsky, who watched him at work in Moscow, was deeply impressed and confesses to becoming a despotic director in imitation of Chronegk. In his opinion, Chronegk, the most genial of men outside the theatre, was obliged to enforce iron discipline in order to achieve the precise coordination of resources that the Duke's complex scenarios demanded. It was this, he felt, that led to a neglect of work with individual actors, who in consequence remained indifferent performers. But in any case the recruitment of star actors was avoided at Meiningen, for fear that outstanding talents might impose themselves and destroy the overall ensemble. On occasions famous artists were employed to play particular roles, but they were designated 'honorary members' of the company, never 'guests', and were expected to fit in with Meiningen production methods and conform with company discipline.[6] In his memoirs Ludwig Barnay recalls his initial reaction when he first came to Meiningen in 1872 to play the Marquis de Posa in Schiller's *Don Carlos*:

> I was both amazed and furious with the rehearsals, since I felt that they wasted a great deal of time on absolute non-essentials: the loudness or quietness of a speech, the way some non-speaking actor should stand, getting a tree or a bush in the right spot, or effectively lighting it. The actors were given long lectures, virtual treatises on the mood of a scene, the significance of a specific incident to the drama, yes, even on the emphasis of a single word. This caused the rehearsal to be stretched out endlessly in a manner quite unfamiliar to me, since other directors staging *Don Carlos* were satisfied with telling an actor whether he should enter and exit right or left and on which side of another actor he should stand. The rest was left to the will of God and the power of Schiller's genius.[7]

However, once Barnay had seen the results of this painstaking process in performance, he was completely won over; he soon returned to Meiningen to play Hamlet, followed by many further leading roles over the next twenty years. Amongst his celebrated performances was Mark Antony in *Julius Caesar*, the first production ever to be presented away from Meiningen.

Julius Caesar originally entered the Meiningen repertoire in 1867, and was a striking example of Duke Georg's concern with historical accuracy. The designs were based on sketches by Visconti, the Curator of Ancient Monuments and Director of Archaeological Research in Rome. Not only the settings, based on the remains of the Roman Forum, but statues, armour, weapons, drinking cups and the rest were all modelled faithfully on Roman originals. Just as Charles Kean proudly documented his authentic designs in his programmes, the Duke urged his *Intendant* to publicise the historical credentials of *Julius Caesar* in the local press, as though the stamp of authenticity would validate the work in advance.[8]

However, as we have seen from Barnay's account of rehearsals, this concern with historical accuracy was only one aspect of the Meiningen method. *Julius Caesar* was refined and revised for nearly seven years before it was considered ready to expose to a wider public. Once Karl Frenzel, the leading Berlin critic, had been summoned to give his final approval, arrangements were made and on 1 May 1874 *Julius Caesar* was given its Berlin premiere at the Friedrich-Wilhelmstädtisches Theatre. The impact of the obscure provincial company on the sophisticated

Berliners was immediate and extraordinary, and the planned four-week season had to be extended by a fortnight to meet the demand for seats. *Julius Caesar* was performed twenty-two times, and over the next seventeen years was given in every city where the company appeared. Critics who believed the essence of theatre to consist in star performers acting great roles spoke slightingly of the mediocre talents of the individual actors, and felt that too often on stage the principals were obscured by the mass; but others were overwhelmed by the company's discipline, its strength in depth, and the coordination of effects in the production. Karl Frenzel wrote:

> The treatment of the masses is here brought almost to perfection. When Casca deals the blow to Caesar, the crowd gathered around the Curia emit a single heart-rending cry; then a deathly silence sets in. The murderers, the senators, the people stand a moment before the body of the once-powerful leader, as if paralysed or enchanted. Then a storm breaks forth. One must have heard its tumult in order to know how powerful, how high and how deep the effect of dramatic art can reach. In the following scene in the Forum, magnificent and amazing moments vie with one another – as Antony is raised on the shoulders of the crowd and thus amidst the wildest demonstration reads aloud Caesar's will; as the enraged mob seize the bier with its body and others with torches rush to join them; as at last Cinna, the poet, is killed in the wildest tumult. One feels oneself present at the beginnings of a revolution.[9]

The opposing view is effectively represented by the critic of *The Saturday Review* on the occasion of the company's visit to London in June 1881:

> The admirably drilled crowd has been much and justly praised, but in the earlier scenes it was used too freely. It was allowed to call off the attention of the audience from those who are carrying on the dramatic action of the tragedy. In the scene of Caesar's murder it almost hid the conspirators and was wholly out of place: none but senators should have seen the deed. Loafers, women and children were not allowed to cover the floor of a Roman Curia.[10]

Antoine never saw *Julius Caesar*, but he was deeply impressed by the crowd effects in Schiller's *William Tell*, and shortly afterwards applied similar methods to his own productions at the Théâtre Libre.* What struck him was the capacity of the extras to suggest individual characters rather than a regimented mass, whilst never distracting attention from the salient features of a scene. This he ascribed to the practice of breaking the crowd down into small groups in rehearsals, each of them being led by a member of the company, who frequently included those who played major roles.[11] Their success abroad is the more surprising, given that Chronegk had no language other than German in which to coach a crowd recruited on the spot, often from the local military garrison. Nor was there always much

---

* See pp. 30-32 below.

time: when they came to London in 1881 they arrived on the Friday and opened with *Julius Caesar* the following Monday.[12]

As we have seen, enthusiasm for the Meininger in London was far from unanimous; some older critics looked back twenty years or more to Charles Kean and claimed that he had done it all before; others, in a country that still spoke of the 'stage manager' rather than the producer or director, saw the actor's theatre under threat; others were ready enough to indulge their anti-German sentiments with patronising references to 'teutonic thoroughness' and 'military precision'. However, the six weeks' season at Drury Lane aroused lively interest and, whatever the English precedents, it undoubtedly left its mark on the crowd work and lighting of Irving, and on Frank Benson, who in forming his Dramatic Company in 1883 announced in his programme that it would be 'conducted on the Meiningen system'.[13]

The influence of the Meininger on Benson was limited by the small scale of his actor-managed touring company, and hardly extended beyond the sharing of minor roles by all the actors (Benson himself excluded). The deeper impact of Duke Georg's methods was observed on the continent – particularly, as we shall see, in the work of Antoine and Stanislavsky, and also at the Freie Bühne, which opened in Berlin under Otto Brahm in 1889.[14] Meiningen's originality is precisely assessed by Lee Simonson, the noted American designer and director:

> His career inaugurated a new epoch in theatrical production and made the subsequent development of modern stage-craft possible because he eventually convinced every important director in Europe . . . that the fundamental problem to be answered by the scene-designer is not, What will my setting look like and how will the actor look in it? but, What will my setting make the actor do? More than this, he made plain that the dramatic action of a performance was an organic whole, a continuous pattern of movement, complex but unified like the symphonic rhythms of orchestral music. At the end of his career the dynamic relation of a mobile actor and an immobile setting in continuous interaction was an accepted axiom. And it is upon the assumption that experiments in production have proceeded since his day.[15]

The vital principle that the Duke established was that 'the primary function of the theatre is to depict movement, the relentless progress of the action'.[16] This may seem to be stating the obvious unless we consider the prevailing method, which was to have set speeches interspersed with moves designed more or less arbitrarily to shift the actors around or off the stage, or spectacular interludes regularly punctuating historical plays. Whilst it is true that such scenes at Mark Antony's funeral oration in the Meiningen *Julius Caesar* were admired as sheer spectacle, they proceeded logically from the dramatic action; by contrast, the triumphal entry of Bolingbroke into London that Charles Kean inserted as an entr'acte into his 1857 production of *Richard II* was prompted by no such demand in Shakespeare's text.

It has been suggested that much of the resistance encountered initially by the Meininger in Germany was born of critics' desire to protect the reassuring calm and symmetry of Classicism against Romantic turbulence and disorder.[17] The Duke's production sketches give a clear idea of the restless compositions that he sought on stage, and he was precise in setting forth the principles he wished to see followed:

In the positioning of actors in relation to each other parallels are bad. If the placing of one single actor parallel to the footlights, in the face-on position, is unfortunate, it is a positively ugly sight when two or more actors of about the same height take up such a stance. Movement of the actors parallel to the footlights should also be avoided. If, for instance, the actor has to move from downstage right to downstage left, then let him try discreetly and unobtrusively to break the straight line, which, on the stage, is never the best path.

When there are three or more actors in one scene they should never stand in line. They must stand at an angle to one another. The distance between several actors must always be different. If they all stand the same distance apart, this looks dull and lifeless, like figures on a chess board. . . .

The height of the heads of those who stand next to one another in crowd scenes should be varied. Where appropriate the various individuals should stand on different levels; if the situation permits it, some can kneel, while others stand nearby, some bending forward, others standing upright.[18]

To add to the plastic possibilities of the stage setting, whenever possible, the floor was broken into different levels. Thus in Kleist's *Hermannsschlacht* (*The Battle of Arminius*) when the Roman generals come to parley with the German chieftain in his native forest, they were forced to clamber over hummocks and fallen tree trunks in order to reach his hut, thereby emphasising their vulnerability and the barbarism of the world they were invading. In the same production, the overwhelming might of the Roman occupation was graphically conveyed:

What is necessary for a setting that is completely true to the will of the poet is that it summon up the impression of an overpowering mass of troops. How did the Meiningers accomplish this? . . . The scene depicted a square in a Germanic city. Strong wooden fences enclosed the houses. A large hill, shaded by the local linden trees, holy to the Germans, stood to the left. Near it, only a small path led further into the settlement. Through this lane, which was at the most wide enough for only four men abreast, the military troop of Roman legionnaires pushed, pressed, and crowded themselves, while the hill and the fronts of the houses were thickly crowded with watching Germanic folk.

Obviously not in modern military form, the troops marched into the village, clad in simple, dark gray armor and helmets, and carrying their bundles of luggage on spears. It was an especially happy thought on the director's part to send the army diagonally from the foreground to the back through the narrow lane, so that no faces, but only the backs of coats of mail could be seen: as if an iron stream pressed, surged, and swirled along the way towards Teutoburg.[19]

This expressive use of the setting is illustrated once more by the Meiningen treatment of the attack on the English camp in Act Two of Schiller's *The Maid of Orleans*:

> The attack on the English camp in the second act always constituted a cross for the director of a realistic production. Here again the Meininger principle of narrowing the stage proved itself. 'A place circumscribed by rocks,' reads Schiller's stage direction. The Meininger placed the rocks around a steep defile. As the curtain rose, we saw the weary rear-guard of the defeated English forces streaming down the narrow opening in the row of rocks. Several horsemen were trying to drag out of this place a huge, unyielding wagon with all sorts of rescued army goods. They succeeded in doing so, but only as far as the right foreground. Then, their strength completely gave out; they collapsed and sank swiftly into deep sleep. Gradually the stage emptied and the generals could begin their conversion. This wagon was in no way merely decoration; its purpose was later to mask the greatest part of the attacking French soldiers, so that one could not accurately gauge their number. At the same time, its movement by the soldiers brought concretely before the eyes of the audience the utter exhaustion of an army in headlong retreat.[20]

From these examples it is evident that, whereas originally Duke Georg may have been concerned largely with questions of historical exactitude, he came eventually to an understanding of the expressive power of the stage picture, using the elements of composition to convey the inner tension of the drama. At the same time, he was concerned to preserve the naturalistic illusion: frequently, a sense of life continuing beyond the limits of the stage was conveyed by confining the space, and giving the picture a 'natural' frame (in the examples above, by using rocks, over-hanging trees, a wooden fence, the baggage wagon). The same natur-alistic principle moved the Duke to wrestle with the problem of painted backdrops; in Schiller's *William Tell*, in an attempt to create depth and perspective, he even used bearded children to simulate labourers working upstage on a fortress. The results did not impress him, and the experiment was not repeated.

But the principle of creating an environment with which the actor could establish a natural relationship held good, and led inevitably to a far more natural style of acting. It is significant that Antoine commented enthusiastically on the Meininger's ability to concentrate their attention on each other rather than on the audience, even to the extent of speaking their lines whilst facing upstage. This was a principle that both he and Stanislavsky adopted to considerable effect.

A similar evolution took place in the approach to costume at Meiningen. It was not enough that costumes were authentic to the last detail: they had also to be *worn* correctly, to be *clothes* rather than costumes. Not only did the Duke ensure through his research that both under- and over-garments were cut correctly (as well as employing his own armourer), but he prepared annotated drawings for his actors to show them how they should comport themselves. Occasionally, the result was absurd, such as when an already bulky Brutus was swathed in many yards of authentic woollen toga. But sometimes it led to the telling reappraisal of a stereotype; for example:

> When Barnay set out for Meiningen in 1873, to play the role of Petruchio in a production of *The Taming of the Shrew* in renaissance costume, he evidently expected – despite his prior knowledge of Meiningen regulations – to be able to wear his own thigh-length leather riding-boots, spurs and all: for the military dress of the Thirty Years War was the customary way of expressing 'manliness'. Only after taking up the matter with the Duke himself did Barnay give way – and then he began to discover that the costume he had been given demanded a reconsideration of his interpretation of the role, a more subtle and more spiritual form of masculine dominance than the whip-cracking aggression of his original conception.[21]

It is no coincidence that all the examples cited so far have been from plays by Schiller, Kleist and Shakespeare. Together with their later nineteenth-century German epigones, they comprised the bulk of the Meiningen repertoire. However, in 1876 the Duke turned to Ibsen, though once more to historical drama in the shape of his Norwegian epic, *The Pretenders*. It was presented in Berlin on 3 June, less than two months after a performance of *The Vikings at Helgeland* in Munich, which had been the first production of Ibsen outside Scandinavia.

The Duke devoted much attention to *The Pretenders*, having visited Norway to study the terrain and gather source material. Visually, the production (especially the battle scenes) was compelling enough to sustain it for nine performances before the end of the short season. Ibsen himself came up from Munich to see it and was deeply impressed, describing the performance as 'brilliant and spectacular'. Unquestionably, the Berlin premiere was important in introducing Ibsen to Germany and other productions soon followed. However, *The Pretenders* itself did not last long in the Meiningen repertoire, and it was never performed elsewhere on tour.[22]

It has been suggested that Ibsen was encouraged by what he saw of the Meininger in 1876 to develop the style of detailed naturalism that his next play, *The Pillars of Society*, was to reveal when it was published the following year. Be that as it may, he had at least seen one company that might do justice to that style.[23] As things turned out, however, ten years were to elapse before Duke Georg returned to Ibsen.

The publication of the German translation of *Ghosts* in 1881 had caused a furore, leading to a total police ban on all public performances of the play. In April 1886 there was a solitary 'dress rehearsal' before an invited audience of writers, theatre people and journalists in Augsburg, but the critical response was so hostile that it merely led to a reinforcement of the ban. However, Duke Georg was determined to put it on, and he could hardly be prevented from doing so in his own Duchy. Even so, public resistance to the play in Meiningen was strong, and it was only by issuing free tickets to his court officials that the Duke was able to secure a full house to impress Ibsen and the numerous critics who made the journey. He took his customary care with the production, basing his somewhat grandiose version of Mrs. Alving's home on details of Norwegian middle-class life supplied by Ibsen. The cast of five was rehearsed for nearly three weeks from morning till late into the night and the premiere on 22 December was a spectacular success. To guard against disturbances, the entire police force of Saxe-Meiningen (all six of them) was posted around the theatre, but they were not needed, and the play was given a further uneventful performance six days later. Ibsen himself was delighted with the fidelity of the production.

Plans were made to take *Ghosts* on tour to Berlin the following Spring, but this time police authority was not outranked and the play was banned. The following December the Meininger gave it one further performance in Dresden, only for the police to ban it yet again. After that, the production was seen only once more, in Copenhagen in 1889.

The Duke and Chronegk had demonstrated that their company was not wholly dependent on historical tableaux and mass spectacles. In March 1888, *An Enemy of the People* was staged at Meiningen. By that time, theatres throughout Germany were beginning to put on Ibsen's plays – thanks, in no small degree, to the pioneering efforts of Duke Georg and his company.

In July 1890 the Meininger completed their second tour of Russia, and shortly afterwards Ludwig Chronegk's health finally broke down under the physical and mental strain of seventeen years' touring. He died the following year at the age of fifty-three. Although the Court Theatre continued to function at Meiningen, the company undertook no further tours, and the Duke's active involvement soon ceased.

Inevitably, the name of Duke Georg has become associated with the historical set-pieces in which the Meiningen productions abounded, and theatre historians have pointed out that in many of his effects he was anticipated by Charles Kean and earlier English directors.[24] Certainly it is true that if one searches through the annals of the theatres of England, France and Germany, one can find precedents for most of Georg's 'innovations'. But there was about his undertaking a seriousness, a breadth of vision and, crucially, a freedom from the customary constraints of money and custom, that elevated it to an altogether new plane.

Through the good fortune of his position of authority, the Duke was able to assume an over-view of the production process that subsequent directors would have to win for themselves through prolonged struggle. In addition, he was able to use the Court Theatre as a proving ground for his productions throughout the winter season, thereby benefiting from what was in effect an extended series of dress-rehearsals. The refusal to accommodate star-performance was born partly of a commitment to the idea of an ensemble, and partly of practical necessity: it would have been impossible to retain highly-paid actors throughout the winter in Meiningen, not only because they would not tolerate such an obscure engagement, but also because the box-office could not support their salaries. Whatever the inadequacies in performances this led to, the effect was revolutionary and far-reaching; as early as 1880 one German critic observed: 'the virtuoso actor has now given way to the virtuoso director'.[25]

It is to the Duke's credit that he enlisted Ellen Franz and Ludwig Chronegk as his collaborators. It left him free to exercise overall artistic control, which he did both with the eye of a trained and talented artist and with a serious concern for literary values. As a result, the Meiningen productions had a coherence that proceeded from the play's content, not merely from the period setting, and even less from some stylistic preconception. To the selection and interpretation of plays Georg brought a perception and originality that was rare amongst directors of the period. Hence, his respect for Shakespeare, whom he insisted on staging in original and uncut versions; his championing of Heinrich von Kleist (1777-1811) whom he rescued from obscurity with memorable productions of *The Battle of Arminius*, *Prince Friedrich of Homburg* and *The Enchantress*; his numerous revivals of Schiller; and finally, of course, his early recognition of Ibsen.

It is ironic that, given the overwhelmingly historical bias of its repertoire, the Meiningen Theatre should have laid the basis for the future interpretation of naturalistic drama. The reason is that with its preoccupation with the external elements of environment and its effect on the individual, plus the insignificance of that individual in relation to the crowd, Meiningen came to embrace what was in effect a deterministic view of human behaviour; and it was determinism that was the founding principle of naturalistic art. This was the immediate legacy of Meiningen, but beyond it there extended a vision of production that was to bestow on the stage director a power and a responsibility that he had never before possessed. In this sense, Duke Georg can be regarded with justification as the first of a new breed in the theatre.

2. *Antoine and the Theatre Libre*

We have seen how in England, and more decisively in Germany, the movement towards stage naturalism was in the first instance a response to the prevailing taste for the 'picturesque' in history, geography, and nature. At its best this was a reflection of the Romantic impulse in the arts, the urge to transcend mundane life through the aesthetic experience; but at its worst it was no more than 'museum culture', the magpie instinct of an acquisitive age. In this movement France led the way; the Revolution broke the austere hold of classicism, and the beginning of the nineteenth century saw the 'pièce-à-spectacle' firmly established on the Parisian stage. In 1830, the tumultuous premiere of Victor Hugo's *Hernani* announced the dramatic triumph of Romanticism and its passion for historical truth, which promised to extend beyond outward appearance to character and behaviour. But the popular demand for *la couleur des temps* remained powerful, and Hugo, de Vigny, Sardou, the elder Dumas and others were ready enough to meet it. Ironically, Alfred de Musset, the one dramatist of the period of unquestionable genius, shunned the theatre after the failure of his first play in 1830 and published his work for reading only. Significantly, it was not until after his death in 1857 that with the rise of realism he gained belated recognition. His masterpiece *Lorenzaccio*, published in 1834, was not properly appreciated until the Théâtre Nationale Populaire revival of 1951; in common with Pushkin's *Boris Godunov* and Büchner's *Danton's Death* and *Woyzeck*, similarly products of the Shakespearian revival in Europe, *Lorenzaccio* is a work that might have changed the course of theatre history had it been recognised in its day for its true qualities. As it was, the Romantic movement in French drama ran its course in fifteen years, bequeathed no plays of consequence to posterity, and did little to alter the shape of theatre practice or the demands of the theatre-going public. As early as 1836, the predominant tone of the century was expressed by Eugène Scribe in an address to the Académie Française:

> You go to the theatre for relaxation and amusement, not for instruction or correction. Now what most amuses you is not truth but fiction . . . The theatre

is therefore rarely the direct expression of social life ... it is often the inverse expression.[1]

Thus spoke the genius of the well-made play, who with his follower, Victorien Sardou, perfected a commodity that sold throughout Europe by precisely matching the demands of the age. The picture is well drawn by John Henderson:

The theatre in the nineteenth century was a reflection of the society in which it flourished. The age of immense economic expansion which followed the Industrial Revolution favoured the growth of a mercantile middle class, and this class demanded for its entertainment a theatre in which it saw an idealised picture of its own qualities, a theatre that was moral, comfortable, and thoroughly predictable–an antidote, in short, to the unseemly noise of the Romantic rebel. When a certain number of bourgeois dramatists perfected formulae for satisfying these tastes the temptation was to produce endless variations of a form that was known to please; and the development of theatrical entertainment into a fruitful commercial pursuit was equally responsible for discouraging innovation. At the end of the century the drama had not only become divorced from reality; it had lost contact with the poetry of life, with artistic values and had become a sterile, mechanical process.[2]

The advent in the 1850's of the 'problem play' by such authors as Alexandre Dumas *fils* and Émile Augier did little to affect the situation; despite their ostensible concern with social problems, the presentation remained diverting, and their attitude implied an affirmation of bourgeois values. Both formal and social equilibrium were carefully preserved, and the demands of the public were respectfully met.

In terms of stagecraft, the well-made play had no need for innovation, since formally it became as rigidly fixed as classical drama. In acting, the cardinal qualities were style, precision, and personality. Of Sarah Bernhardt, the very embodiment of the age, Shaw wrote in 1895:

She is beautiful with the beauty of her school, and entirely inhuman and incredible. But the incredibility is pardonable, because, though it is all the greatest nonsense, nobody believing in it, the actress herself least of all, it is so artful, so clever, so well recognised a part of the business, and carried off with such a genial air, that it is impossible not to accept it with good-humour ... She does not enter into the leading character, she substitutes herself for it.[3]

But whilst the French theatre degenerated into an after-dinner diversion, the French novel was setting new standards in psychological penetration and the meticulous documentation of modern life at all levels of society. Between 1830 and 1850 Honoré de Balzac completed *La Comédie humaine*, his 'agglomeration of species' which amounted to almost one hundred novels. Similarly Émile Zola's *Rougon Macquart* cycle, completed in twenty volumes between 1869 and 1893, traced 'the natural and social history of a family under the Second Empire'; it included all his best known works such as *L'Assommoir*, *Nana*, *Germinal*, *La Bête humaine*, and *La Terre*. Under the direct influence of the philosopher, historian and critic, Hippolyte Taine, Zola sought to employ the laws and methods of science in the creation of literature. He embraced Taine's system of *race*, *milieu*, *moment* and echoed his slogan 'Vice and virtue are simply products, like sugar and vitriol.'

Several leading novelists turned their hands to the theatre without success: Flaubert's sole effort, *Le Candidat* (1874) was given only four performances; Daudet's *L'Arlésienne* was found too unconventional in structure; the Goncourt brothers wrote several historical dramas that had to wait twenty years or more before Antoine appreciated their qualities;* Balzac treated the stage more as a means of paying his debts than an opportunity for innovation.

Zola, on the other hand, found his belief in determinist objectivity offended by the falsity of the theatre, and resolved by personal intervention, both in criticism and in play-writing, to effect its reform. In the preface to his first major play, his own dramatic adaptation of his novel *Thérèse Raquin* (1873), he wrote 'I have the profound conviction that the experimental and scientific spirit of the century will prevail in the theatre, and that therein lies the only hope of reviving our stage.' He was to be proved right, but not until fifteen years later, and far more through his inspiration as a theorist and critic than his achievements as a dramatist.

Zola came to the theatre armed with the confidence of a celebrated and contentious novelist. The problem as he saw it was the translation of naturalistic technique into stage terms, of reconciling the scientific objectivity achieved in the novel with the degree of artifice unavoidable in the theatre. 'It would be absurd–he wrote in 1876–to suppose that one can transfer nature to the stage: plant real trees and have real houses lit by a real sun. We are forced into conventions, and must accept a more or less complete illusion instead of reality.'[4]

By this time, the mechanics of illusion on the French stage were as ingenious as anywhere in Europe, but Zola contended that so long as they furnished mere backgrounds they were worthless: 'It is man who should be the sum total of the effect; it is in him that the overall result should be observed; the sole purpose of realistic decor should be to lend him greater reality, to locate him in the atmosphere proper to him.'

Zola was concerned with the forces that shape the lives of ordinary, unremarkable people, but in forgoing the unlimited panorama of the novel, he accepted the need for compression and dramatic impact, and was prepared to emphasise his characters' exceptional traits rather than

* See p. 31–32 below.

what made them typical. His declared aim in the Preface to *Thérèse Raquin* applies equally to his plays in general:

> Given a strong man and an unsatisfied woman, to seek in them the beast, to see nothing but the beast, to throw them into a violent drama and note scrupulously the sensations and acts of these creatures ... I have simply done on two living bodies the work which surgeons do on corpses.

The fallacy is surely plain: in working on corpses, surgeons do not select only those with abnormalities, whereas Zola depicted his characters and ordered their experiences precisely in order to emphasise their abnormality. This emerged in practice: *Thérèse Raquin* tells of the drowning of the sickly Camille by his passionate wife, Thérèse and her lover, Laurent; the couple then marry, but find their passion turning to hatred under the burden of remorse; they try simultaneously to kill each other, then finally take poison together. There is much that relates the play to the most lurid and improbable melodrama, not least the closing scene in which the paralysed Madame Raquin miraculously recovers the power of speech and condemns the guilty pair. Nevertheless, *Thérèse Raquin* was unprecedented in its depiction of the power of sexuality and of passion seething beneath the surface of idle conversation. Zola enclosed the drama in a single 'dark and humid' room. Here again, theatrical effect took precedence over mere reportage: the room's atmosphere served to heighten the sense of the couple's entrapment, but it had nothing to do with environment in the determinist sense of the word.

The point is made even more clearly by *L'Assommoir* (staged in England as *Drink*), again a play taken from the novel, and adapted for the stage in 1879 by Busnach and Gastineau under Zola's supervision. The grim story of alcoholism amongst the working-class was compressed into nine 'tableaux' of the most detailed realism with, for example, washerwomen washing real laundry with real soap in real hot water, or the perfect representation of the *assommoir* itself, the bar with patrons drifting in and out. Both Zola and the Paris public, who kept the play running for over three hundred performances, were deeply impressed by this exact reproduction of life, yet the fundamental error persisted: in order 'to add some dramatic interest to the play' Zola authorised the strengthening of the theme of jealousy, thereby rendering the tragedy personal and melodramatic and obscuring its origins in social conditions.[5]

Zola's work generally is characterised by a moral indignation at prevailing conditions in society, yet he is reticent in identifying causes beyond the imperfect nature of the human species. He rightly castigated the moralistic sermonising of Dumas *fils* and the other exponents of the 'problem play', but had he stood less rigidly on his principle of scientific detachment and related his case-histories to a wider social reality he might have found a structure and a dynamic for his dramas which was not merely formal and derived from conventional models.

For all its shortcomings, the production of *L'Assommoir* at the Théâtre de l'Ambigu in 1879 did more than any other single event to bring naturalism to the attention of the French theatre public. Both through his critical writings and through the staging of his work, Zola did much to widen the horizons of the theatre for dramatists and directors. In his authoritative study *Zola and the Theatre*, Lawson Carter writes:

> Whereas the romantics had rebelled against the stereotyped mould of classicism, the naturalists rebelled against stereotyped formulas of morality and rhetoric which frustrated efforts to bring a greater measure of truth to literature and the drama . . . Zola's doctrine, dependent upon the alliance of science and literature, was in a sense merely a primitive expression of modern naturalism, which has discarded his scientific pretensions. Yet the alliance was necessary in its time. The scientific spirit was needed to regenerate literature and the drama, and to free them of conventions and taboos. To Zola belongs the credit for this temporary, yet fertile, mating.[6]

For all the eloquent passion of Zola's critical writings and all the furore created by his plays in the theatre, the crucial breakthrough was not achieved: in the boulevard theatres the stage-director remained answerable to his backers and took risks at his peril, whilst the attitude of the state theatres is accurately conveyed by the celebrated remark of Jean Perrin, director of the Comédie-Française: 'I need no new authors. A year of Dumas, a year of Augier and a year of Sardou is enough for me.' The fact that *L'Assommoir* got put on and then succeeded was due in no small measure to the name of Zola. Unknown dramatists of whatever talent could draw on no such credit, and so were forced to write in a manner calculated to please if they were to stand any chance of performance. The need was for a playwright's theatre: a theatre that would protect the right to fail, was talented enough to guarantee serious standards, yet small enough to function without the aid of capricious benefactors or mercenary backers. This is precisely what came into being in Paris in 1887, the prototype of all the free, independent, art, studio, basement, fringe and lunchtime theatres, which have since initiated most of the advances of any consequence in twentieth-century drama.

At the age of twenty-nine André Antoine worked as a clerk with the Paris Gas Company. A frustrated actor who at eighteen had been rejected by the Conservatoire, he belonged to the Cercle Gaulois, one of several amateur dramatic societies that functioned in Paris. Their work was safe and unexceptional, until Antoine was given the idea by an aspiring dramatist of putting on an evening of unperformed plays. In no time, Antoine found himself with a complete programme of one-act plays, including an adaptation by Léon Hennique of a story by Zola called *Jacques*

Damour, first published in 1880. Due largely to the presence of Zola's name in the programme, the venture was taken up by the press and it was widely publicised. The immediate effect was ominous for Antoine and his friends: alarmed at the scale of the project and the scandal attaching to Zola's name, the conservative Cercle Gaulois took fright and withdrew all support save the hire of its theatre in the Passage de l'Elysée-des Beaux-Arts in Montmartre, which was owned by the society's president. The simple wooden building had no foyer and seated an audience of 343. But this primitive venue was evidently to the liking of the initiates who found their way there. The eminent critic Jules Lemaître reported 'One could shake hands with the actors across the footlights, and stretch one's legs over the prompter's box. The stage is so small that only the simplest scenery can be set up on it, and so near the audience that scenic illusion is impossible.'[7] For the setting of *Jacques Damour* Antoine borrowed the furniture from his mother's dining room, and pushed it to the theatre in a handcart. Denied the use of the stage until the performance, Antoine rehearsed his company in a billiard room behind a nearby café; for this concession Antoine had to agree to buy drinks in the café at each rehearsal. Obliged by the Cercle Gaulois to find a different name to cover their disreputable undertaking, the new company settled on Théâtre Libre.

After rehearsals graced by the attendance and good will of Zola and other like-minded writers and critics, the inaugural programme was given a preview before an invited audience on 29 March 1887 and a single press performance the following night. Of the four one-act plays in the programme, only *Jacques Damour* was successful. Antoine played the title role of the exiled communard who returns home to find that his wife, believing him dead, has remarried. It was a personal triumph for Antoine, and one critic was moved to declare 'If the naturalist theatre produces many plays like this one, it can rest easy about its future.' Due to two other premières on the same evening, few critics were present, but those who were reported favourably. A week later, the illustrious national theatre, the Odéon, requested the play, having rejected it only a few months previously. Through this alone the existence of the Théâtre Libre became validated and a pattern established for the years to come.

Antoine had not dared to look beyond the single programme and was taken unawares. In his memoirs he writes, 'I did not have the slightest plan of becoming a professional actor or director, and I should have laughed indeed if anyone had predicted to me that we were going to revolutionise dramatic art.'[8] Two months later, a second programme comprising two more new plays was given two performances to invited audiences, mostly from the artistic world, and this time a full complement of critics. The main item was a three-act verse comedy by Émile Bergerat called *La Nuit bergamasque*, derived from Boccaccio and built round traditional *commedia* characters. Far more interest was aroused by the one-act sketch, *En famille* by Oscar Méténier, which preceded it. It was a vivid and authentic account of life in the Paris slums, centering on a description of the guillotining of a friend of the family. It was uncontrived naturalism, which owed nothing to traditional conventions, and it moved the august critic Sarcey to comment 'Perhaps this is the theatre of the future. I hope to have gone before it arrives'. One particular innovation worth mentioning was the rejection of foot-lights and the complete lowering of house-lights during performance: unprecedented in France, if familiar enough at Wagner's Bayreuth and elsewhere.[9]

Thanks mainly to the sensation caused by *En famille*, the response to the evening was enthusiastic and Antoine could think realistically of a full programme for the following season. Taking his life in his hands, he resigned from the Gas Company and even refused an invitation to join the Odéon Theatre as an actor.

To safeguard its artistic freedom and to protect itself against the censor it was vital that the Théâtre Libre remain a subscription society. After a summer spent delivering thirteen hundred prospectuses by hand, Antoine had just thirty-seven subscribers and huge bills to meet, but after the reopening in October the number swelled to over three thousand. These sensational events were more than the modest Cercle Gaulois could stand, and the Théâtre Libre was forced to move right across Paris to the Théâtre Montparnasse in the Rue de la Gaité. Thus, after just three programmes, Antoine was in a position to hire and fill a theatre of some eight hundred seats.

Antoine always insisted that the Théâtre Libre was not simply a naturalistic theatre, but literally 'free', and dedicated to all unperformed drama of whatever genre. Over the years his repertoire embraced farce, melodrama, historical pageants, verse drama, mime, even a shadow-play; but most representative of the theatre's style was the *quart d'heure*, the brief one-act 'slice of life', inaugurated by *En famille*, which belonged to the genre called *comédie rosse*. The term *rosse* is untranslatable but it implies, in the words of one critic, 'a sort of vicious ingenuousness, the state of mind of people who have never had any moral sense and who live in impurity and injustice like a fish in water'.[10] Typical was Jean Jullien's *Serenade* staged by Antoine as part of his second programme in Montparnasse. The play concerns a complacent bourgeois husband who accepts that his wife and his daughter share the family tutor as their lover; at the end of the play he welcomes the tutor into the family as his son-in-law, with no indication that this will change the situation in any way.

The advantages of the *quart d'heure* were several: its simple, episodic form helped Antoine to develop an intimate style of natural acting; it enabled him to devise programmes containing the work of young aspiring dramatists alongside full-length plays by established authors, whose names would ensure public support; it could be staged with a minimum of resources, and fostered the development of behavioural naturalism in writing which focussed attention on the motivation and interaction of character rather than external physical details; finally, it exposed the needless contrivances and complications of the full-length formula play.

Strindberg, who closely followed developments in France, acknowledged his debt to the *quarts d'heure* staged by Antoine, and wrote a number himself, such as *Pariah, Simoom, Playing with Fire* and *The Stronger*, before he arrived at his 'new formula' with *The Father* and *Miss Julie*.

At the same time, Antoine took every opportunity to stage major full-length works. The sensation of the 1887-88 season was his production of Tolstoy's *The Power of Darkness*. In this tragedy completed in 1886 Tolstoy gives a vivid account of Russian peasant life in the grip of drink, ignorance, superstition, and avarice. Tolstoy based the play on an actual murder case in the Tula Province and so authentic are the play's setting and dialogue that the tragedy emerges as the inevitable outcome of a brutal existence. On publication in Russia the edition of 200,000 copies sold out immediately, and the play was promptly banned from performance by the Tsarist censor. Thus, Antoine's production on 10 February 1888 was the world première. It was also the first of a series of foreign plays that enhanced the reputation of the Théâtre Libre and opened up the French stage to new and vital influences. This was a task that was to be performed by the independent theatre movement in every country, making repertoires multi-national as they had never been before.

Antoine's concern with authenticity made him reject the play's existing translation and commission a new one, engaging a Russian consultant to check the details of dialect. It was the first time that a word-for-word translation, as opposed to adaptation, of a foreign text had been staged in France. Similarly, although forced to adapt the settings from available stock, he was able to obtain costumes and 'real Russian objects' from the emigré community. Impressed though the audience was, it is unlikely that externally *The Power of Darkness* compared with the standards achieved at Meiningen. Even so, the *Revue des Deux Mondes* commented 'For the first time a setting and costumes truly borrowed from the daily customs of Russian life appeared on the French stage without comic opera embellishments and without that predilection for tinsel and falsity that seems inherent in our theatrical atmosphere.'[11] But what assured the production's spectacular success was the total conviction of the acting by a cast headed by Antoine as the old peasant Akim and including two clerks, an architect, a chemist, a travelling salesman, a wine-merchant, a dressmaker and a book-binder.

Such was the interest aroused by *The Power of Darkness* that Antoine was persuaded by the Russian community to give for the first time a performance for the general public, which was followed by three more in Brussels. By the close of the season Antoine had put on seventeen new plays and established an international reputation for the Théâtre Libre. In February 1888 *Le Figaro* wrote 'The Théâtre Libre has become a Parisian institution, not because of an idle whim of fashion, but because it responds to a desire of the public, a desire in the field of drama, to branch off from the beaten tracks where tradition has driven its ever deeper ruts.'[12] Yet despite this recognition and despite packed houses for every performance of *The Power of Darkness*, Antoine was, as he was always to be, deeply in debt.

In the summer of 1888 the Théâtre Libre moved again, this time to the Salle des Menus-Plaisirs, a theatre in the centre of Paris on the Boulevard de Strasbourg. Antoine planned a season comprising eight evenings of previews, eight first-nights before subscription audiences, and twenty-five public performances. The disadvantage of the new theatre was that, with a total of seventeen productions to mount, there was no longer a stock of scenery on which to draw. Commenting on this, Antoine wrote 'More and more, discussions over our presentations are turning from the values or the tendencies of the work given to questions about interpretation or setting. There has been more debate about such matters than I would ever have thought possible.'[13] This seems to indicate quite clearly that Antoine's search for scenic truth proceeded from the heart of the drama rather than from any fascination with external effects. In July 1888 he saw the Meiningen Company on tour in Brussels and recorded his impressions in a long letter to the critic Sarcey. He found much to admire in their work, notably the carefully rehearsed crowd scenes and the capacity of the actors to play oblivious to the audience, with back turned if need be. These points he resolved to emulate, but at the same time he found plenty to criticise, in particular 'the garish and oddly designed settings', the 'foolishly rich' costumes, the lighting effects, 'often striking, but handled with epic naivete'. The acting he found 'adequate and nothing more'.[14] Two productions in the first season on the Boulevard de Strasbourg reflected the influence of the Meininger on Antoine, both of them being seen by him as 'revivals of the historical play through the methods of the realistic school'.

They were *The Death of the Duke of Enghien* by Léon Hennique and *The Motherland in Danger* by the Goncourt brothers. *The Death of the Duke of Enghien* was presented in December 1888. In three tableaux, it was a factual account of the pursuit and arrest by Napoleon's agents of the counter-revolutionary Duke of Enghien, and his court martial and execution at Vincennes. William Archer wrote: 'It is an attempt to put an historic episode on the stage in its unvarnished simplicity, without any involution of plot or analysis of motive.'[15] What distinguished it from the *grands spectacles* of the Romantic period was the complete absence of grandiloquent heroics and costume for costume's sake. Like the Meininger, Antoine's actors wore *clothes* that emphasised their characters and their situation in the drama instead of conforming to the picturesque image in the popular imagination. Thus the clothes of the Duke and the Princess de Rohan emphasised the misery of their exile, whilst Napoleon's envoy wore a simple frock-coat instead of a general's uniform'.[16]

The most spectacular aspect of the production was the lighting. In the final tableau Antoine used candle-light alone, with the house in complete darkness. During the cross-examination of the Duke the actors were seen as little more than silhouettes. When the court retired to consider its verdict, the prisoner fell asleep, slumped at a table. A soldier returned, roused him and led him outside. The stage was left empty and a volley of shots was heard. William Archer commented ' ... nothing is left to the imagination but what it claims as its right – for it must be remembered that the most thrilling spectacle in real life will not move us save through sympathetic imagination.'[17]

Archer had seen the Théâtre Libre when it visited London for a week in February 1889. As well as *The Duke of Enghien*, the programme at the Royalty Theatre included *Jacques Damour* and *En famille*. Whilst the public response was sympathetic enough, the critics were mostly patronising or simply uncomprehending; *The Times* described Antoine's theatre as 'the happy hunting ground of the ultra-realistic or fin-de-siècle dramatist who specially affects the horrible and the revolting'.[18]

Antoine himself was keen to gain as much experience as he could from his stay. When the company returned to Paris, he remained in order to see Irving's production of *Macbeth* at the Lyceum. He thought little of Irving himself and made no comment on Ellen Terry, but he was deeply impressed by the settings and, in particular, the lighting effects which seemed to him beyond the dreams of the Parisian stage.[19] His comments are typical of his own modesty and open-mindedness, and at the same time indicate the relatively slender resources available to his own company.

Antoine's receptivity to the ideas of other directors was demonstrated a month after his return from London when he staged *The Motherland in Danger* by Edmond and Jules de Goncourt on a scale and in a style much indebted to the example of the Meininger, and with chiaroscuro lighting effects reminiscent of Irving's *Macbeth*. Like *The Duke of Enghien*, which Hennique had dedicated to the Goncourt brothers, *The Motherland in Danger* was more a series of tableaux (in this case, five) than a coherent drama. Completed in 1867, it had been refused by the Comédie Française because its glorification of the Revolution made it unacceptable during the conservative reign of Napoléon III. Though published in 1873, it had never been staged, and it was left to Antoine to present it in celebration of the centenary of 1789. His production excelled in milling crowd scenes, for which he employed two-hundred meticulously schooled extras, in its pictorial beauty and its historical accuracy. However, the play's interminable dialogues were not redeemed by their documentary exactitude, and robbed the action of all dramatic tension. Furthermore, the critics pronounced Antoine's company 'inadequate for the noble genre', a verdict that reflected exactly the prejudicial attitude towards style that Antoine was seeking to break down. Ironically, it seems to have been a view of the production shared even by the arch-naturalist Edmond de Goncourt himself.[20]

Following the usual subscription première, twenty-five public performances were planned for *The Motherland in Danger*, but attendances were poor and it was repeated only five times. So yet again, after a costly production Antoine was left with a heavy deficit. It was not to be his last attempt at mass spectacle, but for the present the Théâtre Libre's programmes reverted to a more familiar formula. In May 1890 Antoine once again introduced a major foreign dramatist to the French stage, this time Ibsen, with a production of *Ghosts*.

By now, the success of the Théâtre Libre had led to the formation of independent theatre groups elsewhere in Europe. The first was an experimental theatre founded by Strindberg in Copenhagen in March 1889 for the performance of his own plays. It closed after only four performances. Of far greater significance was the the Freie Bühne, which opened in Berlin in September of that year under the direction of Otto Brahm. To open his campaign for the 'new theatre' he too chose *Ghosts*, already staged by the Meininger in 1886 but still banned from public performance in Germany.* Similarly, when the Independent Theatre (sub-titled 'Théâtre Libre') under J. T. Grein opened in London with *Ghosts* in March 1891, it succeeded in drawing attention to itself with the predictable rumpus provoked by what *The Times* described as 'the lugubrious and malodorous world of Ibsen'.

Antoine was familiar with *Ghosts* at least as early as the summer of 1888, when he mentioned it in his letter on the Meininger to Sarcey. However, he delayed two years in bringing it to the stage for two reasons: firstly, as Francis Pruner suggests, he was anxious for the critical furore aroused by the publication in 1889 of the French translation to abate at least to the point where a performance would not be dismissed out of hand; secondly, he was dissatisfied with the available text and took the trouble to commision a reliable new version for which he obtained Ibsen's

*See pp. 19-20 above.

authorisation. In both respects, he revealed his characteristic concern for the interests of the author rather than the quick *succès de scandale*. This same concern, in fact, led him to make his one error of judgement in the production: anxious to secure the French public's indulgence for the forbidding Norwegian dramatist, and in particular to avoid provoking religious antagonism, he cut the part of Pastor Manders so much that it lost all coherence and several critics even accused the actor of rendering unpleasant the one *sympathetic* character in the play.

The preponderant reaction to *Ghosts* varied between boredom and confusion, though the agony of the closing scene was powerful enough. Recalling his own performance as Oswald, Antoine writes: 'I . . . underwent an experience totally new to me – an almost complete loss of my own personality. After the second act I remember nothing, neither the audience nor the effect of the production, and, shaking and weakened, I was some time getting hold of myself again after the final curtain had fallen.'[21] In contrast to the confusion of the French critics, two foreign visitors were deeply impressed. George Moore, the English naturalist writer and critic wrote:

> Antoine was superb in the part of Osvalt. The nervous irritation of the sick man was faultlessly rendered. When he tells his mother of the warnings of the French doctor, at the moment when he loses his temper at her interruptions – she seeks not to hear the fearful tale – Antoine, identifying himself with the simple truth sought by Ibsen, by voice and gesture, casts upon the scene so terrible a light, so strange an air of truth, that the drama seemed to be passing not before our eyes, but deep down in our hearts in a way we had never felt before. 'Listen to me, mother. I insist upon your listening to me,' he says, querulous already with incipient disease. And when comes the end of the first act, when the mother, hearing the servant-girl cry out, goes to the door, and seeing the son kissing the girl, cries, 'Ghosts, ghosts!' what shall I say, what praise shall we bestow upon a situation so supremely awful, so shockingly true?[22]

The Swedish poet and active propagandist of Scandinavian literature, Ola Hansson, was impressed by the authenticity of Antoine's performance:

> His portrayal, both in its general conception and in all its incidental details, was altogether convincingly Scandinavian – to such a degree that as a Scandinavian I needed to look around at the theatre surroundings and the audience to remind myself that I was not at home in some familiar, native setting. Yet in the actual manner of his portrayal Antoine revealed himself as the representative of true Gallic naturalism. His body, his clothes, his movements, his gestures, even the way his hair was combed, were all those of a Scandinavian at home; yet the transparent, clear simplicity with which these qualities were conveyed was wholly Gallic in nature. There was a lucidity such as one observes in nature in

late Autumn when the leaves are rotting in the woods and the scent of death hangs over the fields; it was a clarity as gentle yet as unremitting as death.[23]

Interpreting Hansson's poetic imagery and reading the rest of his lengthy appraisal, one gets the impression of a performance that observed every naturalistic detail yet was vividly expressive of the play's inner poetic meaning. Antoine himself felt sufficiently encouraged to return to Ibsen the following year with a production of *The Wild Duck*. To judge from the few impressionistic reports that survive, it seems to have posed even more insoluble problems than *Ghosts*. Having come to terms at length with naturalism, the public and critics were now being led a stage further into the realms of symbolism. Their response on the first night at the Théâtre Libre was, literally, to quack like ducks, though by the end they fell silent and received the final act in admiration, if somewhat puzzled.

But despite the coolness of *The Wild Duck's* reception, Antoine, like Duke Georg and Otto Brahm in Germany, had brought Ibsen before the public eye, and over the next five years twelve further plays by him were staged in various theatres in Paris. In order to stave off the ever-present threat of bankruptcy the Théâtre Libre undertook a number of extensive tours around France and to Belgium, Holland, Italy and Germany. In the course of these *Ghosts* was among the most successful productions, and altogether was given over two-hundred performances.

The 1891-92 season was given over entirely to French plays, but in 1893 Antoine resumed his policy of introducing significant works from the foreign avant-garde. In January of that year he gave three performances of *Miss Julie*, the first production of Strindberg in France. At that time, Strindberg had received little recognition as a dramatist: apart from his own short-lived attempt to found an independent theatre in Copenhagen, the Freie Bühne had staged *The Father* with moderate success in 1890 and had given one single public performance of *Miss Julie* in 1892 that provoked such vehement protests that it was immediately dropped from the repertoire. Some years earlier Strindberg had sent Antoine his own French translation of *The Father*, but despite his professed enthusiasm for it, Antoine had never succeeded in accommodating it in his repertoire. Evidently, he had his doubts too about *Miss Julie*, for he describes it in his *Memoirs* as 'a curious play by Strindberg' (November 1892). However, he took the trouble to have Strindberg's lengthy preface to the play translated and distributed in advance of the premiere to his subscribers and the critics. It was a curious decision, since Strindberg had written it five years previously, and most of the innovations that he advocated had by now been achieved by Antoine and his followers elsewhere. It also proved injudicious: Antoine neglected to date the piece, and the French critics didn't take kindly to being lectured on the current state of the theatre by a mere Swede (though Sarcey believed him to be Norwegian), and objected to Strindberg's criticism of the 'over-simplified view of people' in the great Molière.

Thus the evening was blighted before it began, and the audience's humour was not enhanced by the two worthless items that made up the triple bill with *Miss Julie*. In his *Memoirs* Antoine writes '*Miss Julie* made an enormous sensation. Everything stimulated the audience – the subject, the setting, the packing into a single act an hour and a half in length of enough action to sustain a full-length French play. Of course, there were sneers and protests, but it was, after all, something quite new.'[24] To judge from the first-night critics, there was little but sneers and protests: they speak of 'this latest bout of tiresome silliness', 'international pornography', 'an irritating evening with a wind of insanity blowing from the North', 'an adulterous mixture of Zola and Ibsen'. Even some writers who were associated with the Théâtre Libre suggest that the audience made little effort to comprehend Strindberg's blend of naturalism and symbolism. Francis Pruner rightly observes that even *Ghosts* had been ill-received at first; but the fact remains that whereas *Ghosts* survived to receive over two-hundred performances, *Miss Julie* was never staged publicly at the Théâtre Libre, and was given only two further invitation performances on tour. By now, the continual struggle for survival was causing Antoine's energies to flag. After a finely orchestrated production of Hauptmann's vast social drama *The Weavers* in May 1893, he began to look for ways of winding up the company. Further foreign tours were undertaken to balance the books, but October 1894 found Antoine and his company of fifteen stranded in Rome and hopelessly in debt. He extricated himself somehow, but at the cost of turning over the Théâtre Libre to another management under which it survived until 1896.

After a time Antoine took over the Théâtre de Menus-Plaisirs again and, renaming it the Théâtre Antoine, continued his policy of promoting new writing. In 1906 he was appointed artistic director of the Odéon, where he worked until 1914. After that he gave up the theatre for the cinema, making a number of screen versions of books by Hugo, Dumas, Zola and others. For the last twenty years of his life he was a respected film and theatre critic. He died in 1943 at the age of eighty-six.

When Antoine founded the Théâtre Libre in 1887, his principal aim was to provide a stage for new and unperformed drama. When he visited London in 1889, he said in an interview:

> The aim of the Théâtre Libre is to encourage every writer to write for the stage, and, above all, to write what he feels inclined to write and not what he thinks a manager will produce. I produce anything in which there is a grain of merit, quite irrespective of any opinion I may form of what the public will think of it, and anything a known writer brings me, and exactly as he hands it to me. If he

writes a monologue of half-a-dozen pages, the actor must speak those half-dozen pages word for word. His business is to write the play: mine to have it acted.[25]

In his seven years at the Théâtre Libre Antoine put on 111 plays, most of them previously unkown in France. The care he took over their selection and presentation, his refusal to capitulate in the face of critical onslaughts, and his determination to educate rather than pander to popular taste all support his claims as a *playwright's* director. Certainly his greatest successes were achieved in the field of naturalism, and he never ceased to acknowledge the support and inspiration of Zola, but above all, he showed the world what a theatre could do when freed from the constraints of custom and profit.

3. The Symbolist Theatre

On 24 August 1890 the eminent critic of *Le Figaro*, Octave Mirbeau, announced the arrival of a new dramatic genius. He was the little known twenty-eight years old Belgian poet, Maurice Maeterlinck, and his brief tragedy *La Princesse Maleine*, was described by Mirbeau as 'The most inspired work of our time, the most extraordinary and the most un-affected, comparable with, and – dare I say it – superior in beauty to all that is finest in Shakespeare.' In fact, Maeterlinck was not nearly so obscure as Mirbeau claimed, but his extravagant eulogy had its effect and the Paris avant-garde theatre hastened to stage *La Princesse Maleine*. As we have seen, Antoine was in no way bound in his loyalty to naturalistic drama, and he soon announced the inclusion in his repertoire for 1890/91 of Maeterlinck's brief, heavily significant tragedy of corrupt kings and queens, acted out in towers, passages, and forests.

However, by February the following year Antoine seems to have had second thoughts; in his *Memories* he writes '... I really don't have the materials, costumes, settings, or actors at hand to do [*La Princesse Maleine*] ... The truth is that I don't think that this would suit the nature of the theatre, and I would be undertaking a venture which would only betray the author.'[1] Antoine's work had barely reached its zenith by 1891, but his reluctance to meet the challenge of Maeterlinck indicates his limits, and points to a shift that had already overtaken the arts at large and was now to affect the theatre, tardy as ever in its response to innova-tion.

In France the Symbolist Movement came to its peak in the decade following 1885, but its influence extended throughout Europe and can be traced beyond the First World War. In the Introduction to *The Heritage of Symbolism* Maurice Bowra writes 'Seen in retrospect the Symbolist Movement of the Nineteenth Century in France was fundamentally mystical. It protested with noble eloquence against the scientific art of an age which had lost much of its belief in traditional religion and hoped to find a substitute in the search for truth.'[2] But it was not so much the theory of Naturalism that the Symbolists rejected; rather, it was the tawdriness of bourgeois life, the lack of higher values, that the Naturalists seemed content to reproduce in their work. The Symbolists were reacting against an age in which a series of public scandals culminating in the Dreyfus Affair in 1894 exposed the humbug and philistinism of the Third Republic. Stéphane Mallarmé, one of the greatest of the Symbolist poets and their principal theorist, said in 1891 'In a society lacking stability, lacking unity, it is not possible to create stable definite art. From this imperfect social order, which in its turn is an expression of spiritual disquiet, is born the vague need for individuality of which present literary phenomena are the direct reflection.'[3]

What was the aim of the Symbolists' 'search for truth'? To quote the critic Guy Michaud, 'to seize through the relativity of existence the essence of the universe . . . to transcend the individual poetic act and attain a higher reality'.[4] The formulation is appropriately vague, for the Symbolists denied the possibility of definition in a universe that could at best be perceived indistinctly through the medium of artistic inspiration. Their ultimate belief was in a cosmology contingent not on moral or mathematical but on aesthetic principles.* They saw the poet's task as 'to follow an intuitive sense with which he is endowed and to perceive (in existence) analogies, correspondences, which assume the literary aspect of the metaphor, the symbol, the comparison, or the allegory'.[5] It is important to remember that the Symbolist poets used words not as signs to fix and define experience, but as evocations of a reality beyond that perceived by the senses, 'enabling the self to escape from its limitations and to expand to the infinite' (Marcel Raymond). The notion of patterns and interrelationships in the external world, called 'correspondences', intimating a superior ideal world, first entered poetry with Baudelaire, and was expressed in his sonnet _Correspondances_, published in _Les Fleurs du mal_ (1857).[6] Seeking to overcome the limiting specificity of language, the Symbolists looked to music, and in particular to the music of Richard Wagner. They found that in most respects he had anticipated their thinking; thus, in 1864 in his Notes to _Parsifal_ he had written: 'The highest work of art must put itself in the place of real life, it must dissolve this Reality in an illusion, by means of which Reality itself appears to us to be no longer anything but an illusion.' As early as 1861, a year after the Paris premiere of _Tannhäuser_, Baudelaire published a long essay on Wagner, praising his ability 'to penetrate to profound and essential reality whose _confused words_ the poet sometimes overhears'. Neither music nor poetry alone, he said, is capable of expressing this reality; music does not speak clearly enough to our intellect, and poetry not delicately enough to

---

* Compare Nietzsche's statement in his early work _The Birth of Tragedy_ (1872): 'The only way that existence and the world can ultimately be justified are as an _aesthetic_ phenomenon.' It was not until the late 1890's that Nietzsche's writings became known in France.

our sensibility. Wagner's *Musikdrama* was a union in which 'one of the two arts comes into play at the point where the other reaches its limits'.[7] Despite the passionate advocacy by Baudelaire and other devotees, philistinism and chauvinism, exacerbated by the Franco-Prussian War of 1870–71, combined successfully to keep Wagner from the Paris stage until some years after his death in 1883; after the failure of *Tannhäuser* in 1860, his works were given only as concert extracts. But this did not prevent the composer's music and theoretical writings from having an enormous effect on the Symbolist Movement, due largely to the publication between 1885 and 1888 of the monthly *La Revue Wagnérienne*.

The *Revue* published accounts of productions of Wagner abroad and discussed his theories concerning the *Gesamtkunstwerk*, the total synthesis of the arts in the form of music-drama. In 1876 Wagner had opened the Festspielhaus in Bayreuth, embodying his idea of a theatre for the future: a single, steeply raked auditorium kept in darkness during the performance; the orchestra pit a 'mystic chasm' buried beyond the audience's sight; no visible prompter's box; complex overhead lighting with footlights abolished; his operas alone performed for an annual festival season to an audience of initiates. All these elements were designed to promote direct communion between the audience and the experience enacted on stage, to restore the shared ritual of the Ancient Greeks. Yet what was actually depicted on the Bayreuth stage and what Wagner stipulated in his written stage-directions constantly thwarted the spectator's imagination with banal representations of grassy banks, swans pulling boats, swords in trees, and dragons' heads.

It took the genius of the great Swiss theoretician and designer Adolphe Appia to pull the production of Wagner from the morass of tawdry operatic convention. In his writings, particularly *Die Musik und die Inscenierung*, published in 1899, Appia showed with detailed designs how Wagner could be staged in terms of space, light, shape, colour and rhythmic movement, all dictated by the mood, the sub-text of the drama. Rejected indignantly by Wagner's widow, Cosima, and held back by his own extreme reticence, Appia made little direct impact on the theatre during his lifetime. However, his influence as a theorist was profound, notably on Meyerhold in Russia as early as 1907*. When Wagner's grandsons, Wieland and Wolfgang, took over Bayreuth in 1951, Appia's vision was at last applied to the composer who had inspired it, and Wagner was freed from the clutches of the nineteenth century.[8]

Great as the Symbolists' veneration of Wagner was – and veneration is not too strong a word – it was directed more towards his spiritual example than his practical proposals for the theatre. This was hardly the result of disenchanting visits to Bayreuth, which most of them, including Mallarmé,

* See p. 125 below.

never saw anyway, but rather because they feared the encroachment of music on the drama, which they saw as the rightful province of poetry. In 1885 the *Revue Wagnérienne* published an essay by Mallarmé entitled 'Richard Wagner: Rêverie d'un poète français'. Described by Mallarmé as 'half article, half prose-poem', it was more an act of homage to the composer, a meditation on him, than a detailed exegesis of his ideas, and indeed revealed Mallarmé's knowledge of Wagner's theoretical writings as far from complete. Mallarmé expressed his astonished admiration for Wagner's grandiose plans for the transformation of the theatre into a temple where the masses would participate in a sacred rite. He endorsed his idea of the *Gesamtkunstwerk* that would reject direct representation and play on the power of the imagination to convey inner experience. Yet he could not accept music as the means of expressing ultimate experience, and asserted the independence of poetry. In fact, he defended the purity and autonomy of every artistic genre, arguing that whereas they might reinforce and complement one another, they must not be fused into a complete synthesis. In part, Mallarmé was writing as a poet in defence of the poet's rights, but we must remember too that in 1885 the French stage could offer nothing that suggested that Wagner's extravagant visions were in any way realisable. As Symbolism moved into its ascendant towards 1890, the poets continued to dally with their theories and visions of an ideal drama, composing nothing that was staged and next to nothing that was even stageable. What is more, they were hesitant to entrust their work to the theatre, preferring the play for reading, or '*spectacle dans un fauteuil*'. In 1890, Maeterlinck wrote in *La Jeune Belgique*:

> The majority of the great poems of humanity are not stageable. *Lear, Hamlet, Othello, Macbeth, Antony and Cleopatra* are not to be realised and it is dangerous to see them on the stage. The day we see Hamlet die in the theatre, something of him dies for us. He is dethroned by the spectre of an actor, and we shall never be able to keep the usurper out of our dreams ... The staging of a masterpiece with the help of human and unpredictable elements is a contradiction. Every masterpiece is a symbol and the symbol will not tolerate the active presence of man ... The absence of man seems to me unavoidable.[9]

In place of man Maeterlinck envisaged 'a shadow, a reflection, a projection of symbolic forms, or some being with all the appearance of life though not actually living'. The previous year he had subtitled *La Princesse Maleine* 'a little play for puppets'. Both the puppet and the shadow play were now seen as serious alternatives to the all-too solid human actor, and a number of new theatres devoted to them were opened in Paris. Introducing the *Petit Théâtre de la Galérie Vivienne* in 1888, Paul Margueritte wrote:

> While the name and the over-familiar face of an actor in the flesh impose upon the audience an obsession which makes illusion impossible or very difficult,

impersonal puppets, creatures of wood and cardboard, possess a quaint and mysterious life. Their appearance of truth is surprising, worrying. In their essential gestures is contained the complete expression of human feelings.[10]

What Margueritte was implying with 'their appearance of truth' (*leur allure de vérité*) is unclear, but certainly the puppet demonstrates that it has no need of the *outer* truth of external appearance in order to convince the spectator of the *inner*, spiritual truth. This of course presumes the ability of the artist to employ his perception and his art to trigger the spectator's power of association and imagination, or, in other words, to adopt the play as a projection of his *own* imagination. The spectator is placed in an active role, whereas in the theatre of illusion he is no more than a passive recipient. Extend this principle to costume, settings, sound, music, lighting, and you have a theatre of conscious convention in which the spectator is not distracted by any divergence from external reality because no attempt is made to sustain an illusion of it. In such a theatre the actor, if only he will surrender his precious personality for the sake of the total experience, can virtually become a puppet, but he will be compensated by acquiring the puppet's disturbing power. This was the role he came to assume in the theatre of Craig and Meyerhold after the turn of the century. But the crucial experiments began now in 1890, and it was the puppet and shadow theatres, not to mention the revival of mime, that pointed the way ahead.[11]

As Antoine's failure to stage *La Princesse Maleine* indicates, there was by 1891 a growing divergence between the Théâtre Libre's methods of staging, the style of acting it fostered, and what was intimated by the theories of the Symbolists. The need for a poets' theatre was clear, and the need was met eventually in 1893 by the foundation of the Théâtre de l'Œuvre. But before that various small amateur groups flourished briefly, of which the only one that needs to be considered is the Théâtre d'Art, founded by the seventeen-year old poet Paul Fort in 1890.* Like the Théâtre Libre, it was composed mainly of amateurs and gave occasional programmes, usually performed twice in whatever hall or theatre that could be secured. It was a precarious enterprise which produced ten programmes altogether in rather less than two years.

Paul Fort signalled his ambition in January 1891 with a performance of Shelley's unwieldy verse tragedy, *The Cenci*, first performed in London by the Shelley Society in 1886.[12] It was a ramshackle production which terminated in some disorder at two o'clock in the morning. Nothing daunted, Fort announced shortly afterwards in the press that henceforth 'under the patronage of the masters of the new school, Stéphane Mallarmé, Paul Verlaine, Jean Moréas, Henri de Régnier, Charles Morice', the

* Called initially 'Théâtre Mixte'.

Théâtre d'Art would become 'absolutely Symbolist'. Fort's claim was demonstrated convincingly two months later when in an evening of four plays plus the recital of a poem by Mallarmé he presented *The Girl with the Severed Hands*, 'a mystery in two tableaux' by Pierre Quillard. This static dialogue on the conflict between sensuality and chastity, in which 'the action takes place anywhere, preferably in the Middle Ages', was more a recitation punctuated with gestures and poses than a dramatic action. The characters on stage declaimed in melodious verse and at times sang in chorus. They were separated from the audience by a gauze and moved slowly and rhythmically in soft lighting against a backdrop of gleaming gold decorated with the stylised figures of angels and framed with red drapes. On the forestage there was a narrator in a long blue tunic standing at a lectern, who described in heightened prose the action, the locations, and the inner thoughts of the characters.[13]

Thus the sovereignty of the work was secured, leaving the spectator free to create his own pictures in his imagination. In Pierre Quillard's words, the theatre became what it was always meant to be, 'the pretext for a dream'. Quillard was a close adherent of Mallarmé, and it was Mallarmé that the audience hailed as the inspiration of the production. For the first time, Symbolism had been seen to have its effect in the theatre, opening up a new world before the poet, and calling the assumptions of the Naturalists into question. In May Pierre Quillard wrote a letter to *La Revue d'Art dramatique*, which was published under the heading 'On the absolute pointlessness of accurate staging'; in it he argued that 'Naturalism, that is to say the representation of a particular incident, a trivial and accidental document, is the very contradiction of theatre'. Far from creating illusion, he continued, naturalistic settings can only destroy it, because they merely inhibit the pictures that can be seen by the mind's eye. The stage must neither suggest nor describe the location of the action; instead, it must be 'a pure ornamental fiction that creates the illusion by virtue of the analogies with the drama suggested by the lines and colours'. The ruling principle of Symbolist theatre, Quillard concluded, was as old as the drama itself: the willing complicity and collaboration of the spectator in the play.[14]

In the same letter Quillard had enunciated the formula that Paul Fort was to adopt as his credo: 'The word creates the setting and everything else.' This was true enough, yet equally the contribution of the painter to the new theatre was to prove of vital importance. The much admired back-drop for *The Girl with Severed Hands* was the work of Paul Sérusier. As we have seen, it was in no way depictive but instead evocative through its colour, composition and imagery of an ideal spiritual world. It was around this time that the Symbolist Movement in painting, headed by Paul Gauguin, found literary spokesmen to interpret its work to a wider public, and the affinities with poetry became clear.[15] Hence, it was logical that an alliance should now be formed on the common ground of the theatre, and Sérusier was soon followed to the Théâtre d'Art by Bonnard, Denis, Ranson and others of the '*Nabis*' (or prophets), as they were called.

Like Sérusier's back-drop for *The Girl with Severed Hands*, their contributions were modest in scale and discreet in intention, partly because they shared his view of the theatre, and partly because of the extremely limited resources that Fort could command. Even so, their work with Fort, and more importantly later with Lugné-Poe, led directly to a transformation in the role and importance of the stage designer.

In May 1891 two special benefit matinees were arranged by Fort for Paul Verlaine and 'the splendid Symbolist painter' Gauguin. The lengthy programme consisted of four recited poems, and five one-act plays. The event aroused considerable critical interest, thanks mainly to the inclusion of Maeterlinck's one-act drama *The Intruder*; due to Antoine's failure to stage *La Princesse Maleine* it was the first production of the Belgian poet. The action of the play is set in a remote house with doors opening onto a garden. As night falls, the family gathers about the lamp with their eighty-year-old almost blind grandfather, awaiting the arrival of the father's sister, a nun. In neighbouring room the mother lies ill after a difficult childbirth. Through the open doors comes the sound of wind in the treetops, a carpenter sawing, the gardener sharpening his scythe, the nightingale's song, the leaves falling, the cool wind freshening. The family tries to ward off its fears with desultory conversation. The lamp flickers and dies; the clock's ticking marks the relentless passage of time; the old man senses the approach of some danger, the arrival of some uninvited guest. As the clock strikes midnight, the child cries out for the first time, the blackrobed sister appears in the doorway and makes the sign of the cross. The mother is dead. There is little dialogue and long pauses, with a constant pattern of muted sounds. This fragile piece is typical of Maeterlinck's theory of *la tragédie immobile*, which rejects what he calls '*le tragique des grandes aventures*' as superficial, arguing that the truly tragic is to be found in the simple fact of man's existence.* Reviews give no indication of how Paul Fort treated *The Intruder*, but his earlier production of Quillard's play and the orchestration of Maeterlinck's text give a good idea of how it might have been. In any event, it was the one unquestioned success of the programme, and the critical reception was favourable enough to indicate that the staging of Maeterlinck might not be so impossible as he himself had suggested. When the following season opened in December the programme included another of Maeterlinck's 'plays for puppets', *The Blind*, directed by Adolphe Retté and the young actor, Aurélien Lugné-Poe, who had played the Grandfather with great

* See p. 47-48 below.

success in *The Intruder*. He performed this time as well, taking the role of
one of the twelve blind people lost in a forest at night who are unaware
that their guide, an aged priest, has died in their midst.

This rather ponderous allegory seems to have produced a powerful
effect, despite complaints that little could be understood from the actors'
soft, unexpressive intoning and little was visible in the bluish semi-
darkness that shrouded the action. But as usual at the Théâtre d'Art, the
effect was marred by the sheer length of the programme and by the
inclusion of items that verged on the hilarious in their pretensions. On
this occasion, the last of the five items was a 'symphony of spiritual love
in eight mystic devices and three paraphrases' adapted by Paul-Napoléon
Roinard from eight chapters of Solomon's *Song of Songs*. Pursuing Baudelaire's doctrine of correspondences and Wagner's idea of an artistic
synthesis to their limits, Roinard had devised a scenario in which the
poetic dialogue was augmented by a complex orchestration of music,
colours and scents, one for each 'device'. The depleted audience, which
had stayed on until one o'clock in the morning for this event, lost patience
as it found itself enveloped by an increasing confusion of olfactory sti-
mulants, and finally the symbolists came to blows with their opponents.[16]
Surprisingly enough, the Théâtre d'Art survived this debacle and in February 1892 Fort presented the French premiere of Marlowe's *Doctor
Faustus* in a translation that was unanimously condemned and a production that exposed the paucity of his resources. On this occasion, the
evening terminated not far short of three o'clock with a clumsy recitation
of Rimbaud's great poem *Le Bateau ivre* that outraged the few spectators
who had stayed on to honour the memory of the poet who had died three
months earlier. At the end of March, after one further disaster, '*le théâtre
des poètes*' closed its doors for the last time.

Fort's productions were far too uneven to persuade Mallarmé and his
fellow Symbolists to entrust their fragile masterpieces to the theatre; with
few exceptions, they retreated to the safety of the printed page, and today
none of their works survive except as literary curiosities. But, as we have
seen, Fort's theatre broke the hold of Naturalism and caused a revolution
in stage design; it also led directly to the opening of the Théâtre de l'Œuvre,
the one French Symbolist theatre of real consequence. Born in 1869,
Aurélien Lugné-Poe established himself at an early age in the Paris avant-
garde theatre. While still at school in 1886, he helped found the amateur
Cercle des Escholiers, a serious enterprise which over the years introduced the new work of a wide variety of authors. Lugné-Poe then trained
as an actor at the Conservatoire and concurrently, between 1888
and 1891, appeared at the Théâtre Libre in a large number of small
parts, going on tour with the company to London and Brussels. In
1891 he made his debut at the Théâtre d'Art where his performances

in *The Intruder*, and *The Blind* helped him to win the confidence of Maeterlinck.

Lugné-Poe had already undertaken a number of productions for Les Escholiers, but none of them as demanding as Ibsen's *The Lady from the Sea*, which they performed on 16 December 1892. Choosing to emphasise the mysterious community that exists in the play between Ellida Wangel and the sea, and depicting her as a phantom in a long white robe, Lugné-Poe encouraged Georgette Camée, Paul Fort's leading actress, to employ the solemn movements and monotone delivery used for Maeterlinck at the Théâtre d'Art. As Ellida's husband, the down to earth, rational Doctor Wangel, he himself appeared grave, remote and entranced, the manner he was to assume for many of his roles in Ibsen and which earned him Jules Lemaitre's description 'the somnambulist clergyman'.[17]

As with most productions of this period, scarcely any precise details appeared in print, but it is certain that *The Lady from the Sea* was coherent enough to gain a sympathetic hearing for the symbolist view of Ibsen. A month after the performance the critic Henri de Régnier published an appraisal that precisely summarises that view:

> Ibsen has invented one thing which is unique to him: characterisation in depth. In his characters there are hidden eddies of the soul which suddenly flow into a vortex and reveal in their tortuous spiral the most secret dreams. That which is latent and unconfessed in them becomes apparent, and beyond the normal and superficial being we discover another laid bare, much more strange and much more true. The characters are like their own spectres.[18]

Jean Jullien, though well disposed towards Lugné-Poe, was less impressed by his approach. In his opinion, 'The play's interpreters were wrong in wishing to create an atmosphere of mystery around the characters with their hieratic gestures and lyrical intonation. True, it is an allegory – he said – but it is a living allegory; so let them be played as living people.'[19]

The difference between the two views is between a mystery that lies within the play beneath what is explicit, and which the multiple means of the theatre can convey to the audience, and a mystery that is superimposed on the play like a colour-wash in order to cloak the characters in an aura of Nordic romanticism, elucidating nothing and inferring more than may in fact be there. So whereas *The Lady from the Sea* offers grounds for interpreting Ellida and The Stranger, who returns to claim her, in the manner of Lugné-Poe's production, the whole point is lost if the 'real' world of Dr. Wangel is treated in the same way. Time and again, he fell into the same error, and it is interesting that years later both Meyerhold and Craig did the same.*

In 1893 there was talk of both the Théâtre d'Art and the Cercle des

* See pp. 87–88, 117–118 below.

Escholiers presenting Maeterlinck's recently published *Pelléas and Mélisande*. But Fort's credit was exhausted, and the Escholiers were daunted by the problems it posed; so eventually, Lugné-Poe staged it independently with the author's close collaboration. It was given a single matinee performance on 17 May. The tragedy of the innocent young couple kept apart by Mélisande's enforced marriage to Golaud, the ageing half-brother of Pelléas, is told in stylised prose and set in the familiar Maeterlinck landscape of an old castle hidden in the depths of a forest. The production was in the style now become familiar, with the characters moving and intoning as though in a dream. The settings were designed to evoke the world of the action in a sombre range of blues, green and greys, with two stylised backdrops representing the castle and the forest. The costumes were designed according to Maeterlinck's detailed instructions and based on the work of the fifteenth-century Flemish painter Hans Memling and the English illustrator Walter Crane. Altogether, the collaboration between Maeterlinck and Lugné-Poe was harmonious. Their correspondence shows clearly that however mystifying the drama may have seemed in performance, Maeterlinck's own understanding of his characters' behaviour was precise and psychologically coherent.[20]

The production was well enough received for Lugné-Poe to present it in Brussels the following month with the same cast and to revive it frequently in subsequent years. But although *Pelléas* led him directly to found the Théâtre de l'Œuvre with most of the same company, and although it remained in the repertoire, he was not truly satisfied with it and staged only one more play by Maeterlinck, the one-act tragedy *Intérieur* in 1895.* Alone amongst the dramatic works of French Symbolism, *Pelléas and Mélisande* survives in regular performance today; but it is in the form of the opera, completed ten years later by Claude Debussy, who was present at the original performance.

The Théâtre de l'Œuvre was founded in the Summer of 1893 by Lugné-Poe with the assistance of the painter Edouard Vuillard and the young poet and critic, Camille Mauclair. Lugné-Poe was specific in his Symbolist loyalty and the new venture was conceived, to quote Jacques Robichez, as 'a theatre of multiple resonances, a theatre where the greatest virtue of the actor will be to efface himself'.[22] Despite the participation of Vuillard, the artist's task was still to be the furnishing of discreet decorative backgrounds, on the principle that 'it is poverty that creates the true wealth: that of the spirit'.

However, a new aim was declared which indicated an important departure from Symbolist orthodoxy. It was, in Lugné-Poe's words, 'to stir up ideas', by which he meant using the stage to take issue with the

---

* Together with *Rosmersholm* and *The Master Builder* both productions were presented on tour in London in March 1895.[21]

forces of social and political conservatism. This principle was born as much of a desire to reach a wider audience as of any clear political belief; it showed the influence of Mauclair on Lugné-Poe, and was reflected particularly in their choice of foreign dramatists, who dominated the first season's repertoire. Announcing their plans, Lugné-Poe added '... and if the anticipated masterpiece from France materialises, it will close our first season'. Who would have guessed that the only French play he would ever stage that really did turn out to be a kind of masterpiece was the scandalous *Ubu Roi?**

The organisation of the Théâtre de l'Œuvre was similar to that of the earlier independent theatres. Productions were staged roughly at monthly intervals through the season, with a dress rehearsal and a single performance of each in whatever theatre was available, plus occasional brief tours abroad. Unlike the *Théâtre Libre* and the *Théâtre d'Art*, however, most of the programmes consisted of a single full-length play. In addition to Vuillard, Lugné-Poe was friendly with two other prominent artists of the *Nabis* group, Maurice Denis and Pierre Bonnard. In 1890 they lived together in a studio in the Rue Pigalle, and Lugné-Poe did much to publicise their work as well as that of Gauguin. A number of the group were now to design settings and lithographed programmes, notably Vuillard, Denis, Ranson and Sérusier. Whilst a number of the programmes survive,[23] there are no photographs of the settings and only one sketch (by Toulouse-Lautrec for the Indian play, *The Terra-cotta Cart*, 1895) – which is probably an accurate indication of the occasional nature of the artists' work as they saw it. Besides, as Robichez suggests, the fact that the critics made little comment on the settings in Lugné-Poe's productions seems to confirm that they were as non-specific as symbolist doctrine demanded. Speculating on their appearance, Robichez writes:

> ... it seems likely that the settings were painted in the same spirit as the lithographed programmes. On them, the words are like an extension of the drawing and they blend together in a mass with predominant shadows. Similarly, we can imagine the theatre's Scandinavian settings devoid of all clear-cut lines and all precise detail, bathed in a semi-darkness that obscures the surfaces, and first discloses and then swallows up the characters who emerge from its depths.[24]

In fact, after three or four years, Lugné-Poe did not even commission a new setting for every production, so that Ibsen would have been played each time against the same background, whatever the play. Beginning with *Rosmersholm* in October 1893, there were three productions of Ibsen in the opening season, plus works by his compatriot Björnson (*Beyond our Power I*), Hauptmann (*Lonely People*), and Strindberg (*Creditors*). On the occasion of the première of *The Master Builder* in April 1894,

* See Chapter Four.

Maeterlinck published a preview article in *Le Figaro* which later formed
the basis of his influential essay 'Everyday Tragedy' (1896):

> Hilda and Solness are, I believe, the first characters in drama who feel, for an
> instant, that they are living in an atmosphere of the soul; and the discovery of
> this essential life that exists in them, beyond the life of every day, comes fraught
> with terror ... Their conversation resembles nothing that we have ever heard,
> inasmuch as the poet has endeavoured to blend in one expression both the inner
> and the outer dialogue. A new and indescribable power dominates this som-
> nambulistic drama. All that is said therein at once hides and reveals the sources
> of an unknown life. And if we are bewildered at times, let us not forget that our
> soul often appears to our feeble eyes to be but the maddest of forces, and that
> there are in man many regions more fertile, more profound and more interesting
> than those of his reason and intelligence.[25]

This reading of *The Master Builder* seemed of more relevance to
Maeterlinck's own plays; it was angrily contested by many of Ibsen's
supporters, questioned by the Danish writer Herman Bang who acted as
Lugné-Poe's adviser, and dismissed by the playwright himself. However,
it did much to influence Lugné-Poe's production and all his subsequent
work. How did he set about revealing 'the essential life' of Ibsen's
characters? Evidently in much the same style as he had interpreted *The
Lady from the Sea* and *Pelléas and Mélisande*:

> ... by distancing himself as far as possible from reality, by lending every line,
> however banal, an undertone of mystery. These were phantoms moving about
> the stage (though as little as possible), whilst the real characters were in the
> wings. Few gestures, a flat and plaintive tone of voice, weak yet impressive.
> Beyond the dimmed footlights it was as though a man in a trance was apologising
> for being there and indicating to the audience that at the same time as he was
> speaking his lines another person elsewhere was speaking different lines that
> were far more interesting and significant.[26]

Lugné-Poe applied this method to the numerous major roles he played,
which in the first two seasons included Rosmer in *Rosmersholm*, Dr.
Stockman in *An Enemy of the People*, Solness in *The Master Builder*,
Allmers in *Little Eyolf*, Brand, Johannes Vockerat in Hauptmann's *Lonely
People* and Giovanni in Ford's *'Tis Pity She's a Whore*. His company was
part-professional, and frequently he hired actors from the regular theatre
to strengthen his cast. This made it impossible for him to develop a
uniform company style, even supposing he had been capable of it and the
actors had been willing, but accounts suggest that he was exceptional in
his manner of interpretation. As regards settings and costumes, the few
performances normally given of each play made 'poverty' as much a
matter of financial expediency as aesthetic principle. One of the extras in
An Enemy of the People recalls:

We wanted to produce the effect of a change of clothes. The only way open to us was to raise our coat collars, lower the brims of our hats, swap round our overcoats or even wear them inside-out. We tried to affect age by wrinkling our brows, hunching our backs, and assuming disillusioned scowls. Artificial though these metamorphoses were, the boss pronounced them satisfactory.[27]

From this description, it is not hard to see why Lugné-Poe preferred dim lighting. For his own Scandinavian roles, he invariably wore a long frock-coat, a stand-up collar, and a waistcoat buttoned to the chin. This was generally accepted as an authentic Norwegian fashion, and was even copied by the young Symbolists in their dress.

Faced with ludicrous details of this sort, one is tempted to doubt the validity of Lugné-Poe's whole enterprise. But the fact remains that in this first phase of its existence, the Théâtre de l'Œuvre functioned successfully for six seasons, undertook numerous foreign tours, and staged no fewer than nine of Ibsen's plays. What is more, two productions passed the scrutiny of Ibsen himself. During the company's first Scandinavian tour in October 1894 he attended performances of *Rosmersholm* and *The Master Builder* in Oslo. On *Rosmersholm* he made little comment, but was rather offended because in the last scene Ulrik Brendel's entrance was lit 'by electricity'. He said he did not want 'any stupid mysticism' in his plays. However, the performance of *The Master Builder* two nights later was a triumph. Since the play's publication in 1892 it had not received a successful production in Scandinavia, but now at last Ibsen was satisfied. Following the performance he said to Herman Bang: 'That was the resurrection of my play.' Subsequently, Ibsen persuaded the King of Norway to decorate Lugné-Poe with a gold medal, which according to him was pawned many times to help finance productions.[28]

During their first meeting, Lugné-Poe was deeply impressed by Ibsen's tactful but pointed remark that 'an author of passion must be played with passion and not otherwise'. 'In an instant, with one word – he recalls – Ibsen made us alter the whole character of our interpretation, which until then had been languid and rather sing-song.' To judge from Bernard Shaw's reaction, Ibsen's advice had certainly had its effect by the time the company appeared in London six months later. In *The Saturday Review* of 30 March 1895 he wrote 'M. Lugné-Poe succeeded because he recognised Solness as a person he had met a dozen times in ordinary life, and just reddened his nose and played him without preoccupation'.[29] Another London critic described his performance as 'violent and almost brutal in manner, jerky and hard in delivery, and curiously abrupt in demeanour', whilst Suzanne Depres' Hilda was a 'loud-voiced brazen girl, utterly unmysterious,' and a 'Hilda translated into everyday prose'.[30] When *John Gabriel Borkman* was given its French premiere in November 1897, the designs were executed by the Norwegian painter Edvard

Munch; their evocation of an authentic Nordic atmosphere seems to have set the tone for the whole production, and Lugné-Poe's restraint and stylistic control were generally praised. Revivals of earlier Ibsen productions that followed *Borkman* reflected a similar balance, and won the praise even of visiting Scandinavian critics. However, the revival of *An Enemy of the People* in February 1899 proved to be the last at the Théâtre de l'Œuvre, for that summer financial pressure forced Lugné-Poe to terminate its existence as an independent art theatre. Thereafter, as a more conventional theatre run on commercial lines, it continued to function for a further thirty years.

We have considered Lugné-Poe's productions of Maeterlinck and Ibsen, and the 1896 performances of *Ubu Roi* will be discussed in the next chapter. Besides these works, Lugné-Poe introduced to his audience a wide-ranging repertoire which included examples of Classical Sanskrit drama, Jacobean tragedy (*Tis Pity She's a Whore*, in a translation by Maeterlinck), Oscar Wilde's *Salomé*, Strindberg (*Creditors* and *The Father*, but curiously none of his symbolist works), Hauptmann, Gogol, and many more. But with Ibsen more than any other dramatist, he demonstrated how much more an actor can suggest than he actually says, and how little the stage needs to furnish for the spectator to picture a world in his imagination. Whatever absurdities his Symbolist doctrines and his limited resources may have led him to perpetrate, and even if he failed to create a single masterpiece, Lugné-Poe still succeeded in giving new significance to the ideas of style and convention, and this was to have far-reaching effects on the theatre at large.

4. Alfred Jarry

In 1893, around the time when Lugné-Poe and his friends were planning to launch the Théâtre de l'Œuvre, the rarefied atmosphere of Mallarmé's soirées in the Rue de Rome was stirred by the turbulent arrival of Alfred Jarry. Aged twenty and newly defaulted from the course in *rhétorique supérieure* at the exclusive Lycée Henri IV, he announced himself in Paris literary circles 'like a wild animal entering a ring'. His dwarfish bow-legged figure was soon a familiar sight at the weekly receptions held by the Symbolist journal *Le Mercure de France*, and in April 1893 the monthly review *L'Echo de Paris* awarded his fragment *Guignol* the prize for the best new piece of prose by a young author. Jarry added rapidly to his reputation with a succession of works in prose and verse, as well as co-publishing two finely produced art reviews which included a number of his own woodcuts. All these achievements were carried off with a mixture of adolescent tomfoolery, recondite erudition, and an undeniable sense of style. Not that Jarry owed any of these qualities to the forcing-house of Paris: he appears to have been endowed with them by the age of fifteen when he entered the Rennes *lycée* in his native Brittany. There he brought his anarchic talents to bear on Monsieur Hébert, a luckless pedant who struggled to teach him physics. Together with his elder brother, Charles, and a classmate, Henri Morin, Jarry composed a satirical playlet, *Les Polonais*, in which Hébert featured as 'le Père Ebé', king of an imaginary Poland, who was subjected to the most degrading indignities. The sketch was expanded into a play for marionettes and performed at the boys' homes in their 'Théâtre des Phynances'.[1] This and a second script were the prototypes for Jarry's *Ubu the King* and *Ubu the Cuckold*, in which 'le Père Ebé' was transformed into the definitive Père Ubu.

Once in Paris, Jarry devoted just as much energy to his outrageous private life as to his varied artistic activities. In his fine study of the period, *The Banquet Years*, Roger Shattuck suggests that with the death of Jarry's mother in 1893 the only stabilising force in his unruly existence was removed and he took a more or less conscious decision to retreat into a state of permanent adolescence in both his art and his life, obliterating the distinction between the two and demonstrating in his excesses an absolute disdain for survival, both social and biological. By degrees, and with the aid of absinthe and ether, he assumed the gross attributes of his creation, Ubu. By 1896 he had published six different fragments of the *Ubu* cycle; in the Spring of that year *Ubu the King* itself was published in Paul Fort's monthly review, *Livre d'Art*, and then in June in its final form as a book.

At the same time Jarry mounted a carefully planned campaign to get the Ubu plays staged at the Théâtre de l'Œuvre. He plied Lugné-Poe with copies of his published works, and succeeded in getting himself employed as his secretary and general factotum. Playing on Lugné's current enthusiasm for the Elizabethan theatre, he was careful to emphasise the Shakespearian elements in *Ubu the King*. Certainly, as its epigraph implies, there are evident parallels: for instance, Ma Ubu encourages her husband to assassinate King Wenceslas rather as Lady Macbeth urges Macbeth to slay Duncan; in Act Two Queen Rosamund begs Wenceslas not to attend the Grand Review, just as Calpurnia in *Julius Caesar* warns Caesar against going to the Senate; and Boggerlas is sworn to vengeance by the ghost of his Father, just as Hamlet is on the battlements of Elsinore.

But it is not so much the specific literary references in the play that matter, as the general lampooning of heroic attitudes and of the order they glorify. Here Jarry is true to the spirit of anarchic comedy, and indeed Ubu himself recalls both Pulcinella and the Capitano from the traditional *commedia dell'arte*, as well as their Shakespearian cousins Falstaff and Pistol. Moreover, he wields his various phynance hooks and physick sticks to the same knockabout effect as the bat of Harlequin and the club of Punch. This is not merely a scholarly question of genealogy. What Jarry was doing with *King Ubu* was restoring to the theatre the clown and his licence to confront the world with its own brutishness. The innocent physics teacher satirised by Jarry and his school-friends in their puppet plays had become inflated by degrees into what Maurice Nadeau has described as 'the bourgeois of his time and still more of ours, (who) coagulates in himself the cowardice, the ferocity, the cynicism, the disdain for the mind and its values, the onnipotence of *la gidouille* (the belly) ... the prototype of a class of tyrants and parasites, the extent of whose misdeeds Jarry, dead too soon, was unable to contemplate'.[2]

Commonly, laughter is thought to afford the audience a comforting sense of its own superiority over the characters on stage. But Jarry envisaged something quite different. After the first performance he wrote:

> I intended that when the curtain went up the scene should confront the public like the exaggerating mirror in the stories of Madame Leprince de Beaumont, in which the depraved saw themselves with dragons' bodies, or bulls' horns, or whatever corresponded to their particular vice. It is not surprising that the

public should have been aghast at the sight of its ignoble other self, which it has has never before been shown completely. This other self, as Monsieur Catulle Mendès has excellently said, is composed 'of eternal human imbecility, eternal lust, eternal gluttony, the vileness of instinct magnified into tyranny; of the sense of decency, the virtues, the patriotism and the ideals peculiar to those who have just eaten their fill.' Really, these are hardly the constituents for an amusing play, and the masks demonstrate that the comedy must at the most be the macabre comedy of an English clown, or of a Dance of Death. Before Gémier agreed to play the part, Lugné-Poe had learned Ubu's lines and wanted to rehearse the play as a *tragedy*. And what no one seems to have understood – it was made clear enough, though, and constantly recalled by Ma Ubu's continually repeated: 'What an idiotic man! . . . What a sorry imbecile!' – is that Ubu's speeches were not meant to be full of witticisms, as various little ubuists claimed, but of stupid remarks, uttered with all the authority of the Ape.[3]

As Jarry suggests here, Lugné-Poe had little idea of what he was taking on. But Jarry himself was quite clear; as early as January 1896 he set out his requirements in a letter to Lugné-Poe:

1) Mask for the principal character, Ubu; I could get this for you, if necessary. And, in any case, I believe that you yourself have been studying the whole question of masks in the theatre.
2) A cardboard horse's head which he would hang round his neck, as they did on the medieval English stage, for the only two equestrian scenes; all these details fit in with the mood of the play, since my intention was, in any case, to write a puppet play.
3) One single stage-set or, better still, a plain backdrop, thus avoiding the raising and dropping of the curtain during the single act. A formally dressed individual would walk on stage, just as he does in puppet show, and hang up a placard indicating where the next scene takes place. (By the way, I am absolutely convinced that a descriptive placard has far more 'suggestive' power than any stage scenery. No scenery, no array of walkers-on could really evoke 'the Polish Army marching across the Ukraine.')
4) The abolition of crowds which usually put on a terrible collective performance and are an insult to the intelligence. So, just a single soldier in the army parade scene, and just one in the scuffle when Ubu says 'What a slaughter, what a mob, etc . . .'
5) Choice of a special 'accent,' or, better still, a special 'voice' for the principal character.
6) Costumes divorced as far as possible from local colour or chronology (which will thus help to give the impression of something eternal): modern costumes, preferable, since the satire is modern, and shoddy ones, too, to make the play even more wretched and horrible.[4]

Once installed in the Théâtre de l'Œuvre, Jarry took over its publicity and made himself generally indispensable, bicycling the length and breadth of Paris to drum up subscriptions. The staging of *Ubu* became virtually a moral obligation for Lugné-Poe, despite his alarm at the mounting complexity of the enterprise. To represent the figures of the doomed nobles, magistrates and financiers in Act Three Jarry acquired forty life-size tailor's dummies, all in costume. Following the two scheduled performances, they had to be paid for and cluttered the theatre backstage for months afterwards. Then there was a life-size horse for Ubu and masks for all the main characters. On the other hand, the bear in Act Four was dropped, a plan to suspend the actors like puppets from wires was abandoned, and the grandiose orchestra was replaced by the composer Claude Terrasse and his wife at a single piano. The list of artists who had a hand in the decor makes imposing reading: Bonnard, Sérusier, Vuillard, Ranson, Toulouse-Lautrec, and Jarry himself. For the part of Ubu, the celebrated comedian, Firmin Gémier, was borrowed from the Odéon, whilst the perfect Ma Ubu was found in Louise France, an actress of formidable girth, celebrated for her unabashed portrayals of the sleaziest roles and for the repertoire of bawdy songs which she performed around the least reputable bistros and cabarets.

Less than a month before the performance Lugné-Poe was quailing at the prospect of what Jarry was preparing to unleash, but he was finally persuaded by the novelist, Mme. Rachilde, that a good scandal could do his theatre no harm, and indeed 'would furnish marvellous proof of his eclecticism'.[5]

The public dress-rehearsal took place at the Nouveau Théâtre on 9 December 1896 before a packed house of a thousand spectators; of them it is reckoned that not more than a hundred paid for their seats, the remainder being either critics or friends and hangers-on.[6] It was an initiated public, representative of all artistic factions and well primed for a scandal – remember that *Ubu* had already appeared twice in print, and that Jarry himself was a figure of some notoriety. Jarry, garishly made-up like a streetwalker, appeared before the curtain to read a ten-minute introductory address, inviting the audience to see in *Ubu* as many allusions as they pleased, ascribing the production's imperfections to its hasty preparation, and concluding 'the action which is about to start, takes place in Poland, that is to say Nowhere'.[7] The curtain parted to disclose a spectacle no less curious than that of Jarry himself; a somewhat bemused Arthur Symons wrote:

> ... the scenery was painted to represent, by a child's conventions, indoors and out of doors, and even the torrid, temperate, and arctic zones at once. Opposite you, at the back of the stage, you saw apple trees in bloom, under a blue sky, and against the sky a small closed window and a fireplace ... through the very midst of which ... trooped in and out the clamorous and sanguinary persons of the drama. On the left was painted a bed, and at the foot of the bed a bare tree and snow falling. On the right there were palm trees ... a door opened against the sky, and beside the door a skeleton dangled. A venerable gentleman in

evening dress . . . trotted across the stage on the points of his toes between every scene and hung the new placard on its nail.[8]

For all its scatology and provocations, the play was well enough received up to Act Three, when the umpteenth '*merdre*' (shite) drew the first protest from the audience. Breaking point was reached finally at the Fortifications of Thorn when one of the actors was made to simulate a castle-door opening. It was too much for Antoine, who rose from the stalls to voice his protest. Then for a full fifteen minutes the whole theatre was in an uproar and near to blows, both for and against the play. Gémier finally restored order by dancing a frenzied jig and collapsing exhausted across the prompter's box. The audience cheered and received the rest of the performance in relative peace. Contrary to most reports, it was on the second night that the very first '*merdre*' in Act One raised howls of protest, and by that time Gémier had equipped himself with a motor-horn to restore order.[9]

To the theatre historian, it seems almost too good to be true that Antoine, the champion of naturalism, should have initiated the demonstration against Jarry's wilful flouting of the laws of illusion. But eyewitness accounts in general tend to emphasise its *formal* eccentricities; we have seen how Arthur Symons was struck by the 'child's conventions' of the scenery and puzzled at 'the venerable gentlemen (who) trotted across the stage on the points of his toes between every scene and hung the new placard on its nail'. W. B. Yeats was similarly confused (the more for knowing little French), and in his *Autobiographies* wrote: 'The players are supposed to be dolls, toys, marionettes, and now they are all hopping like wooden frogs, and I can see for myself that the chief personage, who is some kind of king, carries for a sceptre a brush of the kind that we use to clean a closet.'[10] Yeats would probably have been even more mystified if Jarry had been able to carry out his original intention of attaching actual strings to the actors' bodies. As his production plan to Lugné-Poe demonstrates,[11] Jarry's intention was to explode illusion with every means at his disposal. Hence, although he was himself a great lover of puppets (recalling that the original version of *Ubu* was written for them), it was certainly not out of admiration for them that Jarry got his actors to simulate their jerky movements on the stage; rather, it was conceived as one further element of incongruity to confuse the audience. In other words, the scenario (without which the text alone is meaningless) was devised to confound every expectation that the audience might bring to the theatre. Whatever Jarry might have written about *Ubu* as a satire on bourgeois manners, he stood little chance of directly offending the moral sensibility of his highly sophisticated public. The only way to assail them was through their sense of *theatrical* propriety, and in that Jarry unquestionably succeeded. Yeats concludes his recollections:

> 'Feeling bound to support the most spirited party, we have shouted for the play, but that night at the Hotel Corneille I am very sad, for comedy, objectivity, has displayed its growing power once more. I say, after S. Mallarmé, after Verlaine, after G. Moreau, after Puvis de Chavannes, after our own verse, after the faint mixed tints of Conder, what more is possible? After us the Savage God.'

Yeats hardly needed to understand French to realise that an assault was being mounted on the audience's artistic taste. Jarry and the actors deployed lines, characters, settings and music to create a situation within the theatre that involved themselves and the audience in direct confrontation, rather than re-enacting, as the theatre of illusion invariably did, a situation presumed to have occurred in some other place at some other time. Ubu-Gémier-Jarry was using his lavatory brush to assail not so much the Palcontents on the stage as the public and critics in the theatre. He was launching the kind of frontal assault that up to then had been the exclusive right of the court-fool, the clown and the music-hall comic. The difference was that whereas they were licensed by convention and pardoned by laughter, Ubu fitted no convention, and, as Jarry pointed out, was not even meant to be funny.

Jarry had long been an habitué of the Théâtre de l'Œuvre; when he set about getting *Ubu* staged, he knew precisely what he wanted, and he was in deadly earnest. Already at the age of twenty-three he had adopted a persona and life-style that expressed total disdain for the customs of orthodox society. Judging the efforts of science, religion, and philosophy to impose order on an absurd universe as wholly inadequate, Jarry set out through his writings to create a system of unreason to match the illogic of existence as he observed it. This system, which Jarry called 'Pataphysics', was given its fullest exposition in *Exploits and Opinions of Doctor Faustroll Pataphysician*, completed in 1898 and published in 1911.[12]

Ubu the King, and for that matter Jarry's entire literary output, might be regarded as an elaborate intellectual hoax, were it not for the fact that they were the coherent expression of a philosophy that Jarry sustained in everything he did, to the point of eventual self-destruction at the age of thirty-four. Conversely, his life and works might be dismissed as marginal, the work of an eccentric or even a psychopath, were it not for the fact that the patterns they reveal adumbrate what may be regarded as *the* major movement in twentieth-century art up to now. When Apollinaire and the Surrealists 'rediscovered' Jarry around 1916, they acknowledged him as the forerunner of all the painters, composers and poets who rejected traditional forms as the false images of a universe demonstrably lacking both system and purpose, the movement that Apollinaire christened *'L'Esprit Nouveau'*. Since Baudelaire and Nietzsche, artists had been asserting their autonomy as the only true interpreters of existence, yet through their works they continued to seek an ultimate order or ruling intelligence, or else to create their own in terms of aesthetic beauty. It took Jarry to express the full implications of an irrational and destructive existence in a form that was equally irrational and destructive. This is really what Yeats meant when he predicted the advent of the 'Savage God'.

His mission accomplished, Jarry quickly made himself scarce from the Théâtre de l'Œuvre after the premiere of *Ubu*, and Lugné thankfully resumed his habitual course. In various forms and through his own person, Jarry continued to elaborate on his creation; but only twice more, both times as a puppet, did Ubu tread the stage again in his lifetime. In 1908, the year following his death, *Ubu the King* was revived briefly by Gémier, but otherwise the play was forgotten until Jarry's rediscovery, which culminated in 1927 with the opening of Artaud's Théâtre Alfred Jarry. Artaud, at least, was shrewd enough to avoid reverential revivals of the Ubu plays, preferring to stage Vitrac and others in the offensive spirit of Jarry; but in the past thirty years or so numerous would-be avant-garde theatres have sought to prove their daring by recruiting popular comedians and staging mildly updated versions in feeble attempts to reproduce the scandal of 1896.

In 1931 Lugné-Poe wrote with belated hindsight in his memoirs: 'If on that first night *Ubu* had been recognised as the revolutionary piece it was later found to be, many things in the theatre might have turned out differently. Where might we have been now?'[13] It is a parochial view: Lugné is right in suggesting that in the French theatre order and rationality long held the stage, undisturbed by Jarry; but elsewhere in Europe dramatists and directors had joined him in revolt, if not with quite the same violence and single-mindedness.

In Vienna, Arthur Schnitzler, whose first play *Anatol* was staged in 1891, frequently juggled with truth and illusion, reality and play, to disorientate his audience and manoeuvre them into adopting his ironic view of a corrupt society. Strindberg, beginning with his trilogy *To Damascus* (1898–1901), presents a bewildering sequence of subjective and ambiguous images, culminating in *The Ghost Sonata* (1907), in which he literally strips the facade from a solid naturalistic house to expose the hidden guilt of its inhabitants.

Most audacious theatrically was Frank Wedekind. Born in 1864 and schooled in the Munich cabarets, he wrote his first play as early as 1886, and *Spring Awakening*, his revolutionary drama about the adult repression of adolescent sexuality, in 1891. Considerably influenced by Georg

Büchner, Wedekind used a similar staccato sequence of short scenes, alternating savagely dramatic confrontations, bizarre portrayals of authority, tenderly lyrical love scenes, and passionate sexual encounters. With the difference that his aim was specifically moral, Wedekind like Jarry deployed style and form in order to disorientate his audience and shake them out of their preconceptions. By the time he died in 1918, Wedekind had written over twenty plays, all of them having as their central theme 'the elemental force of sex and its antagonism to a society hemmed in by hypocritical conventions'. Apart from *Spring Awakening*, this idea is most powerfully expressed in his two Lulu plays, *Earth-Spirit* (1895) and *Pandora's Box* (1902) in which, far from censuring his heroine's promiscuity, Wedekind celebrates her unswerving pursuit of her natural instincts. The Lulu plays were not staged in their entirety in public until after Wedekind's death: in fact, his entire career was punctuated by battles with the censor. However, in November 1906, fifteen years after its publication, *Spring Awakening* was given its first performance at Max Reinhardt's Kammerspiele in Berlin with Wedekind himself as The Man in the Mask, and it was played an unprecedented 321 times.*

It is no coincidence that all these dramatists either directed their own plays or worked in the closest collaboration with the director. Perceiving the universe and society as irrational and contradictory, they felt impelled to create works that were correspondingly irrational and contradictory in their forms, that stood the accepted conventions of theatre on their heads – and to achieve this they sought to exercise the closest possible control over the play in production, lest the theatre be tempted to impose its habitual symmetry on their calculated disorder. Whilst the established theatre continued to offer its reassuring pictures of the world, the New Spirit continued to find its exponents. After his experience of staging Blok's *The Fairground Booth* in 1906, Meyerhold defined it as 'the grotesque'.† As he acknowledged, both as a style and as a view of the world it was nothing new, being traceable in sculpture at least, back to the beginning of the Christian era in Rome.[14] But whereas the grotesque may apply to any art form, nowhere is its effect quite so powerful as in the theatre, because nowhere else has it quite the same scope for assailing and disorientating its audience face to face. It was this cardinal truth that Jarry grasped and demonstrated to literally riotous effect in December 1896.

* See p. 102 below.
† See p. 124 below.

5. Stanislavsky and Chekhov

Of all the independent theatres in Europe that sought to emulate Antoine's Théâtre Libre, none ever approached in fame or influence the Moscow Art Theatre. Founded in 1898, it functions to this day in two imposing theatres in the centre of Moscow, and is universally recognised as the progenitor of psychological realism on the modern stage.

When the Art Theatre opened the Russian stage was as moribund as any in Europe, despite the fact that in terms of stylistic invention and social relevance Russian dramatists were unsurpassed in the nineteenth century. The main reason for this was the existence until 1882 of a state monopoly that forbade the existence of any public theatres in Moscow and Petersburg save those few under the direct control of the Imperial Court. In effect, this meant that only the Maly Theatre in Moscow and the Alexandrinsky Theatre in Petersburg were regularly devoted to the performance of drama. Production, insofar as it existed at all, was a matter of discussion amongst the leading actors; the director was a mere functionary who supervised rehearsals; settings were never more than painted flats taken from stock, plus a few necessary pieces of furniture; costumes were chosen by the actors from their personal wardrobes. It was a situation akin to the rest of Europe, only far worse because there was absolutely no competition to stimulate innovation, and the imperial censor exercised his prerogative not only in the field of morals and politics, but in questions of artistic taste as well.

Following the abolition of the state monopoly, a number of commercial theatres came into being, but until 1898 no manager was prepared to risk anything more than was necessary to ensure full houses, and all experiments were left to amateur societies. The best-known of these was the drama group of the Moscow Society of Art and Literature which opened in 1888. One of its founders was Konstantin Stanislavsky, born in 1863 of a wealthy business family. Stanislavsky (his stage name - he was born Alekseyev) was a devoted and accomplished amateur actor who played major roles in all the Society's productions and from 1890 directed a large proportion of them. Interested in nothing but the theatre, he was quite prepared to help meet production costs out of his own pocket.

Inspired by the example of the Meiningen Theatre, whose work he observed closely during its second visit to Moscow in 1890, Stanislavsky became Russia's first stage-director in the true sense of the word. Slavishly following Ludwig Chronegk's autocratic methods,* he set unprecedented standards in ensemble discipline, scenic illusion, stage effects, and attention to detail. But for all his genius as an actor and as a director of actors, Stanislavsky was never to be the best judge of a play, and apart from his few experiments with Symbolism in the years following 1905, his tendency was to treat every text in terms of literal representation.

In the summer of 1897 Stanislavsky met Vladimir Nemirovich-Danchenko, critic, novelist, and highly successful writer of social dramas, who taught acting at the drama school of the Moscow Philharmonic Society. Deeply concerned at the state of the Russian theatre, Nemirovich approached Stanislavsky with a view to creating a theatre independent of entrepreneurs and state bureaucrats. The two met on 22 June 1897 and talked non-stop from lunch until breakfast the next morning, a total of eighteen hours. In that time they drew up detailed plans for what was to become the Moscow Art Theatre.[1] In brief, the main principles were:

1. Overall policy and organisation to be determined by the needs of the play-text and the actors.
2. Each production to have specially designed settings, properties and costumes.
3. The performance to be treated as an artistic experience, not a social occasion – applause of entrances and exits to be discouraged.

Initially the company was called the Moscow *Popular* (literally 'generally accessible') Art Theatre, in order to reflect the policy of keeping a high proportion of seats at low prices and so to encourage the attendance of a wide audience. In his opening address to the company in 1898 Stanislavsky said:

What we are undertaking is not a simple private affair but a social task. Never forget that we are striving to brighten the dark existence of the poor classes, to give them minutes of happiness and aesthetic uplift to relieve the murk which envelops them. Our aim is to create the first intelligent, moral open theatre, and to this end we are dedicating our lives.[2]

Pious sounding words perhaps, but less than forty years had elapsed since the abolition of serfdom, and in that time little or nothing had been done to improve the spiritual and material conditions of the workers and peasants in Russia. In fact, the Art Theatre kept faith with its liberal and democratic principles, and never courted a coterie public as most other art theatres in Europe tended to do. On the other hand, it avoided any

* See p. 13 above.

overt political commitment, to the extent even of staging no Soviet plays until eight years after the October Revolution.

Thanks to the support of a number of philanthropic patrons (Stanislavsky himself included), the Moscow Art Theatre had a firm financial basis and a rented home at the ramshackle Hermitage Theatre. However, it remained a hazardous enterprise. The young and inexperienced company, most of them either ex-students of Nemirovich-Danchenko or recruited from the Society of Art and Literarature, numbered no fewer than thirty-nine. Furthermore, they were committed to a five-month season of a mere nine productions running in repertoire, whereas other Moscow theatres were offering a different play every few days. As things turned out, the company survived financially thanks partly to further donations and partly to the success of its first production, Count Alexei Tolstoy's historical drama *Tsar Fyodor Ivanovich*, written in 1875 but only now released by the censor for public performance. It opened on 14 October 1898.

When Stanislavsky had staged *Othello* at the Society of Art and Literature in 1896 he had shown how far he was indebted to Meiningen principles by going to Venice in order to sketch costumes from frescoes and to purchase authentic furniture, weapons and brocades. A similar approach was now adopted to the production of *Tsar Fyodor Ivanovich*, but in addition it was given no fewer than seventy-four rehearsals. It also had in Victor Simov a naturalistic designer of outstanding talent.

The role of Simov in the evolution of the Art Theatre's style was crucial. From 1898 to 1906 he was responsible for every one of the company's productions, and in the years following designed many more, right up to his death in 1935. In every case he worked on an equal footing with the director from the earliest stage of the production. He did much to advance the conception of the stage setting as a lived-in space, following the Meiningen example by employing diagonals and varied levels.

When he and Stanislavsky started work on *Tsar Fyodor*, they began by steeping themselves in all available documentary and pictorial sources; next they organised expeditions to the ancient cities of Rostov, Nizhny Novgorod and Kazan in order to absorb the atmosphere of sixteenth-century Russia, to make sketches, and to collect authentic furs, gowns and assorted bric-a-brac. It was to become the company's regular practice: they explored the Tula Province before *The Power of Darkness*, Rome before *Julius Caesar*, and the Moscow doss-houses before *The Lower Depths*.

In other respects, the Art Theatre differed significantly from the Meininger. The work with individual actors was certainly far more painstaking, and the company could draw on a far greater depth of talent. What is more, it had in Nemirovich-Danchenko a literary manager of exceptional sensibility. Even so, in the early days at least, there was a strong tendency to camouflage the inexperience of the young company by over-attention to surface detail, a tendency emphasised by Stanislavsky's naive fascination with the many effects of illusion that advances in stage technology and Simov's ingenuity brought within his reach. However, the level of naturalism achieved at the Art Theatre was a revelation to the Moscow public and did much to establish its early reputation; it was certainly no coincidence that *Tsar Fyodor Ivanovich*, no great play but the one visually spectacular production in the opening season, was easily the greatest popular success.

If *Tsar Fyodor* secured the Art Theatre a public, it was *The Seagull* which enabled the company to find its identity. Nemirovich-Danchenko, who had known Chekhov for some years and was convinced that *The Seagull* had been totally misinterpreted at its disastrous premiere in Petersburg two years earlier,[3] managed to persuade him that his play was vital to the success of the new company. Those actors who were former students of Nemirovich shared his enthusiasm for *The Seagull*; they included Vsevolod Meyerhold, who was to play the aspiring young writer Konstantin Treplev, and Olga Knipper, Konstantin's actress-mother Arkadina in the production, who three years later was to become Chekhov's wife.

Stanislavsky directed the play, with Nemirovich taking a share of the rehearsals. He and Chekhov had met before and had not got on well together. Now Stanislavsky could make little of *The Seagull*; its lack of external drama was remote from his theatrical instinct and, as Maurice Valency has suggested, being himself a member of the merchant class, Stanislavsky:

> ... had no intimate knowledge of the provincial gentry, or the country environment which furnished the background of most of Chekhov's plays. The petty quarrels, the atmosphere of indolence and boredom, the economic exigencies and social amenities of provincial life were alien to his experience, and had to be reconstructed imaginatively. The sense of the mystery of familiar things, the feeling of the supernatural in nature, all the wonder and poetry of the countryside to which Chekhov instinctively responded were quite foreign to his city-bred director.[4]

What Stanislavsky did come to perceive as he studied *The Seagull* before starting rehearsals was that there was a 'sub-text', an inner action concealed beneath its largely uneventful surface. Chekhov himself had said, echoing Maeterlinck, 'Let us be just as complex and as simple as life itself. People dine and at the same time their happiness is made or their lives are broken.'[5] Unconfident of his novice company and encouraged by Chronegk's despotic example, Stanislavsky withdrew for some weeks from Moscow and in seclusion devised a complete *mise-en-scène*, which was intended to convey the play's sub-text. Every detail of the production was prescribed, including the actors' every move, gesture, and vocal inflection. His instructions, many of them illustrated by sketches on his prompt copy, extended even to sound-effects, make-up, costumes and props.[6] A striking example of Stanislavsky's interpretation is the conclusion of Act One. In Chekhov's text we read:

MASHA. I'm so unhappy. No one, no one knows how unhappy I am. (*Lays her head on his breast, softly*) I love Konstantin.

DORN. What a state everyone's in! What a state! And what a lot of love! ... Oh, you magic lake! (*Tenderly*) But what can I do, my child? Tell me, what can I do? What?

CURTAIN

Compare Stanislavsky's prompt-book:

DORN. ... But what can I do, my child? Tell me, what can I do? What? (MASHA *bursts into sobs and, kneeling, buries her head on* DORN'S *knees. A pause of fifteen seconds.* DORN *is stroking* MASHA'S *head. The frenzied waltz* [from the piano in the house] *grows louder, sounds of the tolling of a church-bell, of a peasant's song, of frogs, of a corncrake, the knocking of the night-watchman, and all sorts of other nocturnal sound-effects.*)

Similarly, Stanislavsky mobilised all the theatre's resources to establish the desired mood at the beginning of each act. For instance, at the play's opening near the lake in the park, Chekhov's direction reads: 'The sun has just gone down. Yakov and some other men are working on the stage behind the curtain; they can be heard hammering and coughing.' In the prompt-book we find 'The play opens in darkness, an evening in August. The dim light of a lantern on the top of a lamp post, the distant sounds of a drunkard's song, the distant howling of a dog, the croaking of frogs, the crake of the landrail, the slow tolling of a distant church-bell - assist the spectator to appreciate the sad monotony of the life of the characters. Summer lightning, the faint sound of distant thunder.'

Nemirovich was most impressed with Stanislavsky's *mise-en-scène*, but how close was it to what Chekhov himself had envisaged? As early as 1886 he had written to his brother Alexander '... you can put across a moonlit night by writing that a fragment of broken bottle gleamed like a bright star against a mill-dam; and that the black shadow of a dog or a wolf flashed past.' A very similar image is used by Konstantin in Act Four of *The Seagull* immediately before Nina's return, when he is comparing Trigorin's literary style with his own. In both cases the reference is to short-story writing, and Chekhov's own work in that genre abounds in examples of laconic imagery employed to convey atmosphere or states of mind. But equally Chekhov conceived his plays, and importantly his stage-directions, in the same impressionistic manner. Meyerhold recalls

Chekhov attending an early rehearsal of *The Seagull*; apprehensive at the promise of croaking frogs, humming dragon-flies, barking dogs and crying children, he emphasised the precise selectivity of his imagery, and concluded 'the stage reflects the quintessence of life and there is no need to introduce anything superfluous on to it'.[7]

The production was painstakingly rehearsed for a total of eighty hours followed by three dress-rehearsals, which was an unprecedented time for such a small-cast play. Stanislavsky's directions were followed to the letter, so that even personal idiosyncrasies such as Medvedenko's continual smoking, Masha's smacking of her lips when eating, Dorn's repeated quiet whistling of the same tune, were dictated not by the actor's conception of the part but by the director's master-plan.

Simov's close collaboration with Stanislavsky and Nemirovich ensured that there was a complete unity of purpose in the production's external aspects, and the designer was familiar enough with Chekhov's world to appreciate the atmosphere of down-at-heel gentility that the interior settings needed to convey. The setting for the first two acts in the park (for economy's sake it was used for both) posed a more difficult problem; so powerful is Chekhov's lyrical evocation of the moonlit lake after the close of Treplev's play that no literal depiction of it could possibly match the poetry of the words and sound-effects. Simov did his best with a half-lit tracery of foliage and irregularly placed tree-trunks, but still the setting tended to detract from the illusion, rather than enhance it; the imagination was denied the vision of 'its' lake. In Act Two, with the necessary effect of full daylight, the illusion declined still further. Simov was not helped by the cramped stage of the Hermitage Theatre and limited workshop resources, but ironically, when the play was revived in 1905 in the company's new, fully-equipped theatre, the setting was constructed in much more complete detail and the vital air of mystery dispelled totally.[8]

For all the production's imperfections, the premiere of *The Seagull* on 17 December 1898 was an historic event, commemorated to this day by the seagull emblem which the Art Theatre bears. What were the reasons for its success? Firstly, the audience had never seen everyday life conveyed with such fidelity and delicacy; secondly, the level of intimate ensemble playing was unprecedented; thirdly, and perhaps most important, the mood of the production corresponded precisely to the despondent uncertainty that affected the Russian intelligentsia of the period, but which, incidentally, Chekhov himself neither shared nor intended to convey in *The Seagull*.

He could not be present at the opening night, having been ordered by his doctor to winter in the Crimea, but when he saw the production for the first time the following spring at a private performance hastily

1. *Julius Caesar* (Saxe-Meiningen, 1874)

2. *En famille* (Théâtre Libre, 1887)

3. Programme design by Edouard Vuillard for *An Enemy of the People*
(Théâtre de l'Œuvre, 1893)

4. Poster design by Jarry for *Ubu the King* (Théâtre de l'Œuvre, 1896)

arranged for his benefit, he was not impressed: the hysterical interpretation of Nina appalled him, and he said that Stanislavsky played Trigorin
'like a paralytic ... without any will of his own' and 'needed an injection
of sperm'. However, in a letter to Gorky he did concede that 'On the
whole, the play was not bad, and it gripped me. In places, I could hardly
believe it was I that had written it.' [9]

After the first-night ovations and the enthusiastic notices that followed,
The Seagull was only moderately successful with the public; by the
summer it had been staged only nineteen times, compared with the fifty-
seven performance of *Tsar Fyodor*, and over the next three seasons it was
never given more than thirteen times. When revived in 1905, it received
eleven performances, but was then dropped for good. In fairness, it should
be said that in Russia, at least, it has never been the most successful of
Chekhov's plays, and it was not until 1960 that the Moscow Art Theatre
attempted a new production of it.

The play's true success in 1898 was for the company itself; it gave them
a sense of their own identity, a corporate style which, though still tentative,
held infinite promise. Variously defined by Stanislavsky and others, this
style came down to a rejection of theatrical stereotypes and naturalistic
approximations in favour of a corporate search for the inner psychological
truth of the character's behaviour, directed towards the revelation of that
truth through all the available means of the production. Gradually, this
yielded a seemingly effortless realism in performance, a perfect illusion of
life in progress; but the danger remained that for all the perception of
behavioural detail, the playwright's overall design, what he was saying
through the medium of his characters' actions, could easily be overlooked.

The following season the Art Theatre staged *Uncle Vanya*, Chekhov's
third major play, which he had completed in 1897 and which had already
been staged widely in the provinces with considerable success. The play
is aptly sub-titled 'Scenes from Country Life', for there is throughout a
strong emphasis on such apparent trivialities as the old nurse Marina
knitting, Vanya's mother annotating her magazines, Telegin strumming
the guitar, the Watchman tapping his stick to scare off intruders, and so
on. But far from being mere genre detail designed to evoke a general
mood of rural torpor, these actions invariably point or undercut the inner
drama. And where Chekhov does create moments of dramatic tension in
the orthodox manner, such as the abortive shooting of the Professor, or
Vanya surprising Astrov and Yelena in an embrace, he is careful to stress
their essential absurdity. The contrast with *The Seagull* is striking, for in
that play, despite its muted tone, the confrontations are much more
conventionally 'dramatic' in their conception.

It is not surprising then that the Art Theatre found it easier to capture
the rhythm of everyday life in their production of *Uncle Vanya*, for it is

delineated so much more clearly in the text. After the first dress-rehearsal, Meyerhold, who this time was not cast in the play, wrote to Chekhov:

> The play has been produced amazingly well. Above all, I would single out the artistic restraint of the production as a whole, which is maintained from start to finish. For the first time the two directors have achieved perfect accord: the one, an actor-director of great imagination, albeit prone to a certain unevenness in his productions; the other, a literary director who watches over the interests of the author. And it seems clear that the former is dominated by the latter. The setting does not obscure the picture. Not only is the content of the picture scrupulously preserved, that is, not buried beneath superfluous external details, but by some cunning means it is actually enhanced.[10]

But again, Stanislavsky tended to miss the significance of Chekhov's carefully planted details. At one rehearsal it was suggested that Vanya should be played as an unkempt landowner in muddy boots and a peasant shirt. In his memoirs, Stanislavsky recalls Chekhov's reaction: 'Listen, that's quite impossible. Haven't I written that he wears fine ties? *Fine* ties! Don't you understand that landowners dress better than we do?' And Stanislavsky continues, 'It wasn't just a matter of the tie, but of the whole central idea of the play. The gifted Astrov and the poetically sensitive Uncle Vanya are stagnating in the back of beyond, whilst this dolt of a professor lives in seventh heaven in St. Petersburg, and with others of his kind lords it over Russia.'[11]

They still had difficulty with the subtlety of Chekhov's irony and his tendency to play against conventional dramatic expectations. During rehearsals, Olga Knipper, playing Yelena, felt that Stanislavsky as Astrov was misinterpreting their final scene together in Act Four, and wrote to Chekhov for advice. He replied:

> At your command I hasten to answer your letter ... You write that Astrov behaves to Yelena like a man passionately in love, clutching at his feeling like a drowning man at a straw. But that's not right, not right at all! Astrov likes Yelena, she attracts him by her beauty, but in the last act he knows that nothing will ever come of it, that Yelena is disappearing for ever, and he talks to her in that scene in the same tone as he mentions the heat in Africa, and kisses her quite casually, to pass the time. If Astrov takes that scene violently, the whole mood of the fourth act - quiet and despondent - will be ruined.[12]

Similarly, when eventually he saw the production on tour in Sevastopol and Yalta the following spring, Chekhov objected to the conclusion of Act Three, in which Sonya sank to her knees on the line 'Father, you must try and understand', and kissed the Professor's hands. 'You mustn't do it that way' - he told them - 'After all, it's not a drama. The whole meaning and the whole drama in a person's life is located inside, not in externals. There has been drama in Sonya's life before this moment, and it will resume afterwards; but this is merely an incident, like the shooting.'[13]

However, despite such reservations, Chekhov was satisfied with the production – satisfied enough to abandon his previous doubts concerning his metier as a dramatist and to address himself shortly to a new play, written this time specially for the Moscow Art Theatre.

Meanwhile, after an enthusiastic first night reception, *Uncle Vanya* encountered a mixed response from both public and critics. Many were slow to recognise Chekhov's innovations and found the production wanting by accepted theatrical standards. Eventually, though, it established itself in the company's repertoire and in the end far outstripped *The Seagull* in popularity. For all Chekhov's reservations about Stanislavsky as an actor, he grew into the part of Astrov, and came in time to be regarded as his very incarnation.

By the time the Art Theatre presented *Three Sisters* in January 1901 the company was well-established, with substantially the same actors that had come together in 1898, and with some fifteen productions to its name, including works by Ostrovsky, Hauptmann and Ibsen, as well as Chekhov and Alexei Tolstoy. However, *Three Sisters* was the first play Chekhov had written especially for the Art Theatre, and a number of the roles were conceived by him with particular actors in mind, including Vershinin for Stanislavsky and Masha for Olga Knipper. Even so, he suffered his usual misgivings and dallied nervously over the final draft; in September 1900, he wrote to Olga Knipper from Nice: 'Four responsible female parts, four educated young women; I can't leave them to Stanislavsky, with all my respect for his talent and understanding! I must have at least a peep at the rehearsals.' Similarly he warned Olga against playing Masha too unhappily, because 'people who have long been unhappy, and grown used to it, don't get beyond whistling and are often wrapped up in their thoughts'.[14]

By the time Chekhov returned to Moscow in October he had given up all hope of completing *Three Sisters* for the current season, but the Art Theatre insisted, and at the end of the month there was a first read-through of his rough draft. It left the company nonplussed at Chekhov's insistence on treating the play as a comedy, and the author equally angry at their lack of understanding. Whilst the company wrestled with the text, Chekhov continually revised it, and by the time he returned to Nice in December, Acts Three and Four were still uncompleted. They finally reached Moscow some five weeks before the premiere. Reluctant to surrender all control to Stanislavsky, Chekhov nominated in his absence a certain Colonel Petrov to act as military consultant on the production; he was most anxious that there should be nothing caricatured about the army officers in the play, since he visualised them as cultural missionaries in the remote garrison town. Apparently, the Colonel was scrupulous in his correction of the actors' deportment, whilst finding Colonel Vershinin's seduction of a married woman distinctly unprofessional! Despite

their uneasy relations, Stanislavsky now had the experience of two seasons
playing Chekhov behind him, and his company was far more experienced.
In consequence, he approached *Three Sisters* with greater confidence than
before, even though for most of the time he lacked the collaboration of
Nemirovich, who was abroad. But partly due to the pressure of time, he
once again prepared a detailed scenario, which left relatively little to the
actors' own creative initiative. Meyerhold, who played Baron Tusenbach,
recalls the anguish of being required to rehearse the same move over and
over without any indication from the director as to its motivation.

As rehearsals wore on, the play refused stubbornly to come to life; for
all the ingenious interpretation of its separate components, it seemed to
lack overall meaning. To use the terms that Stanislavsky was later to
define in his 'System', he had failed to grasp the play's 'ruling idea', which
would give each actor the key to the 'through action' of his part. In *My
Life in Art* he describes the incident at rehearsal which revealed the ruling
idea in *Three Sisters*:

> Two or three electric lamps were burning dimly. The stage was in semi-
> darkness. I felt that our position was hopeless. My heart was beating fast.
> Someone began scratching the bench on which he was sitting with his nails and
> the sound of it was like the scratching of a mouse. For some reason it made me
> think of a family hearth; I felt a warm glow all over me; I sensed truth and life,
> and my intuition began to work. It is of course also possible that the sound of
> the scratching mouse combined with the darkness and the helplessness of my
> position had been of some significance in my life before and that I had forgotten
> about it. Who can say what the ways of the subconscious mind are? Be that as
> it may, I suddenly *felt* the scene we were rehearsing. I felt at home on the stage.
> The Chekhov characters came to life. Apparently they were not all wallowing
> in their depression, but were longing for gaiety and laughter. I sensed the truth
> of such an attitude towards the Chekhov characters, and that filled me with
> courage and I realised intuitively what had to be done.[15]

Whatever one thinks about the interpretation of *Three Sisters* that this
implies, the important fact remains that Stanislavsky had grasped the
existence of an emotional sub-text in Chekhov, which might determine
the emphasis on particular detail.

However, this did not mean that Stanislavsky now limited himself to
the letter of Chekhov's stage directions. His prompt book shows that he
built up a complex scenario to express the struggle between the quest for
happiness and the all-enveloping threat of petit-bourgeois philistinism.
Thus, in contrast to the dominant mood of celebration and optimism in
Act One, here is the opening of Act Two:

> It is dark in the living room; the fire in the stove is going out, only a streak of
> light falls from the open door leading to Andrei's room. From time to time

Andrei's shadow flickers in this streak of light; he is walking up and down in his room, recalling his lectures. One can hear Andrei's footsteps as well as the sound of conversation, the monotonous undertone, occasional coughing, sighs, blowing of the nose, the shifting of a chair. Everything falls silent; he stops at his table and leafs through a notebook (the rustle of pages). Perhaps a sound hinting at tears, and once again a blowing of the nose, steps, a low murmuring, and his shadow on the stage. The lamp is about to go out in the dining room; it flares up, then again begins to die out. The windows are frozen over. Snow on the roof. Outside it is snowing. A storm. The piano has been moved and it obstructs the bay window ... The appointment of the room is in Natasha's taste ... A child's blanket, baby sheets, cushions, swaddling bands, and the like are strewn over the sofa. On the table next to the sofa are toys: a little barrel-organ (with a squeaky sound), a harlequin clapping cymbals together. On the floor next to the piano – a large rug; on it are cushions from the sofa, toys – a child's harmonica, a top, a little wagon. On the piano are pieces of material, scissors, a towel.[16]

If this seems an over-literal extension of what is in any case clear in the opening dialogue between Natasha and Andrei, the use to which Stanislavsky later put the toys in order to point the same antithesis between dream and reality was rather more subtle: later in the act, just before Chebutykin's entrance, as Irena began again to talk wistfully of Moscow he made Vershinin play idly with the harlequin, unconsciously undercutting her words with the flat noise of its cymbals; just afterwards, when Vershinin began to philosophise about life in two or three hundred years, his thoughts were punctuated by the squeaks of the barrel-organ being turned by Tusenbach.

In Act Four, Andrei leaves the sisters in the garden to deal with the papers Ferapont has brought and to face the loathsome menage of Natasha, her vulgar lover Protopopov and the pampered Bobik. On Natasha's line 'Say Hullo, Auntie Olia' Stanislavsky interpolated deep bass laughter (obviously the unseen Protopopov's), and the sound of a child playing with a ball which bounced into the garden for a nurse to retrieve. He even contemplated introducing Protopopov in person for a brief moment to pick up the ball:

This would be a marvellous role. Just imagine: suddenly a fat man with a cigar between his teeth would unexpectedly leap from the balcony: he would run after the ball, bending over several times since he could not catch it at once. Then he disappears forever with the ball.[17]

Thus he intended the painful atmosphere of leavetaking which pervades the act to be momentarily disrupted by the intrusion of ponderous hilarity.

In the event, Protopopov remained unseen, but there seems no doubt that in places Stanislavsky upset the play's delicate balance by compulsive over-production. Towards the end of Act Three, Chekhov's stage direction reads 'Natasha, carrying a candle, enters through the door right, crosses the stage, and exits through the door, left, without saying anything.' Stanislavsky proposed a number of intrusions by Natasha, slamming doors, extinguishing lights, and looking for burglars under the furniture. Chekhov wrote to restrain him 'Better if she crosses the stage, in a straight line, without looking at anybody or anything, *à la* Lady Macbeth, with a candle – this would be simpler and more terrible.[18]

During rehearsals, Stanislavsky wisely cut a procession bearing Tusenbach's corpse across the background at the end of the play (which even Chekhov had included in the play's first draft), fearing that it would disrupt the final mood of reconciliation evoked by the sisters. However, consider his treatment of Irena and Tusenbach's leavetaking before the duel:

> The music comes closer. Violin and harp. Tusenbach caresses Irena, smooths her hair, wraps her more warmly in her shawl, kisses all the fingers of her hand. Irena is tense, does not take her eyes off Tusenbach. He pats her on the head. She presses more closely to him. Tusenbach: 'I'm happy' – he becomes much more cheerful, inspirited, livelier. 'It's time for me to go now' – quickly kisses her hand, leaves, takes hold of the gate handle, opens the gate. Irena runs after him with an anxious glance, grabs him by the hand and holds him back. Tusenbach makes an effort to smile. Irena embraces him and nestles close to him. Tusenbach pensively looks off towards the garden.[19]

This is not merely superfluous; it actually blurs the sense one gets from Chekhov's lines of Irena's incapacity to return Tusenbach's love.

But if Stanislavsky's interpretation of the action was still uncertain, the settings which Simov designed in close collaboration with him were far more expressive and integral to the play's structure than anything they had previously achieved; they were perhaps the earliest example of naturalism used in a poetic, metaphorical manner. The basic aim was to establish the provincial ethos in which, to quote Simov, 'colours fade, thoughts become debased, energy gets smothered in a dressing-gown, ardour is stifled by a house-coat, talent dries up like a plant without water'.[20]

For the first three acts Simov constructed not single rooms but a complete section of the Prozorovs' flat: in Act One the sitting room was joined upstage to a small dining room by an archway, glass doors gave onto a landing with a staircase leading down to Chebutykin's quarters, whilst a further door opened onto a terrace. With the comings and goings of the various guests, this created an atmosphere of airiness and animation. In Act Two the terrace was closed off with shutters, a stove was lit on the landing, and the whole setting seemed enclosed; the atmosphere was one of provincial cosiness and rather limited taste – appropriate enough to a town which Chekhov imagined to be some eight-hundred miles to the

East of Moscow. The culminating image came in Act Four with a setting that disregarded Chekhov's specific directions, yet afforded a powerful sense of the sisters' virtual eviction by Natasha and their desolation at the departure of the garrison. The audience saw the entire left-hand side of the stage taken up with the bulk of the house, seen end-on to a street which ran along the setting line. Next to it was a lamp-post with a low wooden fence enclosing the garden where yellowing leaves fell from the birch trees. In the closing scene, the sisters huddled together against the lamp-post behind the fence, dwarfed and excluded by the house which had once contained all their hopes.

Three Sisters remains perhaps Chekhov's most enigmatic play, and the first-night audience on 31 January 1901 became progressively puzzled from one act to the next, receiving the final curtain in near silence. In time, however, it became one of the theatre's greatest successes and remained in the repertoire right up to 1940. Chekhov eventually saw it in September 1901 and wrote: '*Three Sisters* is going splendidly, brilliantly, and much better than the play is written. I've done a little producing, exercising my author's influence on one or two of them, and now it's said to be going better than last season.'[21]

In October 1903 Chekhov despatched the long and eagerly awaited final draft of *The Cherry Orchard*. Stanislavsky replied by telegram 'JUST READ PLAY SHAKEN CANNOT COME TO SENSES IN UNPRECEDENTED ECSTASY – – – SINCERELY CONGRATULATE AUTHOR GENIUS.' Chekhov feared the worst, and proceeded to despatch a series of detailed and illuminating instructions to the company on the casting and interpretation of the roles in the play.[22] When he came to Moscow in December he spent almost every day at the play's final six weeks' rehearsals.

The last collaboration between Chekhov and Stanislavsky was far from harmonious; Nemirovich remained in the background and declined to mediate, having himself fallen out with Stanislavsky over a variety of issues, principally the division of directorial responsibility within the theatre. Chekhov was not able to persuade Stanislavsky to his view of *The Cherry Orchard* as 'a comedy, at times almost a farce'. Stanislavsky felt far too deeply the pathos of the old order passing, and argued 'it is a tragedy, no matter what solution you may have found in the second act for a better life'. Chekhov riposted that there were no tearful people in the play. 'Where are they? Varya's the only one, and that's because Varya is a cry-baby by nature, and her tears shouldn't distress the audience.' The disagreement was not resolved, and three months after the opening Chekhov was still complaining to Olga Knipper about the description of the play on the posters as 'a drama'. Stanislavsky deserves sympathy: after the vision of the orchard that Chekhov has evoked in Act One, it is hard not to be moved by the sounds of its destruction in Act Four, whatever the implications of profligacy and exploitation the orchard might have carried.

Understandably, Stanislavsky seems to have handled the production with an uncertain touch, in places positively enhancing Chekhov's intentions, yet elsewhere missing the point completely. One striking alteration proposed by Stanislavsky which Chekhov actually incorporated in his final published version was the setting of the final act in the same nursery that we see in Act One, rather than in some other unspecified room in the house. Thus it was Stanislavsky and Simov who were responsible for the poignant effect of 'oppressive emptiness', which the text prescribes, and which gains so much from the contrast with the sense of life returning in Act One.

In Act Three, far from treating the 'ball' as an opportunity for filling the stage with extras, as he certainly would have done a few years earlier, Stanislavsky conveyed Chekhov's mood exactly. His prompt-book reads:

> A completely abortive ball. Very few guests. Despite all their efforts they've only managed to drag along the station-master and the post-office clerk ... Silence prevails the whole evening, so that you'd think they'd come along to a funeral. As soon as a dance ends, they all come to a halt, then disperse to their seats along the wall. They sit and fan themselves. The moment someone breaks the silence by running through the room or starting to talk, everyone else is embarrassed and the offender immediately feels guilty at causing the disturbance, and the room becomes even more silent and embarrassed.[23]

In the final scene of the act, following Lopakhin's reeling exit, where Chekhov says 'The band plays quietly', Stanislavsky counterpointed Ranevskaya's bitter tears and Anya's comforting platitudes with the sounds of drunken revelry offstage in a conscious attempt to realise Chekhov's sense of harsh tragi-comedy.

On the other hand, Act Two was entirely at odds with what Chekhov had envisaged, largely because Stanislavsky and Simov chose to elaborate on the details of the setting that he had prescribed, and so destroyed their precisely balanced counterpoint. Chekhov intended the line of telegraph poles, the town on the horizon and the long-abandoned shrine to convey the encroachment of the new industrial age; at the same time, he was emphatic that the setting should be in a steppe landscape, flat under a vast sky, to underline the diminutive stature of the characters and their ambitions. Hence, at one point Lopakhin says 'Oh Lord, you have given us huge forests, immense fields, vast horizons; surely we ought to be giants, living in a country like this ...'

Ignoring this profoundly expressive visual metaphor, Stanislavsky concentrated on motivating his actors and on creating a charming genre picture of Central Russia in the style of Chekhov's painter-friend Levitan. Not content with Chekhov's 'old bench', Stanislavsky substituted 'a mown field and a small mound of hay, on which the scene is played by the group out walking. This is for the actors, it will help them get into the spirit of their parts.'[24] In contrast to the ball scene described above, he is concerned here with the individual character, and the play's wider meaning suffers in consequence. As for the telegraph-poles, the town, and long-abandoned shrine, Stanislavsky wrote to Chekhov:

> Let's hope the scenery will be successful. The little chapel, the ravine, the neglected cemetery in the middle of an oasis of trees in the open steppe. The left side and the centre will not have any wings. You will see only the far horizon. This will be produced by a single semicircular back-drop with attachments to deepen the perspective. In the distance you see the flash of a stream and the manor house on a slight rise, telegraph poles, and a railroad bridge. Do let us have a train go by with a puff of smoke in one of the pauses. That might turn out very well. Before sundown there will be a brief glimpse of the town, and toward the end of the act, a Fog: it will be particularly thick above the ditch downstage. The frogs and corncrakes will strike up at the very end of the act.[25]

Yet again, the fascination of the new technology of naturalism had proved too strong for Stanislavsky. On one occasion, Chekhov said to someone in Stanislavsky's hearing 'I shall write a new play and it will begin with a character saying: "How wonderfully quiet it is! There are no birds to be heard, no dogs, no cuckoos, no owls, no nightingales, no clocks, no harness bells, and not a single cricket." '[26] Stanislavsky indulgently records this in his memoirs written some twenty years later, but at the time he seems to have had little regard for Chekhov's theatrical instinct. In the 1930's Nemirovich-Danchenko wrote 'There is no denying that our theatre was at fault in failing to grasp the full meaning of Chekhov, his sensitive style and his amazingly delicate outlines ... *Chekhov refined his realism to the point where it became symbolic*, and it was a long time before we succeeded in conveying the subtle texture of his work; maybe the theatre simply handled him too roughly.'[27]

It is worth noting that the 1904 production of *The Cherry Orchard* followed directly on a sequence which included Tolstoy's *The Power of Darkness*, Gorky's first two works, *Philistines* and *The Lower Depths*, and a ponderously historicist treatment of *Julius Caesar* by Nemirovich. All four were interpreted in the Meiningen manner, with a heavy emphasis on external naturalism, so it is hardly surprising that Chekhov's allusive imagery in this most complex play was often obscured with superfluous detail.

The premiere of *The Cherry Orchard* on 17 January 1904 was timed to coincide with Chekhov's forty-fourth birthday and name-day, and to celebrate his twenty-fifth anniversary as a published writer. In fast declining health, he was dragged to the theatre half-way through the play, and in the last interval had to mount the stage to suffer endless sentimental eulogies, which he resented almost as much as the performance itself. But however far short of Chekhov's intentions the production fell, it was firmly established as a popular favourite by the time it was presented in Petersburg in April, and in the long run outlasted even *Three Sisters* in the repertoire.

Later in 1904, acting on an earlier suggestion of Chekhov, the Art Theatre finally tackled Maeterlinck's trilogy of one-act dramas *The Blind*, *The Intruder* and *Interior*. They proved a depressing failure, convincing Stanislavsky finally of the need to experiment in new forms. It was this that led directly to the formation in 1905 of the Theatre-Studio under Meyerhold. Even after the Studio's failure, the Art Theatre continued through a series of symbolist productions of Ibsen, Leonid Andreev, Maeterlinck and Hamsun to seek a new means of expression, influenced unquestionably by the work of Meyerhold in Petersburg in 1906–1907.* The collaboration of Stanislavsky and Edward Gordon Craig on the production of *Hamlet*, which finally reached the stage in 1912, was the culmination of this period in the Art Theatre's history.†

Eventually, however, Stanislavsky became convinced that, both in their work on symbolist drama and in their earlier naturalistic productions of Chekhov and other dramatists, the company had concentrated too much on external elements and failed to analyse sufficiently their work as actors. In 1906, following the Art Theatre's first tour abroad, Stanislavsky spent the summer in Finland reflecting on his experiences as an actor and director, and trying to establish rules of cause and effect which would replace hit-or-miss inspiration in the creation of a role. It was now that he began to formulate the principles which later were to form the basis for his 'System'. He recalled that when he first played the part of Dr. Stockman in *An Enemy of the People* he was inspired by the memory of a friend whose refusal to compromise his principles had led to his destruction. On stage this 'emotional memory' invariably inspired in Stanislavsky the necessary 'creative state of mind' to create the character of Stockman. However, he realised that with the passage of time he had forgotten his living memories, and all that remained were the external mannerisms of the character. The problem was to devise a method whereby the emotional memory could be stirred, the creative state of mind reliably achieved, without relying on chance inspiration.‡ By studying the great actors of the day, both in Russia and abroad, Stanislavsky observed that what they all shared on stage was physical freedom, muscular relaxation, and he concluded that this was the first prerequisite of creativity. In time, his

* See Chapter 8.
† See pp. 89–93 below.
‡ Compare the experience of *Three Sisters* described on p. 68 above.

own experience taught him that he was most relaxed when his entire attention was fixed on the stage, with no concern for the audience, and furthermore that it was only then that the audience gave all its concentration to the actor. Thus he developed the concept of what he called the actor's 'circle of attention'.

Finally, he realised that whilst the actor is bound to know that everything around him on the stage is false, he must say to himself: 'But *if* it were true, then this is what I would do, this is how I would react to this or that event.' This sense of truth Stanislavsky called the 'creative' or 'magic *if*', from which proceeded the actor's 'inner justification' for his role.[28]

In attempting to put these discoveries into practice Stanislavsky encountered considerable scepticism within the company. Eventually, he isolated a small group of actors and devoted four months exclusively to experiments which led to the staging in December 1909 of Turgenev's *A Month in the Country*. The play is virtually a conversation piece, set on an idyllic mid-nineteenth century estate, in which the concealed emotions of the leisured inhabitants are catalysed by the arrival of an attractive young stranger. In contrast to all his earlier work, Stanislavsky's *mise-en-scène* was largely static and almost entirely devoid of external effects. The immobility of the production was further emphasised by the settings designed by Dobuzhinsky. Totally unlike Simov's work, they were stylised evocations of the period, a confined symmetrical space which kept the actors in a seated semi-circle for much of the action. Again, the resemblance to the methods developed by Meyerhold in Petersburg was unmistakeable. However, the aim was different, the audience's attention being focussed not so much on the ruling design of the production as on the characterisation and the delicate interplay of emotions conveyed by the merest gestures and facial expressions.*

When *A Month in the Country* was revealed finally to the public it was generally recognised as one of Stanislavsky's most sensitive productions, yet still it failed to win over the majority of the company to his new ideas, which were as yet far from clearly formulated and often fogged by his own dogmatism. For years he was all but an outsider in his own theatre, remote from the company and on uneasy terms with Nemirovich-Danchenko, who now assumed greater responsibility as a director. Stanislavsky's 'System' as it was eventually codified was the outcome of exhaustive experimental work in a virtually separate theatre, the First Studio of the Moscow Art Theatre which was opened in 1912 by Stanislavsky with his close friend and collaborator Leopold Sulerzhitsky. Though he continued to direct occasional productions at the main Art

---

* Compare the description of Meyerhold's production of *Hedda Gabler* on p. 117 below.

Theatre, this and other studios now became the main focus for his activities.

As an actor, Stanislavsky did not make his final appearance until 1928, when at the age of sixty-five he played Vershinin in a performance of *Three Sisters* to celebrate the theatre's thirtieth anniversary. During this performance he suffered a heart attack, as a result of which he devoted the remaining ten years of his life mainly to pedagogical activities and wrote the books which set out the principles of his 'System', published in English as *An Actor Prepares, Building a Character* and *Creating a Role*. Stanislavsky shows little awareness of advances in psychological theory, and his writing has a quaint moralistic tone (particularly in translation); but even so these three books together constitute the most searching empirical study of acting that has yet been attempted, and they are still widely employed in actor-training. Yet they exhibit one crucial defect, a defect which so often flawed Stanislavsky's work as a director: whilst concentrating on the problems of the actor, he seldom considers the production as a total synthesis with a unified objective. What is more, he takes little account of the psychology of the *audience*, assuming that if the individual performances are truthful the spectator will necessarily respond to their truthfulness through a process of empathy. As the work of other directors considered in this book demonstrates, Stanislavsky's proposition is by no means unassailable.

6. Edward Gordon Craig

In the forty years leading up to the outbreak of the First World War the English theatre reached a new level of popularity and commercial success. Between 1880 and 1900 fourteen new theatres opened in London alone, and many existing ones were completely renovated. With their extravagantly gilded and plush upholstered interiors and with the previously uncomfortable pit benches replaced by high-priced orchestra stalls, a night at the theatre acquired a new decorum and sense of occasion, which precisely matched the opulent respectability of the affluent middle-class of late Victorian England. Inevitably, managements that had invested considerable capital in costly new or renovated premises needed a reliable product to sustain their paying audience, and the unfortunate casualty was artistic innovation. Theatre production made no significant move from the position to which Charles Kean, Samuel Phelps, Tom Robertson, the Bancrofts and others had advanced it by the 1860's.[1]

Following the successful London season of the Comédie Française in 1879, there were visits by the Meiningen company in 1881, Antoine's Théâtre Libre in 1889, the Théâtre de l'Œuvre in 1895, and the first-ever Japanese company under Otodziro Kawakami in 1900. Whilst certain of the lessons of the Meininger were absorbed by Henry Irving and Frank Benson, the only other lasting impression was made by Antoine, who was the direct inspiration for the Independent Theatre Society, formed in London in 1891 by J. T. Grein. Like the Théâtre Libre, the Independent Theatre was a subscription society, giving occasional performances of serious new drama, unhampered by the constraints of official censorship and commercial accountability. Whilst there was nothing innovatory or even particularly accomplished about this mainly amateur group's makeshift productions, it can nevertheless claim credit for the first English performance of *Ghosts*, with which it announced itself at the Royalty Theatre in March 1891, and for the introduction to the English stage of George Bernard Shaw, whose *Widowers' Houses* it presented the following year at the same theatre. The Independent Theatre produced twenty-eight plays in seven years, and together with the Stage Society, which succeeded it in 1899, was responsible for establishing what Matthew

Arnold called an 'ethical drama', headed by Shaw, Harley Granville Barker and John Galsworthy.

The only other comparable venture during the period was the Elizabethan Stage Society, created in 1894 by the actor-manager, William Poel, for the purpose of presenting Shakespeare uncut, without scene changes, and on stages corresponding to the Tudor originals. Unfortunately, Poel's achievements as a director were undermined both by the limitations of his largely amateur casts and by his own antiquarian pedantry. Even so, his vision revealed far-reaching possibilities for the staging of Shakespeare without recourse to ornate and irrelevant scenic display.

Up to this point, the mounting of a play had been in the hands of the leading actor or the dramatist, with a stage-manager functioning in a purely auxiliary capacity, and this remained the common practice so long as actor-managers and stars of the magnitude of Irving, Beerbohm-Tree, George Alexander and Mrs. Patrick Campbell held the stage. However subtle Irving's lighting effects were at the Lyceum, however spectacular Tree's pageantry at Her Majesty's, however refined Alexander's domestic interiors at the St. James's, they were all invariably subordinated to the requirements of the principal performers, and seldom revealed any unified production concept.

The man who first gave durable currency to the term 'director' in the English theatre was Harley Granville Barker. At the age of twenty-three, already with eight years' professional acting experience behind him, he joined the newly-founded Stage Society, and in his first season in 1900 he staged plays by Maeterlinck and acted in Ibsen, Shaw and Hauptmann. Over the next four years his range of productions embraced Shaw, W. B. Yeats, Shakespeare, Euripides, and in 1902 his own first major play, *The Marrying of Ann Leete*. During the same period he played major roles in a number of William Poel's productions for the Elizabethan Stage Society. Thus prepared, he launched into full-scale professional management in 1904 in partnership with J. E. Vedrenne at the Court Theatre. Operating a policy of short runs, they presented no fewer than eleven plays by Shaw, hitherto regarded as unactable, and introduced new works by Galsworthy, St. John Hankin, Masefield and Barker himself, as well as leading contemporary European dramatists such as Ibsen, Maeterlinck, Hauptmann and Schnitzler. For four years the Court partnership successfully withstood the financial pressures of London management, and succeeded for the first time in establishing the dramatist, and not the star or the spectacle, as a box-office attraction in his own right.

As artistic director, Barker developed a style of carefully pointed realism allied to balanced ensemble playing and meticulous, uncluttered staging, all strictly determined by the needs of the play. Compared with continental developments there was nothing innovative about the

Vedrenne–Barker management, but it foreshadowed the end of the actor-manager's hegemony, and served as the prototype for the repertory theatre movement that was soon to flourish throughout Britain. From 1912, at the Savoy Theatre, Granville Barker followed Poel's lead and successfully staged Shakespeare with a serious regard for textual meaning and using an apron stage, though with elegantly stylised costumes and settings that owed nothing to period research. As a dramatist himself, Granville Barker naturally saw the function of the director as strictly interpretive, with decor furnishing a tasteful background, and thus he established the dominant mode in the English theatre for decades to come.

By the time the first Court season opened in 1904, Edward Gordon Craig, the man best equipped to challenge this new orthodoxy, had already staged his last production in England. Craig, five years Granville Barker's senior, had an even more precocious theatrical upbringing, first appearing on stage at the age of six, and playing his first speaking part at thirteen on tour in America with Irving and Ellen Terry. Ellen Terry was his mother, and his father was an architect, Edward William Godwin, a highly original theatre designer in his own right.[2] Since his mother and father were not married, Edward Henry Gordon Craig was named respectively after his father, Henry Irving, his godmother Lady Gordon, and in lieu of a legitimate surname, 'Craig' after the island Ailsa Craig chosen by his elder sister, Edith, as a stage name when they were on holiday in Scotland as children.[3]

Craig devoted eight years to learning all aspects of the theatrical trade under Irving's tuition at the Lyceum, spending the summers with a provincial touring company, and graduating eventually to such roles as Hamlet and Romeo. In 1897 he decided to give up acting, partly because he despaired of ever equalling his mentor, and partly because of his growing interest in drawing and painting. For some years he had been a close friend of the artists, James Pryde and William Nicholson, who as 'The Beggarstaff Brothers' had transformed English poster design with their use of woodblocks. Stimulated by their work, by the visionary paintings of William Blake, and by the atmospheric impressionism of James Whistler, Craig produced hundreds of woodcuts and drawings, many of which appeared in *The Page*, a magazine managed and edited by himself from 1898 to 1901.

Meanwhile, Craig retained his interest in the theatre and on a few occasions he tried his hand tentatively at production, modestly following the style of the Lyceum. Then at the end of 1899 *The Page* announced the first production by the newly formed Purcell Operatic Society. It was to be the long-neglected opera *Dido and Aeneas*, composed by Purcell in 1680. The musical director was the pianist, organist and composer, Martin Shaw, and the stage director and designer Edward Gordon Craig. Based

in Hampstead, which in those days was still a village on the outskirts of
London, the Purcell Operatic Society was a small subscription society
devoted to the revival of the music of Purcell, Arne, Handel, Gluck and
other neglected composers, the chief object being 'to select for stage
representation their best works'.[4] In fact, it was Craig who persuaded his
close friend, Shaw, that *Dido and Aeneas* could better be staged than given
as a simple concert performance, despite the simplicity of the plot, which
the programme summarised as follows:

> The Morning breaks. Dido, Queen of Carthage, filled with a Presentiment that
> her love for Aeneas will end in Disaster, refuses to be comforted by her
> Handmaidens. Aeneas enters, and his Words revive her. They leave for 'the
> Hills and the Vales ... to the musical Groves and the cool shady Fountains',
> accompanied by their Train. Meantime the Sorceress and her sisters plot the
> Destruction of these Lovers. They sing –
>
> > 'Harm's our delight
> > And Mischief all our skill',
>
> and it is agreed to send a Messenger in the shape of a God to summon Aeneas
> away. This has the desired effect; the Witches exult, and Dido is left Alone to
> mourn her loss. Her heart breaks, and she dies singing a most glorious Song.[5]

The arrangements were strongly reminiscent of the early days of the other
independent theatre companies: apart from Dido and Aeneas themselves,
the entire company of seventy were amateur, and Shaw and Craig rehearsed them for some seven months in a variety of premises ranging
from private houses to a drill hall. The limitations of the amateur chorus
led Craig to an underplayed style of movement that was to prove one of
the features of the production. During rehearsals he wrote to Martin
Shaw:

> Dances are devilish fishy things for any but professionals to attempt. One dance
> I'll make a dance of arms – white *white* arms – the rest of the scene dark – and
> out of it, the voices – with arm accompaniment – exciting if done well.[6]

The effect was incorporated in the closing scene of the opera at Dido's
death. Reflecting Craig's schooling as an engraver and illustrator, the
entire production was conceived as a sequence of images, evocative rather
than descriptive, and designed to give free rein to the spectator's imagination. The crucial element was light, and Craig's plans required a specially
constructed stage.

The opera was due to be performed at the Hampstead Conservatoire
of Music, which had a stepped concert platform but no proscenium arch.
Using scaffolding masked with grey canvas, Craig constructed a false
proscenium, thirty feet wide and fifteen feet high. His lighting system was
unprecedented: using no overhead lamps or footlights, he incorporated a
concealed bridge in the proscenium, immediately above and behind the

opening, which supported an operator and five electric lamps with coloured filters; there were further floor-standing lamps concealed to either side and spots hidden in boxes standing in the auditorium. Immediately in front of the back-wall were hung a blue and a grey cloth, one in front of the other, and a few feet further downstage, a grey gauze on a stretcher angled forward. The effect of coloured light projected through the gauze onto the two cloths was one of infinite space, in total contrast to the habitual painted backdrop, wrinkled and dimly lit. As Craig's son, Edward, acknowledges, the original idea for this system came from the English-domiciled Bavarian artist, amateur producer and stage theorist, Sir Hubert von Herkomer.[7]

Using this background, and deploying groups of up to forty chorus members on the stepped stage, Craig needed only minimal settings and striking colour contrasts to achieve his desired effects. Haldane Macfall recorded his impressions in *The Studio:*

> In the opening scene, when the love-sick Dido, weighed down by the premonition that evil will come of her love for Aeneas, refusing to be comforted by her maidens, seats herself on the scarlet cushions of her throne, a broad green belt of ivy-clad wall flanking the throne to right and left, the note of doom is struck. Her figure at once gives the dignity of her despair, where she reclines miserably at the foot of the great lilac heavens, bowing her head to her destiny – and the sense of doom seems to grow vast as the heavens at the foot of which she bows in queenly shame.
>
> That was a splendidly composed scene in which, amidst the mysteries of the night, against a background of moonlight, the Sorceress stands high above her sea-devils, who crawl about her feet, and flout and rise and fall, like clouts of raggy seaweed that flap against the rocks at the incoming of the treacherous tide, as she evilly plots the destruction of the lovers, and plans to send a messenger in the guise of a god to summon Aeneas away. It was in this scene that Gordon Craig's fine artistic feeling for black and white did him yeoman service. The dim figures, seen in half-light, compelled the imagination. It is in the final scene that the noblest triumph is achieved. Attended by her kneeling maidens, the woe-begone figure of Dido, wrapped in her black robes, reclines amidst the sombre black cushions of her throne. The disconsolate woman appears with rare dignity at the base of the great lilac background that springs in one vast broad expanse straight upwards to the heavens, large and majestic as the heavens themselves.[8]

The great majority of the critics shared Macfall's enthusiasm for *Dido and Aeneas*, and some were quick to see Craig's approach as the means of rescuing Shakespeare from Poel's dull pedantry and Irving's indiscriminate clutter. W. B. Yeats, who was soon to adopt some of Craig's ideas at the Abbey Theatre in Dublin, wrote:

> He created an ideal country where everything was possible, even speaking in verse, or speaking to music, or the expression of the whole of life in a dance,

and I would like to see Stratford-on-Avon decorate its Shakespeare with like scenery.[9]

In other words, what Craig and Martin Shaw had achieved with a group of Hampstead enthusiasts in just three performances in May 1900 was hailed as the embodiment of the dream that had long tantalised the Symbolists: a perfect fusion of poetry, music, performer, colour and movement. Some ten years earlier, Adolphe Appia had begun to set down remarkably similar ideas for the reformation of Wagnerian production. But, rebuffed by the composer's rigidly traditionalist widow, Cosima, he was to remain an obscure theorist until 1912, when he and his compatriot, Émile Jaques-Dalcroze, began working together at the Institute of Eurhythmics in Hellerau. Although Appia had published his two major works on the staging of Wagner by 1900, Craig apparently knew nothing of him until 1904, and did not meet him for a further ten years after that.[10]

Like all the independent theatres of the period, the Purcell Operatic Society had to rely on benefactors to help balance its books. Despite the critical acclaim the three performances showed a deficit of £180 15s., which was reduced with the help of donations to just over twenty-seven pounds, leaving nothing for Craig and Shaw to show for their seven months' work.

Two months later, they began work on a further production of Purcell, *The Masque of Love*, from his opera *Dioclesian*. After eight months it was presented from 25 to 30 March 1901 at the Coronet Theatre, Notting Hill Gate, in a single programme with a revival of *Dido and Aeneas*, and *Nance Oldfield* by the Victorian dramatist, Charles Reade, which Ellen Terry and others had agreed to perform as a crowd-pulling curtain raiser. This ploy proved successful, for the seven performances showed a profit of over four-hundred pounds, with Craig and Shaw this time receiving a fee of ten pounds each. But the programme was no less an artistic success: with the larger stage of the Coronet, Craig was able to enhance the effects of infinite depth in *Dido and Aeneas*, whilst in *The Masque of Love* he pursued the principle of simplified stylisation still further. Using only a light grey canvas background and stage-cloth, and black and white hessian costumes with occasional touches of green and red, he organised the groups of masked figures into varying geometrical configurations, enhancing their rhythmical movements with pools of coloured light. Again, the plot was of the simplest:

> The Scene is a hall in a mansion. Cupid sends forth children to fetch masks, by which we understand that they are playing at being Gods and Goddesses – Flora, Comus, and the rest. Three groups, representing Blood, Riches, and Poverty, enter at different points; their wrists bound, and they are dragged in, in a typification of the stern mastery of Love. Their fetters are loosened. The rod of captivity becomes a maypole of merriment, whereon a solemn movement

follows – 'Hear mighty Lord!' At the conclusion of this chorus, we hear outside a rustling and the sound of feet, which create mingled fear and expectation. Bacchanals enter, and the maskers flee like startled fawns. A hymn to Bacchus follows, with lively movement of hands and bodies, and an interweaving dance. While the eyes are fed, the measure of a bright country dance enchants the ear, the masque closing with the usual procession.[11]

Reviewing Craig's achievements in 1902, Arthur Symons wrote: 'Mr. Craig is happiest when he can play at children's games with his figures, as in almost the whole of *The Masque of Love*. When he is entirely his own master, not dependent on any kind of reality, he invents really like a child, and his fairy-tale comes right, because it is not tied by any grown-up logic.'[12] Surveying his own career over fifty years later, Craig wrote: '(*The Masque of Love*) proved (maybe) the best thing I ever did on a stage . . . or so I thought it.'[13] It is significant that he says this of a production where he was free to convey sensations and abstractions, unencumbered by the specifics of character, setting and detailed plot. The theatre was rarely to allow him this degree of liberty – with the consequences that we shall see. In March 1902 the *Masque of Love* was revived in a double bill with Handel's pastoral opera, *Acis and Galatea*. Three-hundred pounds profit remained from the week at the Coronet, but Craig and Shaw were unable to secure any further backing of consequence, so they were obliged to hire the little-known Great Queen Street Theatre, which had a lengthy history of failures and whose only virtue was its rent of a mere forty pounds a week. Handel's opera, set at the foot of Mount Etna, has a plot no less accommodating to Craig's fantasy than Purcell's had been:

> The nymph Galatea loves and is loved by Acis, a young shepherd; she is mourning his absence and refuses to join the chorus of other nymphs and shepherds who are singing their delight in the beauties of nature. Acis returns, and the pair resolve never to part again. The chorus warns them of the approach of the giant Polyphemus, who has been seized by a fierce passion for Galatea. Polyphemus kills Acis. The gods, moved by Galatea's grief, change her dead lover into a living spring, whose softly-murmured song of love will float through the valley for ever.[14]

Of course, Craig made no attempt to re-create a Sicilian landscape, even an idealised bucolic one, but once again sought the direct collaboration of the spectator's imagination. Arthur Symons writes:

> . . . the obvious criticism upon his mounting of *Acis and Galatea* is, that he has mounted a pastoral, and put nothing pastoral into his mounting. And this criticism is partly just. Yet there are parts, especially the end of Act I, where he has perfectly achieved the rendering of pastoral feeling according to his own convention. The tent is there with its square walls, not a glimpse of meadow or sky comes into the severe design, and yet, as the nymphs in their straight dresses and straight ribbons lie back laughing on the ground, and the children,

with their little modern brown straw hats, toss paper roses among them, and the coloured balloons (which you may buy in the street for a penny) are tossed into the air, carrying the eye upward, as if it saw the wind chasing the clouds, you feel the actual sensation of a pastoral scene, of country joy, of the spring and the open air, as no trickle of real water in a trough, no sheaves of real corn among painted trees, no imitation of a flushed sky on canvas, could trick you into feeling it.[15]

The tent that Symons refers to was made from hundreds of lengths of upholsterer's webbing, suspended from behind the proscenium arch and draped back over a bar, allowing the characters access as they came and went. Just as simple were the means employed to create Scene Two, called 'The Shadow'. As Acis and Galatea embraced on a formal mound stage-centre, and the chorus dimly seen upstage sang 'Behold the Monster Polyphemus, see what strides he makes', a huge, menacing shadow was projected onto the deep blue backdrop and the lovers were lit by a single cone of red light. The final transformation of Acis into a living spring was effected by a pantomime trick invented by Charles Kean at the Princess's Theatre: holes were pierced in the backcloth and back-lit with revolving perforated discs in front of the lamps, causing the light to come and go, and thus produce a cascade effect.[16]

The few critics who found their way to Great Queen Street were no less admiring than before, but the double-bill could sustain no more than a week's run, at the end of which the broker's men were in the theatre to forestall the removal of anything of value. It was left to Ellen Terry to satisfy the numerous creditors, and a few months later the Purcell Operatic Society wound up its affairs.

In December 1902 Craig and Martin Shaw came together again to work on an amateur production of Laurence Housman's nativity play, *Bethlehem*. Staged in the Great Hall of the Imperial Institute in South Kensington, it resembled *Acis and Galatea* with its broad proscenium opening and lighting arrangement. The play itself was unmemorable, but some of the chiaroscuro effects recalled Rembrandt, on whose etchings Craig had modelled them, and the sense of occasion was enhanced by the entire auditorium being draped with blue cloth to improve the acoustics, thus making it resemble a huge tent. *Bethlehem* was Craig's last work with amateurs, whose devotion and open-mindedness he greatly admired. It was also the first non-operatic production of his mature period, though there was incidental music (arranged by Martin Shaw) as an integral part of it. Like Meyerhold, Craig drew no distinction between actual music and rhythmical speech and movement, and as Denis Bablet points out, it was not by chance that he took as the epigraph for the French edition of his book, *On the Art of Theatre*, Walter Pater's dictum, 'All art constantly aspires towards the condition of music'.

For two years Craig had earned next to nothing from his theatrical labours, and had depended on the endless generosity of his mother. Now he was thirty and she decided it was time to set him up properly in the profession, along with his sister, Edy, who was establishing a highly promising theatrical costumier's business.[17] Furthermore, Ellen Terry herself, now fifty-five, had left Irving, perhaps sensing that the days of the Lyceum style were numbered. She assembled a company and rented the Imperial Theatre. Situated in Tothill Street in Westminster, it was even more remote from the centre of theatrical London than Great Queen Street. Eventually, at Craig's suggestion, it was decided to open with Ibsen's early play, *The Vikings at Helgeland*. Set in northern Norway in the tenth century and taken from the Norse sagas, *The Vikings* is, in Ibsen's words, 'huge, cold, remote, self-sufficient, epic, quintessentially objective'.[18] It was a play ideally suited to Craig's stylised approach; but the part of the implacable warrior-wife, Hjørdis, was both far too young and far too grim for Ellen Terry, and it was only her ambition for her son that persuaded her to take it.

Ibsen's bleak drama prompted Craig to empty the stage of all but the essentials, though those essentials were costly enough, including as they did costumes for a cast of fifty-six, all executed in Edy's workshop, and a host of swords, spears, helmets, shields and other props craftsman-made in wood and metal to Craig's precise instructions. His lighting plans, similar to those for his earlier productions, demanded the complete gutting and re-equipping of the stage, including the construction of a lighting-bridge. For the first time Craig collided with the practicalities of the professional theatre in the person of a business manager who queried every expenditure. Likewise, the company, in contrast to his devoted Hampstead amateurs, demanded to know why he should choose to *interpret* Ibsen rather than merely execute his detailed stage directions. In particular, two of them objected strongly to fighting with massive swords on a rock structure that sloped between thirty and forty degrees, especially as the lighting did not even reveal their faces to the audience. Craig's work with the actors soon degenerated into a running fight; looking back on the production, he wrote to Martin Shaw, who again composed the music: 'You did *The Vikings* – and I did *The Vikings* – and the rest were doing jokes – and never got rid of their skins, much less into any others.'[19] Yet once again, Craig's production was a visual triumph. The American critic, James Huneker, wrote:

Abolishing foot and border lights, sending shafts of luminosity from above, Mr. Craig secures unexpected and bizarre effects. It need be hardly added that these same effects are suitable only for plays into which the element of romance and of the fantastic largely enter. We see no 'flies', no shaky unconvincing side scenes, no foolish flocculent borders, no staring back-cloths. The impression created is one of real unreality. For example, when the curtains are parted, a rocky slope, Nordish, rugged, forbidding, is viewed, the sea, an inky pool, mist-hemmed, washing at its base. From above falls a curious, sinister light which gives purplish tones to the stony surfaces and masks the faces of the players with mysterious shadows. The entire atmosphere is one of awe, of dread.

With his second tableau Mr. Craig is even more successful. It is the feast room in Gunnar's house. It is a boxed-in set, though it gives one the feeling of a spaciousness that on the very limited stage of the Imperial is surprising. A circular platform with a high seat at the back, and a long table with rough benches, railed in, make up an interior far from promising. A fire burns in a peculiar hearth in the centre, and there are raised places for the women. Outside it is dark. The stage manager contrived to get an extraordinary atmosphere of gloomy radiance in this barbaric apartment. He sent his light shivering from on high, and Miss Terry's Valkyr dress was a gorgeous blue when she stood in the hub of the room. All the light was tempered by a painter's perception of lovely hues.[20]

For the closing scene of Hjørdis's suicide on the seashore at nightfall, Craig placed her on a steep rounded white hillock against a huge black expanse of sky. As Denis Bablet observes, the austere symbolism of Craig's production anticipates point by point the style that Wieland Wagner's employed to revitalise his grandfather's music dramas at Bayreuth in the 1950's.

But London theatregoers in 1903 had little desire to see Ellen Terry die on a frozen ice-cap in Tothill Street, and three weeks after the opening night of 15 April she decided to cut her losses by closing *The Vikings* and replacing it as quickly as possible with *Much Ado About Nothing*. With just two weeks for rehearsals, Craig produced a design consisting largely of five eighteen-foot Tuscan pilasters based on designs by the renaissance architect, Serlio. By adding curtains, formal backdrops and balustrades, Craig was able to achieve most of the settings he needed, the exception being the church for Act Three, which was done with curtains and pools of coloured light. Even these economies and the attraction of Ellen Terry giving her much-loved interpretation of Beatrice were insufficient to make the Imperial Theatre a paying proposition, and in June she was compelled to take the company on tour to recoup her losses. Craig blamed the failure of the venture on the ineptitude of his mother's business manager, the lack of vision of his actors, the disruptive influence of his sister's lover, Christabel Marshal,* in the wardrobe – even on Irving's withholding of his support. But mostly it can be ascribed to his stubborn refusal to tailor his visions to practical necessity. Every director of vision in Europe faced similar obstacles, but none was quite so arrogant as Edward Gordon Craig – and perhaps no theatre in Europe was quite so resistant to innovation as

* Her professional name was 'Chris St. John'.

the English theatre. A year later, Craig left England for Germany, never to work at home again for the remaining sixty-two years of his life.

Craig had been invited by Otto Brahm to work as designer on a production of Otway's *Venice Preserved* at the Lessing Theatre in Berlin. The collaboration was doomed from the start: Brahm expected Craig merely to furnish designs, and realistic ones at that, whereas Craig started by proposing extensive modifications to the stage, and ended by persuading the play's adaptor, Hugo von Hofmannsthal, to support his demand to conduct rehearsals. In the event , he contributed only two settings, and those were much modified by Brahm's resident scene painter.

Rebuffed once again by the professional theatre, Craig turned to writing and to exhibitions of his designs to promote his ideas. Between December 1904 and October 1905, his work was seen in Berlin, Düsseldorf, Cologne, Dresden, Munich, Vienna and London, and his short theoretical treatise *The Art of the Theatre* appeared first in German then in English, to be followed in 1906 by versions in Dutch and Russian. In this imaginary dialogue between the 'Playgoer' and the 'Stage-Director' Craig pronounces his formula for the rebirth of the theatre under the presiding genius of the director:

> ... the Art of the Theatre is neither acting nor the play, it is not scene nor dance, but it consists of all the elements of which these things are composed: action, which is the very spirit of acting; words, which are the body of the play; line and colour, which are the very heart of the scene; rhythm, which is the very essence of the dance.[21]

This hastily written booklet said little that Wagner, Appia and the French Symbolists had not said (or even done) already, but its provocative tone captured the mood of the moment and it did more than any of Craig's practical work to establish his reputation as an innovator and to promote the cause of the 'New Theatre' throughout Europe.

In December 1904 Craig saw Isadora Duncan dance in Berlin and they immediately began a passionate affair which lasted nearly two years and produced two children.* Artistically, Craig and Isadora were united by their belief in movement as the essence of drama; his experience of her inspired improvisations on an empty stage to the music of Gluck, Beethoven and Chopin convinced him even more of the degeneracy of the modern theatre and strengthened his resolve to pursue his theatrical dreams through the media of drawing and engraving.

But in 1906 Isadora brought Craig and the great Italian actress, Eleonora Duse, together for him to design a production of *Rosmersholm* which she was planning to put on in Florence. Employing two young house-painters

---

* Both children were drowned in 1913 when the car carrying them plunged into the River Seine.

as his assistants, Craig worked day and night for a week, completely enclosing the stage space of the Pergola Theatre with ordinary sacking painted in overlapping streaks of blues and greens. With the addition of a huge barred window in the background and a few pieces of furniture, the setting needed only Craig's lighting to evoke, not the 'large, old-fashioned, and comfortable living room' specified in the play-text, but rather 'Rosmersholm, a house of shadows' where 'There is the powerful impression of unseen forces closing in upon the place (and) we hear continually the long drawn out note of the horn of death.'[22] Ten years earlier in Paris, guided by Maeterlinck, Lugné-Poe had stumbled falter-ingly towards a symbolist interpretation of Ibsen, and now within a few weeks of each other in Florence, Berlin and Petersburg, Craig, Reinhardt and Meyerhold were treading a similar path.*

Isadora Duncan describes the impact of the performance on 5 December 1906:

> The first evening of *Rosmersholm* an immense, expectant public filled the theatre in Florence. When the curtain rose, there was one gasp of admiration. The result could not have been otherwise. That single performance of *Rosmersholm* is remembered in Florence to this day by connoisseurs of Art.
>
> Duse, with her marvellous instinct, had donned a gown of white, with great wide sleeves that fell at her sides. When she appeared, she looked less like Rebecca West than a Delphic sibyl. With her unerring genius she adapted herself to every great line and to each shaft of light which enveloped her. She changed all her gestures and movements. She moved in the scene like some prophetess announcing great tidings.
>
> But when the other actors came on – Rosmer, for instance, who put his hands in his pockets – they seemed to be like stage hands who had walked on by mistake. It was positively painful. Only the man who played Brendel fitted perfectly with the marvellous surroundings when he declaimed the words: 'When I have been wrapped in a haze of golden dreams that have descended on me; when new, intoxicating momentous thoughts have had their birth in my mind, and I have been fanned by the beat of their wings as they bore me aloft – at such moments I have transformed them into poetry, into visions, into pictures.'[23]

As Duse was playing in repertoire, there were no more performances of *Rosmersholm* in Florence, but on the strength of that single triumph Duse and Craig vowed lifelong collaboration. The following February the production was revived in Nice. When Craig arrived, he discovered that the stage-manager, on finding the proscenium opening much lower than in Florence, had simply sawn two feet off the bottom of the set. Duse found Craig's furious response out of all proportion to the offence, and their collaboration was abruptly terminated. Five years were to elapse before Craig's work was seen on stage again. After the Nice fiasco Craig

* See pp. 101–102 and 117–118 below.

returned to Florence and settled there for the next nine years, taking a lease on the Arena Goldoni, a small open-air theatre built in the Roman style in the early nineteenth century. It served as his workshop and office premises, and was intended to house the School for the Art of the Theatre, whose opening was forestalled by the outbreak of war in 1914. It was here in March 1908 that Craig commenced publication of *The Mask*, a journal devoted to the past, present and future of the theatre, with historical, critical, and theoretical articles, many written by Craig himself under numerous pseudonyms, reprints and translations of important historical texts, plus woodcuts, engravings and other illustrations. Exquisitely designed and produced on hand-made paper, *The Mask* built up a distinguished international subscription list and whilst serving primarily as a mouthpiece for Craig's ideas, it did much to place the discussion of theatre practice on a new level of seriousness. The final number appeared in 1929.

Craig's years in Florence were immensely productive in terms of writing, illustration, research and experiment, but with one exception, every invitation to direct or design was either rejected or ruled out by the totally impractical conditions that he sought to impose. The exception was *Hamlet*, which was revealed to the public of the Moscow Art Theatre in January 1912 after more than three years preparation fraught with personal bickering, financial wrangling and artistic cross-purposes.[24]

Stanislavsky knew nothing of Craig until he met Isadora Duncan when she was on tour in Russia at the beginning of 1908. She gave him a copy of *The Mask* and *On the Art of the Theatre* in a German translation, and at her suggestion Craig was invited to Moscow to consider possible collaboration. That Autumn he spent a month with the company and saw ten of their productions. Before he left, it was agreed that he would stage something by Shakespeare, probably *Hamlet*, though once the play was confirmed, it was Stanislavsky who was named as director, with Craig responsible for designing the settings and costumes. When Stanislavsky began his preliminary rehearsals early the following year, his production concept was rooted in a concrete reality, with Elsinore 'a cold stone prison' which the Norwegians have invaded many times and where 'a rough militarism pervails'. At the same time, there were certain scenes that he visualised in stylised terms reminiscent of Meyerhold's recent work in St. Petersburg. Thus Act One, Scene 2:

> Entrances and exits are destructive – they are no good at all, create a lot of movement and drag things out. On a golden throne sit the King and Queen and at left, beside them, sits the pensive Hamlet ... It must be calm. The characters must be King, Queen, and Hamlet. The rest are only a background of vileness, wealth and density. An enormous throne beneath a magnificent baldachin, where the King and Queen sit, and on a step below or perhaps right beside them, Hamlet. On benches along the wall sit the courtiers and down front in a

trap, back to the audience, stand warriors with spears. The problem is to show the throne, the three characters, and the retinue, the courtiers, merge into one generalised background of gold. Their mantles flow together, and they cannot be perceived to have individual faces. They are rough brush-strokes, saturated with majesty, a background.[25]

In April 1909 Craig returned with his design sketches, and he and Stanislavsky embarked on a scene-by-scene discussion of the text, aided by Leopold Sulerzhitsky, Stanislavsky's faithful assistant who worked for years with him on the evolution of his System. Whilst Sulerzhitsky spoke some English, the only language that the other two shared was a smattering of German. Straightway, Craig announced that Shakespeare was unconcerned with historical reality, and set about developing his own conception of the play as a 'monodrama', with all the action viewed through Hamlet's eyes, ideally with Hamlet himself on stage throughout.[26] Pursuing the idea of Hamlet's fixation on death (and toying with the possibility of introducing a Death-*Doppelgänger* for him), Craig argued: 'All the idea of this play is the struggle between spirit and material – the impossibility of their union, the isolation of spirit in material.'[27] Much as Stanislavsky resisted certain consequences of Craig's interpretation (notably his view of Ophelia as 'stupid and worthless'), he remained fascinated by his novel approach, and after a month it was announced that Craig was to direct as well as design the production – much to the alarm of the company, who had had no access to the discussions thus far, and feared that Craig's method would be incompatible both with the Art Theatre's traditional realism and with Stanislavsky's new system of working with actors.

For some time in Florence, Craig had been experimenting with mobile and variable stage settings, and he decided that *Hamlet* would lend itself to a system of tall screens shifted by stage-hands in full view of the audience. Experiments with iron and solid wooden screens showed that they were far too cumbersome, whereas reed, bamboo and plywood tended to buckle. Eventually, they resorted to simple grey canvas flats; but, as we shall see, even these fell short of practical requirements.

After two or three weeks rehearsing, Craig left Moscow in June 1909. By the time he returned for his third stay the following February, relations with the Art Theatre's board of directors had become soured by Craig's repeated demands for advances of salary, which, with some justification, they suspected were subsidising his other activities in Florence. Even so, he and Stanislavsky remained, at least outwardly, on good terms, and the theatre was extraordinarily indulgent towards his requirements, furnishing two model-workshops for his exclusive use, one containing a large-scale model of the theatre with a complete lighting system in miniature. Whilst Craig, Stanislavsky and their production assistants worked long hours in these workshops, none of the cast were admitted and they grew increasingly suspicious of Craig's intentions. They can hardly have been reassured when after a month in seclusion he addressed them all for the first time together; typical of his opaque utterances was the following:

> To attain tragedy, one must be joyful ... Hamlet is the triumph of love. It is a beautiful song, a wonderful song, through which one figure passes, who surmounts all obstacles. Love is music. Therefore it is difficult to talk about this in words ... The triumph of love, all-embracing love, fantasy and music ... Hamlet is an utter contradiction ... In the course of a single month he ennobled Denmark and Napoleon didn't do that in a life-time ... If the actor thinks less of the content and more of the music of the verse, only then will Shakespeare be possible for him.[28]

By the time Craig left for Florence at the end of April, he had lost faith in the actors, whom initially he had so admired for their intelligence and seriousness; now he complained about their lack of initiative, and felt that he was being denied the leading members of the company.

Plans to put the production on in the autumn had to be cancelled when Stanislavsky fell ill with typhoid fever, and nearly a year elapsed before rehearsals were resumed. Back in Florence, Craig's interest waned as he devoted himself to his new book *On the Art of the Theatre*. In his *Daybook* he wrote:

> I want time to study the Theatre. I do not want to waste time producing plays – for that is vanity – expensive – unsatisfying – *comic* ... This *Hamlet* production for Russia is wasting my time .... I have passed it all – gone on into places where I have really seen *something* – a glimpse of something wonderful. And now I have to return and work at this nothing – this 'producing *Hamlet*'.[29]

At the same time, Stanislavsky was having second thoughts about some of Craig's ideas, and was exasperated by his unpractical attitude and repeated demands for more money. Finally, he decided to resume as director himself, and it was agreed to dissuade Craig from returning to Moscow until the dress-rehearsal stage. Taking advantage of the production to test the principles of his newly formulated System, Stanislavsky now encouraged the actors to seek the inner truth of their roles before proceeding to external details, though the overall shape of Craig's conception was preserved.

In December all performances were cancelled for ten days so that *Hamlet* could be rehearsed non-stop on stage to be ready for the premiere on 5 January 1912.* Craig arrived in time for the first run-through, but half-way through caused such a disturbance with his shouts of dissatisfaction that he was told to keep away until the final dress-rehearsals. When he was allowed to return a week later, he again brought the rehearsal

---

* 23 December 1911 by the old-style Russian calendar.

to a halt with violent complaints about the lighting, blocking and costumes, and the entire lighting design was then revised under his supervision. The final disaster occurred in his absence: one hour before
curtain-up on the opening night after the opening scene had been set up,
one screen fell over, bringing down all the rest. The only solution was to
anchor the screens with ballast, which meant that the plan for shifting
them in full view of the audience had to be abandoned and the curtains
drawn after each scene. Hence, Craig's system of kinetic staging was never
seen by a theatre audience, though as a principle, publicised through the
pages of *The Mask*, it was widely influential.[30] Despite the lengthy scene
changes and four intervals, which stretched the evening to five hours, the
performance was received with fascinated attention by the packed house.
Later, the poet, Valery Bryusov, was to draw attention to the obvious
discrepancy between the stylised staging and the actors' lifelike gestures
and movements, but in those scenes where Craig's intentions approached
realisation the effects were memorable. From Laurence Senelick's
scene-by-scene description here are impressions of the opening court
scene and the finale, the first by Serafima Birman, who played a Lady of
the Court, the second by Stanislavsky, from *My Life in Art:*

> The people were arranged on wooden platforms so as to represent symbolically
> the feudal ladder: at the top the King and Queen, the courtiers below; at the
> feet of Claudius and Gertrude assemble their more intimate henchmen, with
> the less honoured below. The court ladies were dressed in golden mantles as
> were the men, but with plated stomachers. From the slits in the golden skullcaps
> hung long, almost knee-length braided brocade ribbons ... The actors were
> distributed on various planes, their mantles flowed out and gave the impression
> of a monolithic golden pyramid.

. . . .

> Far beyond the arch a virtual forest of spears moving back and forth and the
> banners of the approaching Fortinbras; he himself, like an Archangel, ascending
> the throne at whose foot lie the bodies of King and Queen; the solemn and
> triumphant sounds of a soul-stirring funeral march; the huge, slowly descending
> banners that covered the dead but smiling face of the great purifier of the earth
> who had finally discovered the secret of earthly life in the arms of death. So did
> Craig picture the court that had become Hamlet's Golgotha.[31]

Despite the ovations at the final curtain, all those involved in the
production were well aware of how far short of their original ambitions it
had fallen. Craig wrote to his sister: '... I won't say it will equal the touch
of *Masque of Love* or *Acis*, but it will do its best under the disadvantage
of having cost the management over £14,000'.[32] Years later Stanislavsky
recalled:

> We had wanted to make the production as simple and as modest as possible. Of
> course this modesty was to be a result of rich imagination. There was very

much imagination and simplicity, but the production seemed unusually luxurious, grandiose, affected to such an extent that its beauty attacked the eye and hid the actors in its pomp. This new quality of the stage was a surprise to me. The more we tried to make the production simple the stronger it reminded us of itself, the more it seemed pretentious and displayed its showy naivete.[33]

For all the expense and the initial sensation, *Hamlet* remained in the MAT repertoire for only three seasons and was performed only 47 times, considerably fewer than *The Seagull*, the least successful of the Chekhov productions.

On the day of the premiere, Sulerzhitsky, who had borne the brunt of all the disputes, wrote to Stanislavsky:

> When (Craig) talks about lines, designs, compositions, and even lighting, I feel that this is Craig, but when the question concerns directing, then I don't trust him: be he absolutely right, he is too uninterested in acting.[34]

This is surely true: time and again in his dealings with actors he demonstrated his lack of understanding, his indifference, even his scorn for them, and for this reason it is impossible to regard him as a director in the true, complete sense of the word. Designer of genius, eloquent propagandist, inspired prophet – all these, but never a director in the sense that Stanislavsky, Reinhardt, and Meyerhold were directors. In the second issue of *The Mask* in April 1908, Craig published an essay entitled 'The actor and the Über-Marionette', in which he appeared to advocate the replacement of the actor with some unspecified kind of inanimate figure.[35] In 1924, in his Preface to the second edition of *On the Art of the Theatre* Craig corrected this impression, saying 'The Über-Marionette is the actor plus fire, minus egoism, the fire of the gods and demons, without the smoke and steam of mortality.' Many essays and chapters have been devoted to this subject, seeking to unravel Craig's true intentions. Today, they seem of little practical importance: long before Craig took him up, the puppet, real or symbolic, had become the paradigm for the perfect actor – pliable and non-egotistical, obedient yet expressive. The puppet theatre had returned to vogue in Paris in the 1880's and 1890's; Maeterlinck had written his '*drames pour marionettes*', fearful that his fragile creations would crumble in the hands of the insensitive actor, whilst Jarry with great percipience drew little distinction between the puppet and the live performer. The dance of Isadora Duncan and Loïe Fuller revealed new plastic possibilities for the human body, and the early visits of oriental theatre companies and dance troupes, notably Kawakami and Sada Yacco in 1900-1901, confirmed that plasticity could be allied with expressive discipline. These stimuli, together with the rediscovery of the *commedia dell'arte* and the other traditional popular forms, let to a practical reappraisal of the actor's art – by Meyerhold and his younger contemporaries in Russia, by Appia, Jaques-Dalcroze and Reinhardt in Germany, by Jacques Copeau at the Théâtre du Vieux-Colombier in Paris.[36]

In this movement Craig was a source of inspiration and an important theorist. But the translation of theory into practice which others achieved remained beyond his capacity. His school was never revived after the First World War, and the only further production of note on which he collaborated was Ibsen's *Pretenders* at the Royal Theatre, Copenhagen, in 1926. The outbreak of war in 1939 found Craig in France, where he settled and remained until his death in 1966 at the age of ninety-four.

7. Max Reinhardt in Germany and Austria

No director courted Craig more assiduously than Max Reinhardt: in 1905 he invited him to produce *Macbeth*, *The Tempest* and Shaw's *Caesar and Cleopatra*; in 1908 he wanted him to design first *King Lear*, then the *Oresteia* and *Oedipus the King*. But each time Craig drew back, apprehensive that he would never have a free hand in someone else's theatre. In Reinhardt's case he was probably right to refuse: for all his lifelong fascination with spectacle, Reinhardt was above all an *actor's* director, whose respect for the performer would surely have proved irreconcilable with Craig's utopian schemes.

Reinhardt's entry into the theatre was due entirely to his own efforts. Born Max Goldman in 1873 near Vienna, the eldest of seven children of an unsuccessful Jewish business family, he was forced to leave school at fourteen and find work. After three years, first in a factory and then in a bank, he defied his parents' wishes and started to take acting lessons. At the age of eighteen, having assumed the stage-name of Reinhardt, he secured his first professional engagement. A year later, he joined the company of the Salzburg municipal theatre, where he came to the attention of Otto Brahm, founder of the Freie Bühne and now manager of the Deutsches Theater, Berlin's leading theatre. Reinhardt joined Brahm's company in 1894 and remained with him for eight years, playing over eighty roles, most of them in Shakespeare, the German classics, and the modern Naturalistic repertoire.

Eventually, Reinhardt and several other younger members of the company grew tired of the unrelieved grimness of the modern works they were required to perform, and with a number of artists, writers and composers of their acquaintance formed an occasional cabaret group called '*Die Brille*' (The Spectacles). In January 1901, the group was consolidated under the title '*Schall und Rauch*' (Sound and Smoke) and later that year acquired regular premises in the centre of Berlin. Their programmes of musical numbers, sketches and parodies became interspersed with one-act plays by little-performed modern authors, such as

Strindberg, Wedekind and von Hofmannsthal. Eventually, this became their predominant interest, and when in August 1902 the group was renamed 'Kleines Theater' (Little Theatre), it began to devote itself exclusively to full-length new plays. Between September 1902 and April 1903, they presented ten productions, including *Crimes and Crimes* by Strindberg, *Salomé* and *The Importance of Being Earnest* by Oscar Wilde, *Earth Spirit* by Wedekind, *The Lower Depths* by Gorky, and *Pelléas and Mélisande* by Maeterlinck.

Until the end of 1902 Reinhardt was bound by contract to Otto Brahm and could work only unofficially with the Kleines Theater, but in January 1903 he became free to devote himself entirely to the new enterprise and the production of *Pelléas* on 3 April was the first in which he was credited publicly as director. Before that, however, he had been responsible for *Salomé*, a work whose eroticism had caused it to be banned from public performance, and so initially could be given only before an invited audience. Within the confines of the Kleines Theater, which in fact was only a converted hotel room, and enhanced by Max Cruse's claustrophobic three-dimensional setting, *Salomé*, with Gertrud Eysoldt in the title role, was an unprecedented sensation for a Berlin public whose expectations of modern drama stemmed largely from Brahm's sober presentations of Ibsen and Hauptmann. *Salomé* inaugurated a new era of grotesque style, heightened lyricism and undisguised theatricality – all qualities embodied in the person of Gertrud Eysoldt, of whom Julius Bab wrote:

> ... (she) has the sexless, gaunt, pointedly moving body of a boy, the thin, cracked voice of a child, the volatile, grimacing mien of a cat ... Eysoldt produces art so long as her cunning brain directs her weak physique to transform into heroines of weakness those demons that modern authors create through passionately exaggerated stylisation: seductive in impotence, driven by lack of will power, naively dangerous: Salome, Selysette, Lulu ...[1]

In fact, *Salomé* was banned totally after its sensational opening performance on 15 November 1902, and it was nearly a year before the censor yielded to a lengthy press campaign and authorised the production's public performance. Meanwhile, the work that provided the material foundation for Reinhardt's subsequent success was, curiously enough, *The Lower Depths*, Gorky's grim portrayal of down-and-outs in a Moscow doss-house. Reinhardt himself played the pilgrim-philosopher, Luka and shared the direction of the play with Richard Vallentin, Reinhardt working principally with the actors on their roles and Vallentin, the named director, being responsible for the overall mise en scène. Closely following Gorky's highly detailed directions, the production succeeded in creating an intensity of atmosphere that far surpassed anything that Brahm had achieved at the Deutsches Theater, and within two years it had been performed over five hundred times. However, Reinhardt never responded

5. *Tsar Fyodor Ivanovich* (Moscow Art Theatre, 1898)

6. *The Cherry Orchard* (Moscow Art Theatre, 1904)

7. *Spring Awakening* (Kammerspiele Berlin, 1906)

8. *Oedipus the King* (Reinhardt, Covent Garden, 1912)

to Gorky's encouragement to stage any of his later, more overtly political plays, such as *Summer Folk* and *Enemies*.[2] Much as Reinhardt admired *The Lower Depths*, it was a work far closer in spirit to Vallentin, who took a militant, socialist view of the theatre that his partner didn't share. In 1901 Reinhardt declared:

> What I have in mind is a theatre that will again bring joy to people, that leads them out of the grey misery of everyday life, beyond themselves, into a gay and pure atmosphere of beauty. I can feel that people are fed up with finding their own misery again in the theatre and that they are longing for brighter colours and a heightened sense of life.
>
> This does not mean that I want to renounce the great achievements of the naturalistic technique of acting, its never heretofore attained truth and genuineness! That I could not do, even if I wanted to. I have passed through this school and am grateful for having had the opportunity. That strict education to merciless truth can not possibly be omitted from our development ... but I should like to carry this development further, to apply it to other things than the mere description of situations and environments, take it beyond the stale smell of poor people and the problems of social critique; I should like to obtain the same degree of truth and genuineness in the depiction of the purely human in a deeper and more subtle psychological art; and I want to show life from another side than that of merely pessimistic negation, yet equally true and genuine in its gaiety, filled with colour and light.[3]

Before long Reinhardt and Vallentin parted company, but not before the huge popular success of *The Lower Depths* had persuaded the group to acquire a second and much larger theatre, the Neues Theater am Schiffbauerdamm (later to become the home of Brecht's *Berliner Ensemble*). Retaining the Kleines Theater, they opened at the Neues Theater in February 1903, thereby establishing the practice of a company dividing its work between a main house and an experimental stage which has since become commonplace. The second season saw no fewer than twenty-four productions by Reinhardt in the two theatres, including new works by Wilde, Wedekind, von Hofmannsthal, Tolstoy, Shaw, Becque, Maeterlinck, and Strindberg. However, he attached just as much importance to the more insubstanial works in his repertoire, for they frequently offered no less scope to the actor, who was his central concern. What he said in 1901 remained his lifelong credo:

> There is only one objective for the theatre: the theatre; and I believe in a theatre that belongs to the actor. No longer, as in the previous decades, literary points of view shall be decisive ones. This was the case because literary men dominated the theatre. I am an actor, I feel with the actor and for me the actor is the natural focal point of the theatre. He was that in all great epochs of theatre. The theatre owes the actor his right to show himself from all sides, to be active in many directions, to display his joy in playfulness, in the magic of transformation. I know the playful, creative powers of the actor and I am often sorely tempted to save something of the old commedia dell'arte in our over-disciplined

age, in order to give the actor, from time to time an opportunity to improvise and to let himself go.[4]

Many of the great actors who passed through Reinhardt's theatre have testified to his unique ability to draw the best out of them, of his capacity seemingly to efface himself and his own directional intentions for the sake of their performance. Martin Esslin, who worked as a student actor with Reinhardt in Salzburg in 1937, writes:

> Reinhardt's method as a director was essentially one of showing the actors their parts – not by fully acting them out, but by a kind of actor's shorthand, a brilliantly concise indication of the essentials of a given gesture or intonation. Being a superb character actor, Reinhardt was able to show an actor not how he, Reinhardt, would act the part, but how that particular actor or actress should do it in order to give full expression to his or her essential individuality. Watching Reinhardt at rehearsals, it was uncanny to see him turn into a given actress, say Paula Wesseley, and demonstrate to her the way in which she could be more like Wesseley as Gretchen than she had been before. The rehearsal process for Reinhardt thus developed its own peculiar dialectic. Watching a given actor, the character–actor Reinhardt learned to capture that actor's optimum personality and expressive individuality; having mastered this, he reproduced it to the actor who was thus confronted, as it were, with his ideal self in the ideal realization of the part. Thus Reinhardt never imposed his way of acting a part on the actor. He grasped that actor's potential and helped him to see it in watching the director. A profound belief in the miracle of human individuality and the uniqueness and richness of personality was the basis of Reinhardt's artistic creed.[5]

This might suggest that Reinhardt's concern for the actor was a narrow professional one, a wish to protect him against the other contending interests within the theatre. Nothing is further from the truth: it was born of his desire to restore the histrionic dimension to life itself. In 1928 in his celebrated address 'About the Actor', Reinhardt said:

> It is to the actor and to no one else that the theatre belongs. When I say this, I do not mean, of course, the professional alone. I mean, first and foremost, the actor as a poet. All the great dramatists have been and are to-day born actors, whether or not they have formally adopted this calling, and whatever success they have had in it. I mean likewise the actor as director, stage-manager, musician, scene-designer, painter, and, certainly not least of all, the actor as spectator. For the contribution of the spectators is almost as important as that of the cast. The audience must take its part in the play if we are ever to see arise a true art of the theatre – the oldest, most powerful, and most immediate of the arts, combining the many in one.[6]

Thus Reinhardt aimed to immerse his audience in a total theatrical experience, using every means, technological as well as human, that lay within his grasp. After his first season at the Neues Theater, he began to explore methods of replacing the conventional lighting, such as Mario

Fortuny's recently invented sky-dome, a silken canopy suspended high over the stage area onto which diffused light could be directed to create an impression of infinite space. He also installed a large revolving stage, on which he could mount large three-dimensional composite settings.

In January 1905 the revolve was used to spectacular effect in Reinhardt's production of *A Midsummer Night's Dream*, a play to which he returned at least eleven times over the next thirty years. Reinhardt and his designer, Gustav Knina, divided the revolve into two contrasting areas: the 'real' world of Athens, represented by a marble arena, a courtyard before a palace, and a spacious hall for the concluding nuptials – and the wood, at once the natural habitat of the spirit world, a refuge for lovers, and a meeting-place for the mechanicals:

> Veritable trees, not painted but plastic ones, were placed on the stage, and the space below was covered, not with a painted ground-cloth, but with what seemed to be palpable grass, in which the feet sunk among the flowers; while here and there were seen bushes and little beeches growing between the trees, and in the midst of all a little lake mirrored between two hills.
>
> And now (constructed on the revolving stage) all this forest began slowly and gently to move and to turn, discovering new perspectives, always changing its aspect, presenting ever new images inexhaustible as Nature. And while the stage turned and changed, the elves and fairies ran through the forest, disappearing behind the trees, to emerge behind the little hillocks. These beings with their green veils and leafy crowns seemed, in their appearance, to form a part of the forest itself. Puck, who up to that time has been usually dressed in the costume of the fantastic ballet or opera, was covered only with grass and became at last the true elf, who rolled with laughter like a child in the green of the forest.
>
> This was a revelation. Never had such unity between actor and stage decoration been seen. Never before, and in a manner so justified, had one seen the stage setting become an actor of such importance in the play. A new impetus had been given and a new and intense life henceforth entered the modern theatre.[7]

On the one hand, Reinhardt's *Dream* was naturalistic illusion pursued to the ultimate extreme – Meiningen set in motion on the revolve – but on the other, it was the metaphorical expression of the play's own universe in which plant and animal life, mortals and immortals, plebeians and patricians are all seen as parts of one creation. The production became an expressive synthesis, creating its own reality in the spectator's imagination rather than counterfeiting the 'real' world.

Thanks to the translations by Schlegel and Tieck published at the close of the eighteenth century, Shakespeare had long since been adopted by the German reading public as their own, but – the achievements of Saxe-Meiningen notwithstanding – it was Reinhardt who established him before a mass audience in the German theatre. *A Midsummer Night's*

Dream, his first great Shakespearian production, was followed by twenty-one more of his plays in over 2500 performances.

Nothing better illustrates Reinhardt's virtuoso eclecticism than the variety of his approaches to Shakespeare. A few months after his first *Dream*, Reinhardt and his designer Emil Orlik again employed the revolve to create a composite picture of sixteenth-century Venice for *The Merchant of Venice*, complete with canals, bridges, gondolas, the contrasting interiors of the ghetto and the law-courts, the nocturnal idyll of Belmont. Then a year later, again with Orlik, he moved to the other extreme with *The Winters' Tale*, a production strongly reminiscent of Craig's earlier work in London, sketches of which Craig had shown them in his Berlin studio. William Archer describes *The Winters' Tale*:

> I have seen only one of Max Reinhardt's Shakespearean revivals at the Deutsches Theater, Berlin; but that struck me as a marvel of good taste in mounting. The play was *The Winter's Tale*. Almost all the scenes in Sicily were played in a perfectly simple yet impressive decoration – a mere suggestion without any disturbing detail, of a lofty hall in the palace of Leontes. For the pastoral act in Bohemia, on the other hand, a delightful scene was designed, for all the world like a page from a child's picture book ... The whole effect was charmingly fantastic and admirably in keeping with the action of the scene.[8]

Craig's influence was similarly discernible in Reinhardt's production of *King Lear* in 1908, which was treated as 'a wild legend from time immemorial' with the forces of good and evil warring about the central figure of the aged king. Against the austere symmetrical background of Carl Czeschka's settings Reinhardt created a strictly regulated symphony of voices and movement, in total contrast to the romantic lyricism of his *Romeo and Juliet* stated the year before.[9] Unlike many of his contemporaries, Reinhardt never sought to impose an arbitrary style on his productions; invariably what emerged was the fusion of the inspiration he derived from the work in hand and whatever was suggested by the time and place of its performance. Thus, *A Midsummer Night's Dream* could be staged in the vast arena of the Grosses Schauspielhaus in 1921, as an ornate baroque confection in the Viennese Theater in der Josefstadt in 1925, as an open-air pastorale with the Oxford University Dramatic Society in 1933, as a Busby Berkeley extravaganza in the Greek Theatre of Berkeley Campus, California in 1934, and finally in 1935 as a Warner Bros. film starring Dick Powell, Olivia de Havilland, James Cagney, Joe E. Brown, and the eleven-year-old Mickey Rooney as Puck.

The success of Reinhardt's first *Dream* in 1905 provided the impetus that moved his career decisively forward. 1904 had been Otto Brahm's tenth anniversary as artistic director of the Deutsches Theater, but at that point the owner, Adolph L'Arronge, decided that Brahm had had his day, and appointed a popular writer-director, Paul Lindau, in his place. Within less than a year his decision had proved mistaken, whereupon with shrewd opportunism, he approached the thirty-two-year-old Reinhardt, convinced that anyone who could make a box-office hit out of run-of-the-mill Shakespeare must be worth taking a chance with. The offer was conditional on Reinhardt giving up the Kleines Theater, which he did readily enough, leaving Richard Vallentin to seek employment elsewhere.

At the end of the 1905-1906 season the Neues Theater also passed into other hands, but Reinhardt was soon to acquire a new second house. Around this time, he appointed his younger brother Edmund as his business manager, and it was thanks to his extraordinary business talents that Max was able to indulge his every extravagance, both personal and artistic, and steadily expanded his theatrical empire without risk of financial disaster. In December 1905, within three months of the opening production, Edmund had secured sufficient backing for his brother to buy out L'Arronge, and less than a year after that they had acquired the run-down dance-hall next door and transformed it into an elegant 292-seat studio theatre, called Die Kammerspiele (The Chamber Playhouse).

With only three steps and no orchestra pit separating the stage and audience, the emphasis at the Kammerspiele was on intimacy and atmosphere. Rejoicing at the opening production of *Ghosts* on 8 November 1906, Siegfried Jacobsohn wrote 'Not a breath goes unnoticed ... Here are only the characters of the poet, and not the personalities of the actors.'[10]

The impact on him must have been powerful, for remarkably he makes no mention in his review of the setting, which was the work of the Norwegian Expressionist artist, Edvard Munch. Commenting on his design, another critic has written:

> If Reinhardt's first poetical production (*A Midsummer Night's Dream*) had still been treated in a more or less naturalistic way, this grim, apparently realistic piece received a very different treatment ... we had a scene that used outward forms only for the purpose of deepening the central mood of the play by the way in which it arranged its lines: vertical most of them, horizontals, and curves, repeating the play and clash of ideas, as it were, in a play and clash of lines. Symbolic was the way in which the room, although it looked out on a fjord, was shut in like a prison by sharply pointed, threatening mountains, piercing and almost expelling the sky, and, with it, freedom and hope. Every line, every mass of space, height, width – all played their appointed parts in this relentless modern drama of fate, and the figures moving in it, almost as if driven by some unknown force, seemed to be placed there by fate itself. They were like necessary spots in the design of the whole scene, like an accent in a bar of music.[11]

Comparing Reinhardt's treatment of *Ghosts* with Craig's *Rosmersholm* and Meyerhold's *Hedda Gabler*, all staged within the same four weeks in 1906, one gets the sense of a far more successful evocation of the play's mood and inner meaning through a fusion of the acting ensemble and the external environment.*

Within two weeks *Ghosts* was followed at the Kammerspiele by Wedekind's *Spring Awakening*. Owing to its open depiction of adolescent sexuality and its savage lampooning of the teaching profession, the play had suffered a total ban on performance since its publication in 1891; even now the scenes of masturbation and homosexual love in Acts Two and Three had to be omitted, and Reinhardt and Wedekind were required to replace the caricatured names of the teachers with inoffensive ones.[12]

Reinhardt seems to have found no satisfactory solution to the abrupt shifts from innocent lyricism to harsh grotesque that Wedekind's rapid sequence of scenes requires, although technically this was handled successfully enough, thanks to the revolving stage of the Kammerspiele and Karl Walser's sequence of naive expressionistic backdrops. The production's great strength was the simple conviction that the young company brought to the roles of the children, notably Camilla Eibenschütz as Wendla and the great Italian-born Alexander Moissi, then twenty-six, as Moritz. Wedekind himself as the Masked Man was criticised by several critics for the uncertainty of his delivery, but nevertheless admired for what he injected into the atmosphere of the closing scene. For his part, he felt the production had failed to convey the necessary tone; to Fritz Basil, who was later asked to play the Masked Man in Munich, he wrote: 'Until Reinhardt's production the play was looked on as pure pornography. Now they've plucked up courage to see it as the driest school pedantry. But still no one's able to see humour in it.'[13]

When Reinhardt had petitioned the censor to authorise the production, he had argued, somewhat disingenuously, that the high prices and limited capacity of the Kammerspiele would mitigate against any depraving effect that the play might have. In fact, it ran initially for 321 performances, and with revivals in 1918 and 1925 achieved a final total of 615 performances. Reinhardt subsequently presented most of Wedekind's major plays, and between 1906 and 1931 no season passed without at least one of them in his repertoire. Thanks largely to him, by the time Wedekind died in 1918 he had become the most widely performed German playwright, rivalled only by Gerhart Hauptmann.

Once the Kammerspiele was firmly established, Reinhardt devoted rather more of his energies to the Deutsches Theater. The statistics for the period 1905 to 1920, when for a time he ceased to be artistic director, make staggering reading: of 150 works presented at the Deutsches Theater he was responsible for 91, whilst at the Kammerspiele he directed 32 out of 91 productions, making a total of 123 productions in fifteen years, plus

* Compare pp. 87-88 above and pp. 117-118 below.

almost thirty more in other theatres. Altogether, between 1905 and 1930 the works of 353 authors were staged in his various theatres by himself and 96 other directors, 35 of them actors whom he had trained.[14]

As early as 1901, well before the opening even of the Kleines Theater, Reinhardt had outlined his plans for two theatres, one for the classics and one smaller for modern plays; and he added:

> And actually – don't laugh – one ought to have a third theatre as well. I am quite serious about that and I already see it in front of my eyes: a very large theatre for a great art of monumental effects, a festival theatre, detached from everyday life, a house of light and solemnity, in the spirit of the Greeks, but not merely for Greeks, but for the great art of all epochs, in the shape of an amphitheatre, without curtain or sets, and in the center, totally relying on the pure effect of personality, totally focussed on the word, the actor, in the middle of the audience, and the audience itself, transformed into *the people*, drawn into, become a part of, the action of the play.[15]

There were many who shared this dream around the turn of the century, but only Reinhardt himself was to make it come true. In the years leading up to the First World War Reinhardt consolidated the Deutsches Theater's position as the outstanding company in Germany with a series of productions of Goethe, Schiller, and, above all, Shakespeare. But eventually he became impatient to extend his artistic horizon, and in any case the Reinhardt financial empire, as is the nature of all empires, needed to expand. In September 1910 he staged Hugo von Hofmannsthal's adaption of Sophocles' *Oedipus the King* at the three-thousand seat Musikfesthalle in Munich. A fortnight later it was seen at the Renz Circus in Vienna and in November at the Schumann Circus in Berlin, and in 1911 it toured throughout Europe, including Russia. The following year Reinhardt restaged the production with locally recruited companies in their native languages in Budapest and in London at Covent Garden, though speaking neither Hungarian nor English himself. Whilst the performances of individual stars in these mass spectacles, such as Moissi as Oedipus, were remarkable for their definition and audibility amidst the throng of hundreds, Reinhardt was no less scrupulous in his rehearsing of the crowd itself. His son, Gottfried, writes:

> It was promoted to an equal partnership with the protagonist, confronting him on equal terms; no customary static chorus, no actor-led units – going back to the Meiningen tradition – triggered to illustrative movements on cue; it was animated by giving each member a physiognomy of his or her own, even his or her own spoken text, and then again forming whole groupings that expressed themselves with deliberate uniformity through stylization of voice and gesture. In other words, this was not pantomine (except in pantomimes), not ballet (except in ballets), it had no ornamental functions, nor was it a realistic mob miming the emotions of 'plebs,' 'retainers,' of 'spear-carriers' or other

conventional human clusters on the stage; instead, it was an autonomous, freely expressive, dynamic element of the drama.

. . . .

That extras ought not to be 'extra,' is a directorial commonplace today. In the first and second decades of the twentieth century it was, however, considered radical. These crescendi of mass ecstasy, these huddling diminuendi, the ritardandi of dawning, slowly paralyzing horror, the breathlessly expectant accelerandi, the catatonic rests and vivaciously surging alla-breve passages, the muted fade-outs of predestined doom were symphonic. But Reinhardt was not only the conductor of this unwritten symphony. He was its composer.[16]

As an illustration of the method used by Reinhardt to achieve such effects, here is Martin Esslin's recollection of playing a small speaking part in Reinhardt's open-air production of Goethe's *Faust, Part I* in Salzburg in 1937:

Reinhardt's method of directing crowds was based on the conviction that every extra was an actor and must play his part as an individual, fully aware of the objectives and motivations of each of his movements and actions. To achieve this, the crowd was subdivided into smaller groups of not more than fifteen people, each under a group leader who had to oversee the performance of each extra, tell him what his function and objective was in each scene and at each moment. Thus, for the great Easter scene in *Faust*, an action was invented for each group or type of people. The students who went to seek the open air, the groups of girls who wanted to attract the student's attention, the burghers going for a walk with their numerous families, soldiers on furlough fooling around, beadles supervising the crowd, and a multitude of other highly individualized types of characters. Each group was given a carefully devised itinerary that would bring it into contact with given other groups at given points of the set, so that the students pursuing the girls would run into the thief being pursued by the beadle at an appropriate moment in the action, or that, at one point, all would converge on the well and the linden tree to listen to the music of the fiddlers and to dance. All this was completely integrated with the main action, which was Faust's and his assistant's, Wagner's, Easter promenade, in the course of which they muse on the people and their ways. The overall impression to the audience was one of teeming life, comparable to the grouping and organization of one of the paintings of peasant feasts by the Elder Brueghel.

Once this complex pattern had been carefully and painstakingly rehearsed, in accordance with Reinhardt's *Regiebuch*, by his assistant, he himself would appear at the last few rehearsals; and then he worked in detail on the interpretation, not only of the principals but also of the smallest character in the crowd. Gently and quietly he would indicate the movement he wanted or speak the line in the correct intonation. The plasticity and clarity of these directions was truly astonishing. One could not but execute them to perfection, so persuasive and immediately convincing was the direction.[17]

By far the most grandiose, the most costly, and yet the most successful financially of Reinhardt's mass spectacles was *The Miracle*, a drama without words by Karl Vollmoeller, based on the same legend as Maeterlinck's *Sister Beatrice*,* and with an accompaniment of music by Humperdinck, the composer of the opera *Hansel and Gretel*. It was presented originally in association with the impresario C. B. Cochran at the Olympia Exhibition Hall in London on 23 December 1911 before an audience of 30,000. Reinhardt rehearsed his multi-national cast of principals and 1,800 extras in barely three weeks, and supervised the transformation of Olympia into a gothic cathedral at the same time. London was overwhelmed by the sheer scale and extravagance of *The Miracle*, but the habitually insular critics were no less admiring of Reinhardt's taste and artistry than of his stagecraft and organisational genius. In particular his masterly timing was singled out for comment; when the production was revived at the Lyceum in 1932 the part of a cripple miraculously cured was played by the future director, Glen Byam Shaw, who recalls:

> I was brought in on a stretcher, supposedly completely paralysed, and laid out on the front of the main stage. The priest started chanting prayers, and this was taken up by the whole crowd, numbering 250 people. It grew louder and louder. At a certain point I started to move my arms very slowly, and then to drag myself off the stretcher and crawl along the floor towards the Madonna. At this point Reinhardt had arranged for drums to back the noise of the crowd. The noise grew, and I gradually got myself up on my feet and staggered forward a few steps, and then crashed to the ground. At that moment, the noise of the crowd and the drums stopped dead. I pulled myself up again, and crawled along till I reached the steps leading to the niche where the Madonna was standing. I struggled up them, and stood below her, gave an agonized cry, and was restored to health. All that was in complete silence from the moment I fell until I cried out. Then the whole crowd cheered, and the orchestra and choir burst out into a hymn of praise.[18]

The London revival was one of several throughout Europe and the United States, including a run of 298 performances at the Century Theatre, New York in 1924, followed by an American tour which lasted five years.[19]

In 1914 Reinhardt conceived the plan of transforming the Schumann Circus into a permanent German National Theatre. Progress was delayed by the war, but eventually financial backing was secured, again by brother Edmund, and the leading architect, Hans Poelzig, was commissioned to convert the building into a 'Theatre of the Five Thousand'. With an actual capacity of 3,300 and renamed the 'Grosses Schauspielhaus', it opened on 29 November 1919 with Reinhardt's production of the *Oresteia*. The steeply raked auditorium enclosed a deep arena at floor level backed by a raised proscenium stage. This stage had an opening variable from thirteen to twenty metres in width and was twenty-two metres deep, with cyclorama and revolve. The numerous plaster 'stalactites' which hung from the roof of the auditorium and decorated its columns were

* See p. 118–119 below.

designed to improve the acoustics, but extending as a decorative motif into the passages and foyers, they made the vast interior resemble nothing so much as a scene for a Grimms' fairytale.

Into this enchanted cave Reinhardt hoped to attract a new mass audience which, inspired by the momentous political changes of the times, would claim the theatre as its own. Unfortunately, the critics refused to accept that the bizarre decoration and massive dimensions of the building were compatible with a serious drama of ideas, and for all the stirring crowd effects, the audience found the environment uninviting. What is more, Reinhardt's repertoire of such works as the *Oresteia, Hamlet, Lysistrata, The Merchant of Venice, A Midsummer Night's Dream,* and *Julius Caesar* hardly reflected the mood of the Berlin proletariat. Even the revolutionary fervour of Romain Rolland's *Danton* amounted to no more than just another night out. As Kurt Tucholsky wrote:

> Act Three was great in Reinhardt's play –
> Six hundred extras milling
> Listen to what the critics say!
> All Berlin finds it thrilling,
> But in the whole affair I see
> A parable, if you ask me.
>
> 'Revolution!' the People howls and cries
> 'Freedom, that's what we're needing!'
> We've needed it for centuries –
> our arteries are bleeding.
> The stage is shaking. The audience rock.
> The whole thing is over by nine o'clock.
>
> The day looks grey as I come to.
> Where is that People – remember? –
> that stormed the peaks from down below?
> What happened to November?
> Silence. All gone. Just that, in fact.
> An act. An act.[20]

Disenchanted with Berlin, Reinhardt handed over the artistic direction of all his theatres to Felix Hollaender after the 1919-20 season, and for the next nine years worked there only as a guest director. His last two productions at the Grosses Schauspielhaus were Büchner's *Danton's Death* and Jacques Offenbach's operetta *Orpheus in the Underworld,* both in December 1921.[21] With his departure the theatre was given over almost entirely to operettas and spectacular revues; soon the arena was filled with seating to increase the capacity even further, and Reinhardt's dream of the drama and audience as one was obliterated. It was revived in July 1925 for just two performances when delegates to the first congress of the

German Communist Party packed the theatre to see Piscator's political revue, *Trotz Alledem!*.*

Reinhardt left Berlin to return to his native Austria, settling at the Schloss Leopoldskron, an exquisite Baroque stately home outside Salzburg. In Vienna he took over the small eighteenth-century Theater in der Josefstadt, and between 1924 and 1933 made it famous for its sophisticated comedies and farces in the tradition of the *commedia dell'arte*. But his greatest achievement was the creation of the Salzburg Festival, inaugurated on 22 August 1920 with *Jedermann*, Hugo von Hofmannsthal's version of the morality play, *Everyman*. Reinhardt had originally staged it nine years earlier at the Schumann Circus, where it made relatively little impact and prompted even the shrewd Siegfried Jacobsohn to comment: 'a sterile affair that can have no consequence whatsoever. Reinhardt is slowly, or perhaps no longer slowly, losing his touch....'[22] But on this occasion, risking Salzburg's notoriously capricious weather, Reinhardt staged the play out of doors on the Cathedral Square and enlisted the whole city in his production:

> ... We put a simple wooden platform in front of the Cathedral – he writes – and we performed on it without any properties, in broad daylight unaided by darkness when you can use lighting effects and focus the spectator's attention wherever you like. The vagaries of the day, the flight of the pigeons, the threatening storms intruded into our play and lent it a peculiar, ever changing magic.[23]

Martin Esslin describes the performance:

> The play opens with the voice of God, who complains about the sinfulness of mankind and summons his servant Death to bring him the rich Everyman to render account of his life on earth. After the prolog had been spoken, calling upon the audience to be attentive, the voice of the Lord resounded mightily from high up inside the cathedral. When the figure of Death appeared to acknowledge his summons, it was as though one of the statues adorning the facade had come to life. And when, during a rumbustious banquet on the platform, Everyman was being summoned, the voices calling him came from all sides, echoing and reechoing from the towers of the many churches of Salzburg (where indeed they had been posted). There they came: some from nearby, some from afar, some loud and thunderous, some faint and distant. There was even one actor stationed on the walls of Salzburg castle, high above the town. (I remember, as a student of the Reinhardt Seminar, serving as the link between that actor and the performance: I was stationed in the castle and had to watch for a white cloth to be waved from the tower of the cathedral to pass the cue on to the actor who was waiting, megaphone at his lips.) When the time had come for Everyman to die, dusk was falling upon the city (the time of the start of the performance varied to allow for the sunset to happen on cue),

* See pp. 147–148 below.

and the figures of Faith and Good Works that appeared to assist the dying man on his path to Eternity, dressed in white and blue seemed again to be no more than the statues of the facade miraculously come to life. When Everyman's soul was finally received into paradise, the interior of the cathedral lit up, the massive gates opened, organ music and hymns resounded from inside, and all the bells of the city's numerous churches began to peal. By this time night had fallen and the only light came from the dazzlingly lit marble-and-gold interior of the great Baroque church.[24]

With every detail noted in the *Regiebuch* (production book), *Everyman* was revived anually by Reinhardt's assistants, with Reinhardt himself present for the final week or so to polish or modify the production.

In the 1930's Reinhardt utilised a number of other outdoor locations around Europe, none more remarkable than the *Felsenreitschule*, a riding school at the base of the sheer cliff in the centre of Salzburg. Here he presented Part One of Goethe's *Faust*, building a veritable city right up the rock-face for the various locations of the drama, with God and his Archangels at the top and Mephistopheles at the bottom. As Martin Esslin says, it was 'a real realisation of the Baroque concept of the theatre as an image of the whole world on all its levels: Heaven and Hell and, in between, the earth, with life as an endless process of rising and falling from one sphere to the other'.[25]

Both *Everyman* and *Faust* were performed in 1937, but by the following year, the Nazis had annexed Austria, and Reinhardt, being a Jew, was forced to remain in the United States where he had gone to work in the cinema. In 1946 his production of *Everyman* was revived once more in Salzburg, and it is performed there to this day.

Reinhardt spent the last six years of his life in America, founding an actors' workshop in Hollywood and directing a number of plays on Broadway. But much as he took to his country of exile, and revered as he was there, he found himself, in his late sixties, obliged to compete for business in the market-place. As he himself remarked, he was judged 'too sluggish for the dance around the golden calf'.[26] He died in New York on 31 October 1943, five months after his last production.

8.   Meyerhold – the First Five Years

In the years immediately following the turn of the century Symbolism came to its peak in Russian literature, but until 1906 it yielded no drama of any consequence and had little impact on the theatre, where the Moscow Art Theatre remained the sole avant-garde influence.[1] One or two unsuccessful attempts were made to stage Maeterlinck, and both his plays and theoretical writings appeared in translation, notably *Le Trésor des humbles*, containing his essay 'Everyday Tragedy', in 1901.* Whilst stage naturalism was generally condemned by Symbolist critics, the practical problems posed by Symbolist drama itself were hardly tackled, far less solved. This situation was totally transformed within the twelve months beginning November 1906, when Vsevolod Meyerhold emerged as the most controversial director in the Russian theatre.

Like Stanislavsky, Craig and Reinhardt, Meyerhold served a thorough apprenticeship in the theatre. Born in 1874 of German parents in Penza, 350 miles to the south-east of Moscow, Meyerhold graduated with distinction from the drama school of the Moscow Philharmonic Society in 1898. Recently married and left penniless by the bankruptcy of the family distillery business, Meyerhold must have been tempted by the offers of secure and lucrative employment he received from the commercial theatre; but his teacher on the acting course had been Nemirovich-Danchenko, Stanislavsky's co-director at the newly-formed Moscow Art Theatre and, together with other Philharmonic graduates, Meyerhold followed him there. In the first season he played a wide variety of roles, ranging from the young writer, Treplev, in *The Seagull* to Tiresias in Sophocles' *Antigone*. But after four years he was being cast only in minor roles. Although still held in high esteem by both Stanislavsky and Chekhov, as much for his acute intelligence as for his natural talent, he had long since fallen out with Nemirovich, who was hostile towards his radical opinions and, in particular, his commitment to the politically contentious plays of Gorky, which were proving an embarrassment to the company.

When the Art Theatre was reorganised as a joint-stock company in 1902, Meyerhold was not amongst those invited to become shareholders,

* See pp. 47–48 above.

and together with Alexander Kosheverov, a fellow-actor, he announced his resignation. Shortly afterwards, they revealed that they had hired the municipal theatre of Kherson in the Ukraine for the 1902–1903 season. With no previous professional experience of directing, they embarked on a five-month season of seventy-nine productions (a quarter of them one-act plays), including works by Chekhov, Gorky, Ibsen, Hauptmann, Tolstoy, and Zola. The local theatregoing public was so limited in size that it demanded a change of play virtually every second night, whilst its taste was profoundly conservative and reacted instantly against any attempt at radical innovation. The new company's style of production was scrupulously naturalistic and closely modelled on the Moscow Art Theatre. Not only did Meyerhold direct the majority of the plays, but he also played many of the major roles, including Ivanov, Treplev, Astrov, and Baron Tusenbach in the four Chekhov plays.

In his second season at Kherson Meyerhold, now the sole director of the company which had been renamed the 'Fellowship of the New Drama', planned to introduce a series of Symbolist works into the repertoire, but was immediately rebuffed by his audience. Even when he moved with his company to Tiflis, the capital of Georgia, for the 1904–1905 season, he still found himself obliged to stage some eight new productions a month to sustain the box-office, and the audience was still liable to object and react violently against anything experimental. So even though Meyerhold contrived to introduce to the public such innovators as Wedekind, Strindberg, Schnitzler and Maeterlinck, it became clear to him that there was as yet no future for experimental theatre outside Moscow and Petersberg.

By March 1905 Meyerhold's reputation as an exponent of 'The New Drama' had grown sufficiently to persuade Stanislavsky that he was the man to become artistic director of the newly-formed Theatre-Studio attached to the Moscow Art Theatre. With considerable resources, a young company, talented designers and musicians, and a whole summer to prepare the first four productions, Meyerhold set about creating a theatre that would realise the symbolist ideal of a total artistic synthesis. Initially, a repertoire of ten productions was planned, of which the first four (all directed by Meyerhold) were to be *The Death of Tintagiles* by Maeterlinck, Hauptmann's *Schluck and Jau*, Ibsen's *Love's Comedy* and *Snow* by the Polish Symbolist Stanislaw Przybyszewski.

Like Lugné-Poe at the Théâtre de l'Œuvre, Meyerhold enlisted painters as his stage designers. They included Nikolai Sapunov and Sergei Sudeikin, two of the younger artists of the 'World of Art' group, which had already transformed the settings and costumes of the Imperial opera and ballet in Moscow and Petersburg. Jointly they were entrusted with the designs for *The Death of Tintagiles*. In a short time they had refused flatly to conform to the conventional method of the Moscow Art Theatre of constructing true-to-life models of the exteriors and interiors specified in the play. Following the already accepted practice in opera and ballet, and in any case inexperienced in three-dimensional work, they produced a series of pictures inspired by the theme and atmosphere of *The Death of Tintagiles* and designed for translation into scenic terms in collaboration with the director and scene-painters. Meyerhold's other designers quickly followed suit, and their method became defined as 'stylisation'. Meyerhold gives his conception of the term:

> With the word 'stylisation' I do not imply the exact reproduction of the style of a certain period or of a certain phenomenon, such as a photographer might achieve. In my opinion the concept of 'stylisation' is indivisibly tied up with the idea of convention, generalisation and symbol. To 'stylise' a given period or phenomenon means to employ every possible means of expression order to reveal the inner synthesis of that period or phenomenon, to bring out those hidden features which are deeply rooted in the style of any work of art.[2]

The convention was taken to its extreme in *Schluck and Jau*, for which the designer was Nikolai Ulyanov. Hauptmann's 'ironical masque' about two vagrants ennobled for a day to amuse the gentry was transferred from its original setting in medieval Silesia to a stylised abstraction of the 'periwig age' of Louis XIV. Here Meyerhold describes the treatment of the third scene:

> The mood of idleness and whimsy is conveyed by a row of arbours resembling wicker baskets and stretching across the forestage. The back curtain depicts a blue sky with fluffy clouds. The horizon is bounded by crimson roses stretching the entire width of the stage. Crinolines, white periwigs, and the characters' costumes are blended with the colours of the setting into a single artistic design, a symphony in mother-of-pearl ... The rise of the curtain is preceded by a duet in the style of the eighteenth century. It rises to disclose a figure seated in each arbour: in the centre is Sidselill, on either side – the ladies-in-waiting. They are embroidering a single broad ribbon with ivory needles – all in perfect time, whilst in the distance is heard a duet to the accompaniment of harp and harpsichord. Everything conveys the musical rhythm: movements, lines, gestures, dialogue, the colours of the setting and costumes. Everything that needs to be hidden from the audience is concealed behind stylised flats, with no attempt to make the spectator forget that he is in a theatre.[3]

By the time rehearsals began in June 1905, Meyerhold was firmly committed to the principle of stylisation, and he was faced with the problem of creating a style of acting consistent with it. Before approaching *The Death of Tintagiles* he acquainted himself with all the available literature on the play, paying particular attention to Maeterlinck's own writings and his theory of '*la tragédie immobile*'.* Meyerhold envisaged

* See p. 40, 48 above.

The Death of Tintagiles as '. . . a chorus of souls singing softly of suffering, love, beauty, and death'. He found the style for their realisation in the art of Il Perugino where, he said, 'the contemplative lyrical character of his subjects, the quiet grandeur and archaic splendour of his pictures could be achieved only with composition whose harmony is unmarred by the slightest abrupt movement or the merest harsh contrast'.[4]

To this end Meyerhold sought to develop a style of diction incorporating 'a cold coining of the words, free from all tremolo and the customary sobbing. A total absence of tension and lugubrious intonation.' Conventional histrionic gestures were replaced by 'The inner trembling of mystical vibration (that) is conveyed through the eyes, the lips, the sound and the manner of delivery: the exterior calm that conceals volcanic emotions, with everything light and unforced.'[5]

But, above all, Meyerhold exploited the expressive power of the actor's body. In his music drama Wagner conveys the protagonists' true emotions, the inner dialogue, through the medium of the orchestral score, which is frequently in counterpoint – emotional as well as musical – to the sung libretto. In *The Death of Tintagiles* Meyerhold tried to employ movement, gestures and poses in precisely the same manner in order to suggest the inexorable tragedy of the little Prince trapped and destroyed by the unseen Queen:

> The *truth* of human relationships is established by gestures, poses, glances and silences. Words alone cannot say everything. Hence there must be a *pattern of movement* to transform the spectator into a vigilant observer . . . The difference between the old theatre and the new is that in the new theatre speech and plasticity are each subordinated to their own particular rhythms and the two do not necessarily coincide.[6]

In order to achieve these effects, Meyerhold left as little as possible to chance, prescribing every possible detail, visual and oral, in his prompt copy, often sketching in desired gestures and poses. In this respect, his method was strikingly similar to Stanislavsky's in his early productions of Chekhov, and reflects the same uncertainty in working with inexperienced actors and in evolving a completely new style of production.

For both *Schluck and Jau* and *The Death of Tintagiles* an orchestral score was composed, and every element of the production was intended to be strictly bound by the musical scheme. But whilst it was easy enough to synchronise gestures and movements with the score, the actors found it impossible to rid their diction entirely of lifelike intonation and to think in purely rhythmical terms. As Meyerhold remarks, their task might have been easier had there existed some form of notation to record the required variations in tempo, pitch, volume and expression, thereby ensuring their consistency from one performance to the next. But the root of the trouble lay in the actors' previous training in the realist tradition: as the tension of the drama mounted they would begin once more to 'live' their roles and all thoughts of musical discipline would vanish.

The full extent of the actors' failure to master the new style of declamation did not become apparent until the Theatre-Studio moved into its permanent theatre in Moscow. Then for the first time they rehearsed on a full-sized stage with music and scenery, and this revealed a number of serious problems, beginning with the difficulty in *The Death of Tintagiles* of synchronising the actors' voices with Ilya Sats' score. Worse still, the designers now showed themselves incapable of translating their brilliant atmospheric sketches into three-dimensional scenic terms. Not only did they introduce crude naturalistic details which marred the overall impression of stylisation, but they had failed to allow for the effects of stage lighting, and it altered their original designs beyond recognition. At the beginning of October the first dress-rehearsals took place. Nikolai Ulyanov describes what happened:

> On stage semi-darkness, only the silhouettes of the actors visible, two-dimensional scenery, no wings, the back-drop hung almost level with the setting line. It's novel, and so is the rhythmical delivery of the actors on stage. Slowly the action unfolds, it seems as if time has come to a standstill. Suddenly Stanislavsky demands 'light!' The audience starts; there is noise and commotion. Sudeikin and Sapunov jump up protesting. Stanislavsky: 'The audience won't stand for darkness very long on stage, it's wrong psychologically, you need to see the actors' faces!' Sudeikin and Sapunov: 'But the settings are designed to be seen in half-darkness; they lose all artistic point if you light them!' Again silence, broken by the measured delivery of the actors, but this time with the lights full up. But once the stage was lit, it became lifeless, and the harmony between the figures and their setting was destroyed. Stanislavsky rose, followed by the rest of the audience. The rehearsal was broken off, the production rejected.[7]

To Stanislavsky the problems went deeper than settings and lighting design. Recalling the dress-rehearsal in *My Life in Art*, he writes:

> The director had tried to use his own talent to obscure the faults of artists who were simply clay in his hands for the modelling of beautiful groups and ideas. But with actors deficient in artistic technique he succeeded only in demonstrating his ideas, principles and explorations; there was nothing and nobody with which to realise them in full, and so the interesting concepts of the Studio turned into abstract theories and scientific formulae. Once again I became convinced that a great distance separates the dreams of a stage-director and their fulfilment, that above all else the theatre is for the actor and cannot exist without him, that the new drama needs new actors with a completely new technique.[8]

The opening of the Studio was put back, first to 10 October and then to the 21st. But by then Russia was in the grip of a general strike, and on 14 October all cultural life in Moscow was disrupted by a fresh and violent wave of revolutionary disturbances. Practically all theatres closed and the Art Theatre was turned into a casualty station with actresses from both companies serving as nurses. Five days later, after an imperial manifesto had proclaimed a constitutional monarchy, normal theatrical activities were resumed. However, the opening of the Studio was postponed indefinitely, and very soon Stanislavsky decided to cut his losses by liquidating the enterprise. At a personal cost of 80,000 roubles, which represented half his entire capital, he paid off every member of the company up to May 1906. It was partly to recover this loss that the Art Theatre embarked on its first European tour in February 1906. Even those most passionately committed to the ideals of the Theatre-Studio soon became reconciled to its closure, not least, Meyerhold himself. But in October 1905 it must have seemed a dismal fiasco to all concerned. Nevertheless, its failure stemmed not so much from the fallaciousness of its aims as from the deep-rooted habits and prejudices that frustrated their complete realisation: in effect, stylisation failed because it was not stylised enough. The lessons learnt at the Studio equipped Meyerhold with the experience to achieve the successes that were soon to follow in Petersburg, and led to the establishment of a new movement in the Russian Theatre, a movement to which the Moscow Art Theatre itself remained committed and to which it was soon to contribute with a series of productions culminating in 1912 with the *Hamlet* of Edward Gordon Craig.

Meyerhold remained briefly in Moscow to recreate his original role of Treplev in the Art Theatre's revival of *The Seagull*, but by now he felt a stranger in the company, and at the end of the year he left for Petersburg. After two further experimental theatre projects had failed to attract financial backing, he accepted an invitation to revive his company in Tiflis, where finally he succeeded in staging *The Death of Tintagiles*.

But Tiflis in 1906 was little more than a staging-post in Meyerhold's career: before he returned there he had been invited by the actress, Vera Komissarzhevskaya, to join her Petersburg company and in May he signed a contract with her as artistic director and actor for the 1906-1907 season.

It was about this time that Meyerhold first read Georg Fuchs' *The Stage of the Future*,[9] a work which, as he himself admitted, made the deepest impression on him. Reflecting symbolist thought as far back as Wagner, Fuchs called for the restoration of the theatre as a festive ritual, involving performers and spectators alike in a common experience that would reveal the universal significance of their personal existence. The drama, he writes, has no life except as a shared experience: 'By virtue of their origins the player and the spectator, the stage and the auditorium are not opposed to each other, they are a unity.' To facilitate this unity, he proposes an auditorium similar to Wagner's Festspielhaus at Bayreuth:

a steeply raked amphitheatre capable of accommodating a large audience in the closest possible proximity to the stage. The stage itself is to be wide rather than deep and divided into three ascending strips joined by shallow steps of the same width. The low forestage is located in front of the proscenium opening, extending in a shallow arc into the auditorium. The middle stage is in effect a narrow bridge joining two walls, between which the aperture is normally closed with a backcloth. In the event of the middle-stage being used (for crowd scenes or to facilitate rapid scene changes), a painted backdrop may be hung behind the rear stage, but in order to furnish a flat decorative background rather than to create an illusion of distance or perspective. The main action is concentrated on the shallow plane of the forestage where the performers are meant to stand out against the background like figures in a bas-relief.

In this way, says Fuchs, all attention is focussed on the most profound means of dramatic expression: the rhythmical movement of the human body in space. He reminds the actor that his art 'has its origins in the *dance*. The means of expression employed in the dance are equally the natural means of expression for the actor, the difference being merely one of *range*.'[10] Not only in Ancient Greece but, as the company of Otodziro Kawakami had demonstrated recently on its first European tour, in the Japanese theatre too every movement is dictated by the choreographic rhythm of the action.

For the Japanese there is no part of a production that is not directed towards the enhancement of the overall rhythmical scheme, and this in its turn reflects the inner psychological development of the drama. The text of the play, says Fuchs, is akin to a musical score, to be interpreted by the performers acting in perfect accord.

Fuchs' advocacy of a theatre based on rhythmical movement is close in spirit to what Meyerhold was attempting in Moscow in 1905, and it is significant that they both took as a paradigm the style of Kawakami's leading actress, Sada Yakko, whom Meyerhold almost certainly saw performing when Kawakami's company visited Russia in 1902.[11] But in *The Stage of the Future* Fuchs was more coherent and more radical in his ideas than Meyerhold had been in his experiments at the Theatre-Studio. On the other hand, Fuchs' doctrinaire theories had yet to be tempered by the inevitable compromises involved in bringing a production to actual performance: he conducted his first experiments with the relief stage in May 1906 at the Prinzregenten-Theater in Munich, and it was not until 1908 that it was incorporated in modified form in the new Munich Artists' Theatre.[12]

As well as lending weight to Meyerhold's own views, *The Stage of the Future* drew his attention to certain aspects of the theatre which he had previously overlooked. An early opportunity to examine them offered itself in June when the Fellowship of the New Drama presented a two-week season at Poltava. There, in Schnitzler's *Cry of Life*, Meyerhold consciously modelled the actors' movements on oriental practice, so that their 'moves either preceded or followed their speeches. Every movement was treated like a dance (a Japanese device), even when there was no emotional motivation for it.' But of greatest significance was his utilisation of stage space in a new, more flexible manner:

> In *Ghosts* and *Cain* (by Osip Dymov) the unity of place was stressed (in the latter play contrary to the author's stage directions). The plays were performed without a front curtain. This was facilitated by the exceptionally convenient design of the stage of the Poltava theatre ... it is easy to remove the footlights and cover over the orchestra pit with a floor on a level with the stage; the resultant platform makes a forestage which extends deep into the auditorium.[13]

In 1912 Meyerhold wrote in the foreword to his book *On the Theatre:* 'Even though the theme of the forestage is not dealt with comprehensively in any of the articles below, it will be easy for the reader to see that all the threads of the various themes in this book lead towards the question of the forestage.' It was at Poltava in 1906 that he first glimpsed the significance of what was to become a crucial element in his mature style.

At the beginning of the twentieth century Vera Komissarzhevskaya was generally recognised as the greatest interpreter in Russia of modern dramatic roles, a reputation she had won by her performance in such parts as Nina in *The Seagull*, Sonya in *Uncle Vanya*, Hilda in *The Master Builder* and Nora in *A Doll's House*. In 1902, at the height of her fame she left the Imperial Alexandrinsky Theatre, determined to perform in plays of her own choosing in her own theatre. Eventually, after two seasons touring in the provinces, her ambition was realised when she returned to Petersburg in 1904 and leased the Passage Theatre to house her new permanent company. Her repertoire was similar to that of the Moscow Art Theatre, with a strong bias towards Ibsen, Chekhov and Gorky, and the style of production was very close to the naturalism of Stanislavsky and Nemirovich-Danchenko.

Eventually, Komissarzhevskaya, like Stanislavsky, felt the need to come to terms with 'The New Drama', and like him, was convinced that Meyerhold held the key to it. He had refused her original invitation because it made no mention of acting, to which he still felt an equal commitment, but now he accepted, and joined the company in September 1906.

The first season with Komissarzhevskaya put him under constant strain. After nearly six months' separation from his wife and daughters in Tiflis and Poltava, he soon found himself on the road again. Whilst a new theatre in Petersburg was being refurbished for the company to move into, he was obliged to join them on tour in Lithuania and western Russia in order to rehearse the opening productions for the new season. Vera Komissarzhevskaya's Dramatic Theatre opened in its elegant new home on Ofitserskaya Street on 10 November 1906 with Meyerhold's production of *Hedda Gabler*, the actress herself playing Hedda. It was a production that owed a great deal to the ideas of Georg Fuchs. Although Meyerhold retained the footlights, he achieved what was in effect a 'relief stage' by reducing the acting area to a broad shallow strip, 33 feet wide and only 12 feet deep, at the extreme front of the stage. Nikolai Sapunov designed a single backdrop, featuring a tapestry and a huge cut-out window, with a further cloth (depicting a day sky and, for Act Four, a night sky with stars). The dominant colours were light blue and gold, with a white grand piano, and a divan and huge armchair, both covered in white fur. The aim was to convey the mood of 'a cold, regal, autumnal Hedda', her slender, cool, green-clad figure associated with the throne-like armchair. Similarly, her bumbling pedant of a husband, George Tesman, was dressed in no identifiable fashion, but in a dull grey, loose jacket with sloping shoulders, an absurdly wide tie, and broad trousers tapering sharply towards the bottoms – all designed together with his movements to express the essence of 'Tesmanism'. Judge Brack frequently sat by a pedestal which bore a large rose, one leg crossed over the other and his hands clasped round his knee – the pose of a faun intended to suggest his manipulative, unprincipled character. Much of the action was immobile; for instance, when Hedda and Loevborg are alone for the first time in Act Two:

> Throughout the entire scene they sit side by side, tense and motionless, looking straight ahead. Their quiet, disquieting words fall rhythmically from lips which seem dry and cold. Before them stand two glasses and a flame burns beneath the punch bowl (Ibsen stipulates Norwegian 'cold punch'). Not once throughout the entire long scene do they alter the direction of their gaze or their pose. Only on the line 'Then you too have a thirst for life!' does Loevborg make a violent motion towards Hedda, and at this point the scene comes to an abrupt conclusion.[14]

Meyerhold's intention was that the audience should hear the lines as though they were being addressed directly at them, and should be able to detect the merest change of expression in the characters' faces, thereby sensing the inner dialogue of concealed emotions. Here was a complete realisation of Maeterlinck's 'static theatre', reinforced by Meyerhold's experience of the decorum of eastern stylisation.

Hedda Gabler was received coldly by the public and even those few critics who admired the elegant beauty of the decor considered that it was hopelessly at odds with Ibsen's intentions. They complained that

Sapunov's sumptuous autumnal vision obscured the point of all Hedda's despairing efforts to escape the trap of the narrow conventions and tawdry bad taste of provincial society. Their objections were directed less against stylisation as such than against what was stylised in this instance: the theme should have been, not Hedda's bay mare and liveried footman, but George's slippers and Aunt Julie's new hat.

The criticism seems incontestable: *Hedda Gabler* was a classic example of a production subordinated to the director's ruling obsession. In a recent probing analysis of him, the Soviet critic Alexander Matskin refers to 'the tragedy of Meyerhold's one-sidedness', whereby 'at any given moment he had a single ruling idea that forced his more durable preoccupations to retreat into the background'.[15] In this particular instance Matskin suggests that Meyerhold felt overwhelmed by the weight of genius and erudition he had encountered amongst the Petersburg Symbolists, and tried to compensate by emphasising the formal aspects of his work, the one area in which he felt truly confident. There may well be some truth in this; certainly the Symbolist philosophical debates at this time were of an awesome complexity and abstruseness. But equally, Meyerhold's interpretation of *Hedda Gabler* (to say nothing of his subsequent productions with Komissarzhevskaya) was conceived in part at least as a polemic against the conventional view of Ibsen, stage naturalism in general, *and* the whole materialist philosophy from which it emerged. In this, he was at one with the Symbolists in regarding beauty as an aesthetic protest against bourgeois society. This doctrine was hardly new: as we have seen, it had been expounded at least twenty years earlier by Mallarmé and the French Symbolists;* but nobody, with the arguable exception of Edward Gordon Craig, had succeeded in bringing it to fruition in the theatre before Meyerhold. It is interesting to compare the Petersburg *Hedda Gabler* with two other major symbolist productions of Ibsen staged within the same few weeks: Reinhardt's *Ghosts* in Berlin, and Craig's *Rosmersholm* with Duse's company in Florence.†

Meyerhold's production of Maeterlinck's *Sister Beatrice* on 22 November was an even more programmatic statement of symbolist ideas, intended as it was to soothe the audience with a vision of harmony and to induce participation in a corporate mystical experience akin to the medieval miracle play. It proved to be the one generally acknowledged success that Meyerhold enjoyed with Komissarzhevskaya, and for her in the role of Beatrice her sole personal triumph with him.

Maeterlinck's '*petit jeu de scène*' tells in simple terms the story of a nun, Beatrice, who elopes from a convent with a knight. A statue of the Virgin comes to life and takes the place of Beatrice in the convent so that her

---

* See p. 37 f. above.

† See pp. 87–88, 101–102 above.

absence is never discovered. After many years during which she sinks to the depths of depravity Beatrice returns in search of retribution. But the Virgin returns to her pedestal and Beatrice dies, hallowed by the sisters for her life of selfless devotion.

Maeterlinck sets the play in fourteenth-century Louvain, but again Meyerhold applied the principle of stylisation, seeking to imbue the legend with universality by creating a synthesis based on the style of Pre-Raphaelite and early Renaissance painters. The future director, Alexander Tairov, at that time a member of the company, recalls how Meyerhold modelled poses and complete groupings on reproductions of the works of Memling, Botticelli, and other masters. In the final act the tableau of the sisters holding the dying Beatrice was a conscious evocation of the traditional descent from the cross. Dialogue and movement were treated in the style first developed by Meyerhold to render Maeterlinck's 'static tragedy', *The Death of Tintagiles*. 'The melodious style of delivery and movements in slow motion were designed to preserve the implicitness of expression, and each phrase was barely more than a whisper, the manifestation of an inner tragic experience.'[16]

Meyerhold succeeded in disciplining his actors' movements by the simple expedient of confining them to a strip of the stage in front of the proscenium arch no more than seven feet in depth. Yevgeny Znosko-Borovsky describes the chorus of nuns:

> All dressed as one, with completely identical gestures, with slow restrained movements and following one another precisely, they moved the whole time in profile in order to maintain the repose of a bas-relief; they passed before you like a wonderful design on the grey stone of an ancient cathedral ... Here was a crowd, a mass in which no individual led or constituted a separate life or a separate character who might disrupt the essential idea and impression of the mass. Here was a unity that by its unity, by the rhythm of all its movements, poses and gestures, produced a far deeper impression than a naturalistic crowd split up into separate units.[17]

The décor by Sergei Sudeikin was executed in contrasting tones of blue, green and grey. A simple 'gothic' wall stood almost on top of the footlights, a neutral background designed to throw the actors' figures into plastic relief. Although footlights were used it was contrary to Meyerhold's own wishes; financial considerations frustrated his original intention to link the forestage with the auditorium by a flight of polished wooden steps and thereby make the actors stand farther from the flat background. Once again the resemblance to Georg Fuchs' relief stage was unmistakeable.

Meyerhold's production drew grudging praise from the previously hostile critics, but the acting (with the exception of Komissarzhevskaya) was condemned as lifeless and uneven. Many blamed Meyerhold's system, which, they maintained, reduced the artist to a mere puppet. But probably

Peter Yartsev came as close as anybody to the truth when he wrote the following year:

> (Komissarzhevskaya's) theatre is seeking to express technically forms that the theatre of the future will have to fill out with content. That is why the new theatre concentrates exclusively on the visual side (settings, costumes, group-ings, movements). As yet in the new theatre there is not and cannot be a new actor.[18]

It was the same fault as Stanislavsky had observed at the Theatre-Studio, and it helps to explain why Meyerhold tended to overstress the inanimate aspects of his productions for all the years until it became possible for him to school actors in his own system and eventually create his own company with them. It was not until his production of *The Magnanimous Cuckold* in 1922 that this ambition was fully realised.

Alexander Blok's *The Fairground Booth*,* which Meyerhold staged in a double bill with Maeterlinck's *The Miracle of St. Antony* on 30 December 1906, was both formally and thematically a total contrast to all his previous productions. Born in 1880, Blok was recognised as the central figure amongst the Russian Symbolist poets, but *The Fairground Booth* was his first play. Originally commissioned for another theatre company which failed to materialise, *The Fairground Booth* was written in January 1906 and published three months later.

In the first of the play's 'lyric scenes' an assembly of 'Mystics' awaits the arrival of Death in the person of a beautiful lady. Pierrot, 'in a white smock, dreamy, distraught, pale, with no moustache or eyebrows, like all Pierrots', protests that she is his sweetheart Columbine. She appears, silent and all in white; Pierrot despairs and is on the point of conceding the allegory to the Mystics when Columbine speaks to reassure him. But at once Harlequin, 'eternally youthful, agile and handsome', his costume decked with silver bells, comes to abduct her, leaving Pierrot and the Mystics confounded. The scene changes quickly to a ball with masked couples gliding back and forth. In the centre sits Pierrot, 'on the bench where Venus and Tannhäuser usually embrace'. He tells how Harlequin carried off Columbine in a sleigh, only for her to turn into a lifeless cardboard doll; then Pierrot and Harlequin roamed the snow-covered streets together, singing and dancing to console themselves. There appear in turn three pairs of masked lovers. The first pair, in pink and blue, imagine themselves beneath the lofty dome of some church: a vision of sacred love menaced by a dark figure, the man's double, beckoning from behind a column. Dancing figures disclose the second couple, the em-bodiment of violent passion in red and black; they leave, again pursued by a third, 'a flickering tongue of black flame'. Finally we see courtly love, the knight in cardboard visor and a huge wooden sword, the lady echoing

* In Russian 'Balaganchik', sometimes translated as 'The Puppet Show'.

his portentous phrases. Their dignity is rudely shattered by a clown who runs up and pokes his tongue at the knight. The knight strikes him on the head with his sword; the clown collapses over the footlights crying 'Help! I'm bleeding cranberry juice!', and then jumps up and leaves. A leaping, jostling torchlight procession of masks makes its entrance. Harlequin steps from the crowd to greet the world in the springtime:

> Here nobody dares to admit
> That spring is abroad in the air!
> Here nobody knows how to love;
> They all live beset by sad dreams.
> Greetings world! You're with me again!
> So long your soul has been near to me!
> And now once more I will breathe your spring
> Through your window of gold!

And he leaps through the window. But the view is only painted on paper, and he falls headlong through the hole.

Death reappears, a scythe over her back, and all the masks freeze in terror. But Pierrot recognises her again as his Columbine: the scythe fades in the morning light and colour floods her cheeks. They are about to embrace when 'The Author', who throughout has kept appearing to protest at the misrepresentation of his text, pokes his head between them to acclaim the happy ending of his simple tale. As he is joining their hands all the scenery is abruptly whisked aloft and Columbine and all the masks disappear. The Author withdraws in hurried confusion, leaving the baffled Pierrot to face the audience alone and play a mournful tune on his pipe 'about his pale face, his hard life, and his sweetheart Columbine'.[19]

As early as 1902 in his first major work, the poetic cycle *On the Beautiful Lady*, Blok had invoked the traditional figures of Pierrot, Harlequin and Columbine to convey his intermittent doubts in the constancy of human relations and even the coherence of personality itself. The bold sceptic, Harlequin, and the childlike innocent, Pierrot, came to represent the two conflicting aspects of the poet's own character, whilst Columbine was both the 'beautiful lady', the ideal of perfect womanhood venerated by the Russian Symbolists, and the very counterfeit of beauty, the deception inherent in all outward appearances. In *The Fairground Booth* he exploited the theatre's irony to give his dualistic vision even greater power. Much of the invention was his own, but in Meyerhold he found an interpreter with the power and insight to extend it still further.

The production followed Blok's stage directions almost to the letter: the author's intrusions, the clown bleeding cranberry juice, Harlequin's leap through the paper flat, the vanishing settings, were all conceived by Blok before his collaboration with Meyerhold and appear in the first published edition of the play. But taking his cue from Blok, Meyerhold depicted the assembly of Mystics as a row of cardboard cut-outs with the actors' hands and heads thrust through them, and when they were left confounded by Harlequin's abduction of Columbine, they ducked beneath the table, leaving a row of headless and handless torsos. There was a further crucial refinement: whereas Blok prescribes 'a normal theatrical room with three walls, a window and a door', Meyerhold and his designer Nikolai Sapunov devised a little box-set erected on the stage with a raised stage of its own, with a prompter and all the scenery exposed, thereby lending a further dimension to the play's irony. In the final reconciliation scene this complete setting was hauled aloft into the files, leaving Pierrot alone on the bare stage.

Pierrot was played by Meyerhold himself in a manner that seemed to owe little to any of the numerous sentimental stereotypes who had gone before him. Valentina Verigina, who played the second masked lady in the ball scene, writes:

> On the stage direction 'Pierrot awakes from his reverie and brightens up' (in Scene One), Meyerhold made an absurd wave with both his sleeves, and in this movement was expressed the suddenly dawning hope of the clown. Further waves of his sleeves conveyed various different things. These stylised gestures were inspired by the musical conception of the characterisation; they were eloquent because, I repeat, they were prompted by the inner rhythm of the role. The gestures always followed the words, complementing them as though bringing a song to its conclusion, saying without words something understood only by Pierrot himself ... It was as though he was listening to a song being sung by his heart of its own free will. He wore a strange expression, gazing intently into his own soul.

In the closing scene:

> ... the curtain fell behind Pierrot-Meyerhold and he was left face to face with the audience. He stood staring at them, and it was as though Pierrot was looking into the eyes of every single person. There was something irresistible in his gaze ... Then Pierrot looked away, took his pipe from his pocket and began to play the tune of a rejected and unappreciated heart. That moment was the most powerful in his whole performance. Behind his lowered eyelids one sensed a gaze, stern and full of reproach.[20]

These accounts suggest a style of acting far removed from the *tableaux vivants* of Meyerhold's earlier productions. The abrupt changes of mood, the sudden switches of personality, the deliberate disruption of illusion, the asides to the audience, all demanded a mental and physical dexterity, the ability to improvise, a capacity for acting not only the part but also one's attitude to it. These devices were all waiting to be rediscovered in the tradition of the popular theatre stretching back to the *commedia dell'arte* and beyond. It was this theatre, the theatre of masks and improvisation, that the experience of *The Fairground Booth* led Meyerhold to explore. In this he was shortly to be followed by a number of younger Russian directors, notably Alexander Tairov, Nikolai Evreinov, and Yevgeny Vakhtangov, with practical experiments into every aspect of the traditonal popular theatre from the mystery-play, and the pageant through to the circus and the music-hall. Together, they achieved a revival of conscious theatricality that was to inspire most of the greater achievements of the early Soviet period.

The opening night of *The Fairground Booth* and many subsequent performances provoked memorable scenes in the theatre. Sixteen years later Sergei Auslender recalled:

> The auditorium was in an uproar as though it were a real battle. Solid, respectable citizens were ready to come to blows; whistles and roars of anger alternated with piercing howls conveying a mixture of fervour, defiance, anger and despair: 'Blok – Sapunov – Kuzmin – M-e-y-e-r-h-o-l-d. Br-a-v-o-o-o'
> ... And there before all the commotion, radiant like some splendid monument, in his severe black frock-coat and holding a bunch of white lilies, stood Alexander Alexandrovich Blok, his deep blue eyes reflecting both sadness and wry amusement. And at his side the white Pierrot ducked and recoiled as though devoid of any bones, disembodied like a spectre, flapping the long sleeves of his loose smock.[21]

Blok clearly revelled in the scandal; three weeks after the opening he wrote to a friend: '. . . at this very moment *The Fairground Booth* is being given its fifth performance at Komissarzhevskaya's theatre, and – I would say – successfully since at the first and second performances I took many curtain-calls and they heartily whistled and catcalled at me . . .'[22] For his part, Meyerhold regarded the violent demonstrations as conclusive proof of the production's 'true theatricality'. Almost to a man, the critics were nonplussed by *The Fairground Booth* and dismissed it as a joke in very poor taste. Their response is fairly represented by 'Objective', writing in the Petersburg *Theatre Review*: 'Truly what took place at Vera Komissarzhevskaya's theatre on the 30 December must be regarded as an insult, not only to the theatre, but also to literature, poetry, and dramatic writing; it lies beyond the pale no less of art than of common sense.' As Blok himself later said, there was essentially nothing new in what he was saying in *The Fairground Booth*; the difference was that he was saying it in public rather than in the personal isolation of the lyric. What had previously been the occasional voicing of self-doubt was now an outright rejection of transcendental reality, a sardonic picture of a spiritually exhausted world devoid of constant values. To no small degree Blok's innate pessimism was greatly exacerbated by the sense of dislocation experienced generally by the Russian intelligentsia in the aftermath of the 1905 Revolution. *The Fairground Booth* in Meyerhold's production captured this mood with acute poetic accuracy, and therein lies the main reason for the violently opposed responses to it. For young and disenchanted radicals it became a rallying point, some going so far as to interpret Columbine as a symbol for the long-awaited, but never-to-appear Russian constitution.

Analysing the 'New Spirit' in *The Banquet Years*, Roger Shattuck writes: '... there are subjects about which one cannot be clear without fraud. Every emotion and conviction has its reverse side, and ambiguity can stand for a profound frankness, an acknowledgement of the essential ambivalence of truth and experience, of life itself'.[23] This was as true of Blok and Meyerhold as it had been of Jarry, and it was the impulse that gave their art a crucial new direction away from the resigned immobility of Symbolism.

In 1912 Meyerhold wrote an article entitled 'The Fairground Booth' analysing the lessons learnt from the production of Blok's play and his subsequent experiments. In it he explores the implications of the mask, meaning not so much the traditional mask of the *commedia* as the style of acting that the mask signifies: the emotional self-control and physical dexterity that enable the actor (as he himself had done in *The Fairground Booth*) to assume the various aspects of his part, 'to manipulate his masks', and at the same time to comment – both implicitly and explicitly – on the actions of himself and his fellow-characters, thereby affording the spectator a montage of images, a multi-faceted portrait of every role. He proceeds to identify a close relationship between the mask and the style defined as '*the grotesque*', of which he writes:

> It is the style that reveals the most wonderful horizons to the creative artist. 'I', my personal attitude to life, precedes all else ... The grotesque does not recognise the *purely* debased or the *purely* exalted. The grotesque mixes opposites, consciously creating harsh incongruity, *playing entirely on its own originality* ... The grotesque deepens life's outward appearance to the point where it ceases to appear merely natural ... The basis of the grotesque is the artist's constant desire to switch the spectator from the plane he has just reached to another that is totally unforeseen.[24]

But for Meyerhold, as for Jarry, the grotesque was no mere stylistic device; it emerged from a recognition of the irrational and an acceptance of it on its own terms. Alexander Matskin writes 'Once he had met Blok, it became clear that for Meyerhold the grotesque was not merely *a means of expression*, a way of heightening colours, it was no less than the *content* of that reality, that dislocated world in which he found himself and which formed the subject of his art.'[25]

There were times in the Soviet period when Meyerhold was inclined to play down his affinity with Blok, and certainly their association after 1906 was far from one of unbroken harmony. Nevertheless, *The Fairground Booth* remained a crucial experience for Meyerhold and one that continued to reverberate through his work long after 1917.

Meyerhold's final production of the season on 22 February 1907 was the first performance of *The Life of a Man* by Leonid Andreyev. In five episodic scenes the play traces the course of a man's life from the moment of birth through poverty, love, success, and disaster to death. The figures involved are allegorical, with little or no characterisation and are called 'The Man', 'The Wife', 'The Neighbours', etc. A prologue is spoken by 'Someone in grey, called He', who then remains on stage throughout, invisible to the protagonists, commenting occasionally on the action, and holding a burning candle to symbolise the gradual ebb of the Man's life and his ultimate return to oblivion.

Although impressionistic rather than naturalistic, Andreyev's stage directions are detailed and explicit. But as with *Hedda Gabler* Meyerhold chose to exercise his directorial prerogative. He devised the settings himself, employing a designer merely as an executant; scenic space was handled with an unprecedented freedom, showing that the stylised theatre was no longer a slave to painting and no longer confined to the shallow relief-stage. The key to the entire production was light, for the first time exploited by Meyerhold for its sculptural power. Employing the full stage area, he enclosed it with dull grey curtains to produce a dim, monochrome expanse. The footlights were removed, and single overhead spots used to produce soft pools of light, which disclosed immobile characters grouped around single items of furniture. In order to enhance the Goya-like chiaroscuro effects, the actors make-up was harshly accentuated, and furniture chosen for exaggerated features that would catch the light. The whole production was dream-like, playing on the power of the imagination to supply all that remained invisible. It is not certain when Meyerhold first encountered Adolphe Appia's theories, only that by the time he staged *Tristan and Isolde* at the Mariinsky Opera in 1909 he was thoroughly familiar with Appia's pioneering work *Die Musik und die Inscenierung*, and his rejection of painted flats in favour of the stage treated as actual volume in which light is the interpretive medium.[26] Appia's conception was entirely without precedent and attracted little attention before 1912, when his work was first seen on the stage of Jaques-Dalcroze's School of Eurhythmics at Hellerau. But reading accounts of Meyerhold's production of *The Life of a Man*, it is difficult to believe that he had no knowledge of Appia's theories in 1907.

Although rehearsed for only twelve days, *The Life of a Man* was a great popular success and played to full houses for the last two weeks of the season; Fyodor Komissarzhevsky, the Head of Design at his sister's theatre, described the production as 'the most fully integrated during the first two seasons at Ofitserskaya Street'. Andreyev himself preferred Meyerhold's version to Stanislavsky's at the Moscow Art Theatre soon afterwards, which he said had a refinement akin to Beardsley rather than the Goya-like harshness that he had in mind. Yet so shallow and preten-tious does the text seem today, and so far did Meyerhold diverge from Andreyev's stage directions, that one feels the production's success must have been due to its visual impact rather than to the intrinsic worth of the play itself.

In his essay *On the History and Technique of the Theatre* (written in 1906–1907),[27] in which he describes the origins and development of the stylised theatre, Meyerhold stresses again and again the capacity of the spectator 'to employ his imagination creatively in order to supply the details intimated by the action on stage'. It is a principle that is the very foundation of stylisation; it was demonstrated by all Meyerhold's produc-tion for Komissarzhevskaya, but by none so clearly as *The Life of a Man*. It was precisely because the spectator was shown so little that he saw so much, superimposing his own imagined or remembered experiences on the events enacted before him. In this way the dialogue and characters assumed a significance and a profundity which overcame their intrinsic banality. Time and again in the Soviet period Meyerhold exploited this associative power of the spectator's imagination to transform mediocre literature into the most telling theatre.

By the autumn of 1907 Meyerhold's position with Komissarzhevskaya had deteriorated to the point where his impending resignation was being openly discussed in the press. In particular, Meyerhold resented the fact that the company had gone on tour in the summer with a number of their old productions. For her part, Komissarzhevskaya was bitterly disap-pointed at the rejection of their new work by the Moscow critics, who had ridiculed even her performance in *Sister Beatrice*.

But Meyerhold was far too single-minded to allow the dwindling confidence within the company to curb his experimental zeal. Encouraged by his successes with Blok and Andreyev, Meyerhold wanted to explore still further the flexibility of the stage area. He proposed staging a new play by Fyodor Sologub called *The Gift of the Wise Bees* 'in the round' by building a stage in the centre of the auditorium and seating part of the audience on the permanent stage. Like so many later innovaters in this field he was foiled by local theatre regulations, and it was left to Nikolai Okhlopkov a quarter of a century later at the Realistic Theatre in Moscow to present the first modern productions on a stage completely surrounded by the audience.

Even so, Meyerhold's first production in the autumn was hardly less bold – not only in conception but in subject matter too. In April he had gone to Berlin with Fyodor Komissarzhevsky and whilst there they had visited Max Reinhardt's Kammerspiele. Meyerhold was reserved in his opinion of Reinhardt. Whilst admiring his boldness, he was quick to spot the influence of Craig, criticised the indiscriminate use of Art Nouveau, and deplored the traditional manner of most of the acting. One of the productions he saw was Wedekind's tragi-grotesque of adolescent sexuality, *Spring Awakening*, which was being staged for the first time,* and he resolved immediately to present it in Petersburg.

Surprisingly enough the play was passed by the Russian censor, albeit extensively cut, and was given its first performance at Ofitserskaya Street on 15 September 1907. Meyerhold describes his interpretation in a production note: 'We have looked for a soft, unemphatic tone. The aim is to tone down the realism of certain scenes, to tone down the physiological aspect of puberty in the children. Sunlight and joyousness in the settings to counteract the chaos and gloom in the souls of the children'. Critics and friends of the theatre alike could find little of merit in Wedekind's text, castigating both its style and theme. The one redeeming feature seen in the production was the method of area-lighting, which Meyerhold devised to eliminate constant scene changes and to ensure an uninterrupted sequence of the play's eighteen short scenes, played on no less than four levels. For all its originality, area lighting was a technique accorded little significance by Meyerhold at the time. In fact, *Spring Awakening* seems to have been a production he was anxious to forget, for he makes no mention of it in his survey of his first ten years' work, published in 1913. Nevertheless, the production's episodic structure lent the action both fluency and moments of abrupt contrast of a kind long absent from the theatre. Now that Meyerhold had recognised the limitations of the static drama he was beginning to exploit fully the dimensions of theatrical time and space in a manner that had no precedent on the modern stage. In retrospect, productions such as *The Fairground Booth*, *The Life of a Man*, and *Spring Awakening* appear unmistakably cinematic – cinematic at a time when the cinema itself was little more than filmed theatre. When Meyerhold came to make his first film *The Picture of Dorian Gray* in 1915 he immediately applied his dramatic theories to such telling effect that the result was what Jay Leyda has called '... undoubtedly the most important Russian film made previous to the February Revolution'.[28]

On 10 October 1907 Meyerhold presented Maeterlinck's *Pelléas and Mélisande* in a specially commissioned translation by the prominent symbolist poet, Valery Bryusov, and with Komissarzhevskaya as Mélisande. Despite the production's imposing credentials, it was a total failure which proved decisive in Meyerhold's career. The principal fault lay in the setting, which consisted of a small raised platform in the centre of the stage; the stage floor was removed to furnish an orchestra pit surrounding the platform. Possibly, Meyerhold was attempting to realise within legal limits his frustrated project for a theatre in the round, in which case the whole point was lost by enclosing the platform from behind with painted

* See p. 102 above.

flats. As Meyerhold admitted afterwards, the effect was precisely that of his early productions against decorative panels: the three-dimensional figures of the actors lost all plasticity in their close proximity to the painted background and were so constricted in their movements that they had no choice but to move as automata in obedience to the scheme prescribed by the director.

For Komissarzhevskaya, struggling at the age of forty-three to play the child-like Mélisande, the production was a personal disaster. The only true success that she had enjoyed with Meyerhold was in *Sister Beatrice* almost a year earlier, and her total failure as Mélisande was more than she could bear. Meyerhold was told bluntly that either he must modify his production methods or leave the company. Although Meyerhold conceded little, an uneasy rapprochement was achieved and he continued as artistic director. In an atmosphere of confusion previously announced productions were cancelled, but somehow Meyerhold contrived to rehearse Fyodor Sologub's new tragedy, *Death's Victory*, and it was presented for the first time on 6 November 1907. With this production Meyerhold confirmed his repudiation of what he called the 'decorative stylisation' of *Pelléas and Mélisande* and his earlier work. Georgy Chulkov wrote:

> The settings (devised by Meyerhold) possessed a stylised simplicity and were most agreeable: a broad flight of steps the entire breadth of the stage, massive columns and the muted, severe tones of the overall background facilitated a blend of the visual impressions with the impressions created by the severe and precise style of the tragedy itself... At the very end the orgiastic frenzy of the crowd around the magnificent Algista was imbued with the magic of true theatre. Apparently, at this point the author wanted to cross the sacred line, 'to destroy the footlights'. And it would have been possible to do this ... by extending the steps on the stage into the auditorium,* thereby enabling the action of the tragedy to culminate amongst the spectators.[29]

The critical reception of *Death's Victory* was almost unanimously enthusiastic, and the production was acknowledged as a clear advance in Meyerhold's style. However, Komissarzhevskaya (yet again without a part in a successful production) was not reassured, and three days after the premiere Meyerhold was dismissed from the company.

Meyerhold protested that his summary dismissal in mid-season was a violation of professional ethics and demanded that the affair be submitted to a court of arbitration. However, Komissarzhevskaya's decision was upheld by the court and Meyerhold's place as artistic director was taken by Fyodor Komissarzhevsky.† Only one further production was staged,

---

* Meyerhold maintained that he was prevented from extending the steps down into the auditorium by the caution of the theatre's management.

† Komissarzhevsky later emigrated and made his name as a director in England and the United States.

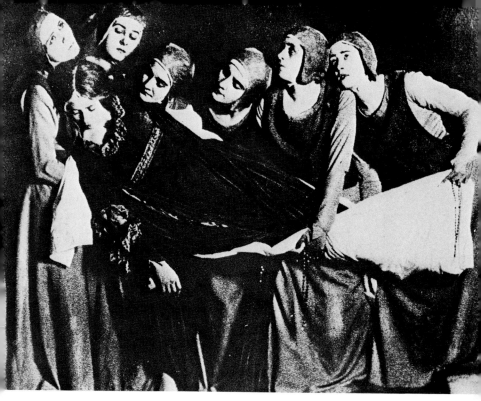

9. *Sister Beatrice* (Meyerhold, Vera Komissarzhevskaya's Theatre, 1906)

10. *Hamlet* (Craig & Stanislavsky, Moscow Art Theatre, 1912)

11. *Earth Rampant* (Meyerhold Theatre, 1923)

12. *Tidal Wave* (Piscator, Berliner Volksbühne, 1926)

and the season ended prematurely on 7 January 1908. The following day Komissarzhevskaya left with a section of her company to visit the United States. She never returned to Ofitserskaya Street; two years later, on tour with her company in Tashkent she contracted smallpox and died at the age of forty-five.

Once again, Meyerhold was forced to retreat to the provinces, but as we shall see, his career was only just beginning and his greatest achievements still lay ahead. Meanwhile, in the space of twelve months with Komissarzhevskaya he had staged no fewer than thirteen productions of formidable complexity, shaken the staid world of the Petersburg theatre to its foundations, and set out most of the ground rules for the rest of his creative life.

9. Meyerhold – Theatre as Propaganda

———————◆———————

On 25 February 1917 in Petrograd the tsarist regime was forced to a final confrontation with a hungry, war-weary proletariat, and the first shots of the Revolution were exchanged. That evening, the Imperial Alexandrinsky Theatre saw the premiere of the most lavish production ever staged in Russia. It was Lermontov's tragic masterpiece, *Masquerade*, and its director was Meyerhold. Nine years earlier, the critics who had exulted at his humiliating dismissal by Komissarzhevskaya had been astounded at his appointment as an actor and stage-director at the Imperial Theatre. But in the face of critical disbelief and the aloofness of a company who ranked stage-directors on a level with carpenters and electricians, Meyerhold had stayed to mount over two dozen productions, eight of them operas. Wisely, he had confined his experimental work to a series of studios, where he schooled young pupils and pursued his research into the *commedia dell'arte* and various other forms of popular theatre. At the Alexandrinsky Theatre and Mariinsky Opera he had formed a close alliance with the celebrated designer, Alexander Golovin, and such collaborations as Molière's *Don Juan* (1910), Gluck's *Orpheus and Eurydice* (1911) and Ostrovsky's *Storm* (1916) were acknowledged as major theatrical events of the pre-revolutionary decade. Nothing, however, equalled *Masquerade*, a production that was almost six years in preparation, required a total of some four thousand design sketches, had a complete orchestral score by Glazunov, and employed a cast numbering over two hundred. The view of the contemporary critics who condemned *Masquerade* as typical of Meyerhold's decadence and megalomaniac extravagance is refuted by Konstantin Rudnitsky in his masterly study, *Meyerhold the Director*; rather, he says, Meyerhold's production 'echoed like a grim requiem for the empire, like the stern, solemn, tragic, fatal funeral rites of the world that was perishing in those very days'.[1] Whatever the truth, *Masquerade* survived all criticism to be performed over five hundred times after the Revolution, right up to 1941.

Within a month of the October Revolution, Meyerhold had identified himself with the Bolshevik cause and in August 1918 he became a Party member. Given his deep involvement in the escapism and aestheticism that typified the arts in the final decade of tsarist power, Meyerhold's new allegiance might appear opportunistic were it not for his earlier involvement with Gorky and the intellectual left, which had been a major reason for his leaving the Moscow Art Theatre in 1902. In addition, we should remember that in 1918 the Bolsheviks were far from secure and any declaration of solidarity with them amounted to a hazardous act of faith, and one which very few artists committed. Hence, in November 1918 the professional theatre's sole contribution to the first anniversary of the Revolution was Meyerhold and Mayakovsky's production in Petrograd of *Mystery-Bouffe*, the poet's exuberant parable of world revolution.[2]

In May 1919, weakened by illness and overwork, Meyerhold was forced to leave Petrograd for convalescence in the Crimea. There he got caught up in the Civil War, narrowly escaped execution by the Whites for alleged subversive activities, and ended up in the political section of the Red Army. In 1920, towards the end of the Civil War, Meyerhold was appointed Head of the Theatre Department of the Soviet Commissariat for Enlightenment, and in that capacity assumed virtual dictatorship over the entire Russian theatre.

Hell-bent on breaking the hegemony of the commercial managements and the former Imperial companies, not to mention settling a few old scores, Meyerhold proclaimed the advent of the October Revolution in the theatre, and sought to initiate a ruthless redeployment of manpower and material resources. But the State, in keeping with its declared policy of preserving artistic traditions, resisted Meyerhold's zealous offensive and after a few months he resigned.

Late in 1920 Meyerhold assembled a young company, took over the Sohn Theatre in central Moscow and renamed it the 'R.S.F.S.R. Theatre No. 1'. The play chosen to inaugurate the new theatre was *The Dawn* ('*Les Aubes*'), an epic verse drama written in 1898 by the Belgian Symbolist poet Emile Verhaeren, depicting the transformation of a capitalist war into an international proletarian uprising by the opposing soldiers in the mythical town of Oppidomagne. It was hurriedly adapted by Meyerhold and his assistant Valery Bebutov in an attempt to bring out its relevance to recent political events.

The first performance, timed to coincide with the third anniversary of the October Revolution, took place on 7 November 1920. The derelict, unheated auditorium with its flaking plaster and broken seats was more like a meeting-hall; this was wholly appropriate, for it was in the spirit of a political meeting that Meyerhold conceived the production. Admission was free, the walls were hung with hortatory placards, and the audience was showered at intervals during the play with leaflets. Also derived from the meeting was the declamatory style of the actors, who mostly remained motionless and addressed their speeches straight at the audience. Critics rightly compared the production with Greek tragedy, which furnished the precedent for the static manner of delivery and for the chorus in the orchestra pit commenting on the peripeteia of the drama. The chorus was assisted in the task of guiding and stimulating audience reaction by a claque of actors concealed throughout the auditorium.

A fortnight after the production had opened, the actor playing the Herald interrupted his performance to deliver the news received the day before that the Red Army had made the decisive breakthrough into the Crimea at the Battle of Perekop. As the applause died down, a solo voice began to sing the Revolutionary funeral march 'As Martyrs You Fell' and the audience stood in silence. The action on stage then resumed its course. Meyerhold felt that his highest aspirations were gratified, and the practice of inserting bulletins on the progress of the war continued. However, such unanimity of response did not occur every night, but usually only when military detachments attended *en bloc* – as they sometimes did, complete with banners flying and bands ready to strike up.

Whilst the more sophisticated spectator was likely to find the conventions crude and the acting maladroit – not to mention the political message oversimplified or even repugnant – the new audience at whom ostensibly the production was aimed could not help but be puzzled by its appearance. The young designer, Vladimir Dmitriev, favoured the geometrical schematisation of the Cubo-Futurist school of artists. His assembly of red, gold and silver cubes, discs and cylinders, cut-out tin triangles and intersecting ropes blended uneasily with the occasional recognisable object such as a graveyard cross or the gates of a city, to say nothing of the soldiers' spears and shields, or the curious 'timeless' costumes of daubed canvas. Furthermore, the overall picture was made to look tawdry in the harsh white light with which Meyerhold sought to dispel all illusion. Defending his choice of Dmitriev as a designer, Meyerhold said:

> We have only to talk to the latest followers of Picasso and Tatlin to know at once that we are dealing with kindred spirits . . . We are building just as they are building .. For us the art of manufacture is more important than any tediously pretty patterns and colours. What do we want with pleasing pictorial effects? What the *modern* spectator wants is the placard, the juxtaposing of the surfaces and shapes of *tangible materials*![3]

His enthusiasm was not shared by the Commissar for Enlightenment, Lunacharsky, who remarked drily: 'I was very much against that piano-lid flying through the sky of Oppidomagne.'

On the same day as the premiere of *The Dawn*, *The Storming of the Winter Palace* was re-enacted at the scene of the original event in Petrograd with over 6,000 participants, plus the cruiser Aurora on the nearby

Neva River and a crowd of over 100,000. The overall director was Nikolai Evreinov. By now, such mass spectacles were regular events on national holidays throughout the Soviet Union.[4] *The Dawn* was the first attempt to establish a comparable atmosphere of mass community within a conventional theatre and with a professional company. It exhibited a number of features that were soon to typify agitatory theatre elsewhere: a text rewritten and staged to give it topical reference, the dismantling of the conventional performer-audience division, the merging of play into collective celebration,* the conscious effort to dispel illusion, the use of a 'modernist' design in an effort to invoke the new spirit of revolution. As Lunacharsky's comment indicates, the Party was more than a little embarrassed by the enthusiastic support it was receiving from the left-wing avant garde. However, Lenin's wife, Nadezhda Krupskaya, writing in *Pravda* had no complaint against the 'timelessness' of the production; what she objected to was the ill-considered adaptation that related the action to a Soviet context and transformed the hero, Hérénien, into a traitor to his class who comes to terms with a capitalist power. Above all, she complained that it was a sheer insult 'to cast the Russian proletariat as a Shakespearian crowd which any self-opinionated fool can lead wherever the urge takes him'.[6] As a direct consequence of Krupskaya's criticism the work was rewritten to render it dialectically more orthodox, but all the original theatrical devices were retained.

With all its imperfections, *The Dawn* depended very much on the mood of the audience on the night for its success, but even so it ran for well over a hundred performances to packed houses. It proclaimed an epoch in the Soviet theatre and is rightly considered a *locus classicus* in the history of the political theatre.

May Day 1921 saw the second production at the R.S.F.S.R. Theatre No 1. It was *Mystery-Bouffe*, completely rewritten to make it relevant to the course of events since 1917. Mayakovsky was present from the first read-through of *Mystery-Bouffe* and added numerous topical couplets right up to the final rehearsal. Among his amendments were the inclusion in the ranks of the bourgeoisie ('The Clean') of Lloyd George and Clemenceau, and the creation of a new central character 'The Conciliator', or Menshevik, who was brilliantly portrayed by the nineteen-year-old Igor Ilinsky in red wig, steel gig-lamps and flapping coat-tails, with an open umbrella to symbolise his readiness for flight. He was a figure derived from the traditional red-haired circus clown. His performance set the key for the whole production: an hilarious, dynamic, caricaturist rough-and-tumble, a carnival celebration of victory in the Civil War in total contrast to the still, hieratic solemnity of *The Dawn*.

---

*Echoing the sentiments of the Symbolist years, Meyerhold called for 'the participation of the audience in the corporate creative act of the performance'[5].

The proscenium which had been bridged by the placing of the chorus in the orchestra pit in *The Dawn* was demolished once and for all in *Mystery-Bouffe*. The stage proper was taken up by a series of platforms of differing levels, inter-connected by steps and vaguely suggestive of the various locations in the action. In front a broad ramp sloped right down to the first row of seats, bearing a huge hemisphere over which the cast clambered and which revolved to expose the exit from 'Hell'. In this scene, one of the devils was played by a circus clown, Vitaly Lazarenko, who entered by sliding down a wire and performed acrobatic tricks. In the final act, set in the new electrified promised land, the action spilled into the boxes adjacent to the stage, and at the conclusion the audience was invited to mingle with the actors on stage.

In this production Meyerhold dispensed finally with a front curtain and flown scenery. The theatre was bursting at the seams, unable to accommodate the kind of popular spectacle that he was striving to achieve, and it was now that the questions arose whose answers he was shortly to seek in Constructivism.

Meyerhold and Mayakovsky were accused once again of futurist obscurity and the production was ignored by all but three Moscow newspaper critics. But despite all opposition, *Mystery-Bouffe* was a far greater popular success than *The Dawn*, and was performed daily until the close of the season on 7 July. In the five months up to the end of May 1921, 154 performances of the two plays in the thousand-seat Sohn Theatre were watched by roughly 120,000 spectators.

Forced to work within the confines of an ill-equipped conventional auditorium, Meyerhold enlisted the designer's assistance to create a new theatrical environment. In the experimental three-dimensional reliefs of the young 'Constructivist' groups of artists he saw the possibility of a utilitarian multi-purpose scaffolding which could be dismantled and erected in any surroundings. This was an important consideration in 1921, for with the introduction of Lenin's New Economic Policy, the state funding of theatres became subject to far more stringent controls, and for a time Meyerhold was deprived of his theatre by the Moscow City Soviet. But in any case, the industrial 'anti-art' of the Constructivists which recognised practicability as its sole criterion and condemned mere representation and decoration, was for him a natural ally in his repudiation of psychological realism and aestheticism.

Even though the constructions designed in 1922 by Lyubov Popova for *The Magnanimous Cuckold* and by Varvara Stepanova for *Tarelkin's Death* showed vestigial representational elements, their function was as machines for acting, springboards to enhance the stunning gymnastic skills of Meyerhold's young actors. By now, he had become Director of the newly formed State Higher Theatre Workshop in Moscow, and it was there that he developed the system of practical exercises for actors called 'Biomechanics' and based, he claimed, on recent experiments in the scientific organisation of labour in America and Russia. There seems little doubt that Meyerhold couched his system in fashionable 'industrial' terminology in order to discredit the rival methods of other directors, principally Stanislavsky and Tairov, which he dismissed as unscientific and anachronistic. But this need not detract from the intrinsic value of Biomechanics as a means of fostering physical discipline and self-awareness in the actor. The system of twenty dramatised solo and group exercises or 'études', many of them derived from traditional circus and *commedia dell'arte* stunts, became indispensable to the dynamic style of theatre which Meyerhold now developed.[7] Eventually, the practical success of biomechanics was largely responsible for the introduction of some form of systematised physical training into the curriculum of every Soviet drama school. A final comment on Meyerhold's conception of the actor's art is supplied by something he said in 1913:

> It is well known that the celebrated actor, Coquelin, began with externals when working on his roles, but does that mean he did not experience them? The difference here lies only in the method, in the way one studies a part. What it boils down to is this: talent always experiences a role deeply, whereas mediocrity merely enacts it.[8]

Meyerhold's productions of Crommelynck's *The Magnanimous Cuckold* and Sukhovo-Kobylin's *Tarelkin's Death*, the one a Belgian surrealist bedroom farce written in 1920 and the other a nineteenth-century satire on tsarist police-state methods, were 'political' in the sense that the style of their performance was an expression of the youthful optimism prevailing in the Soviet Union after the long drawn-out horrors of the Civil War. The bare back-wall of the stage against which both were performed, together with the tawdry auditorium of the Sohn Theatre, served only to emphasise this quality: the sheer verve and agility of the young company succeeded in obliterating the surroundings from the spectator's consciousness, demonstrating, as it were, the power of man over his environment.[9]

In March 1923 it was announced that on his completion of twenty years as a director and twenty-five years in the theatre altogether, Meyerhold had been awarded the title of 'People's Artist of the Republic'. He was the first theatre director and only the sixth Soviet artist overall to be so honoured. Yet on the very day that this distinction was being celebrated in the improbable setting of the Bolshoi Theatre, the electricity at Meyerhold's theatre was cut off because they could not pay the bill, and yet again Meyerhold was forced to go cap-in-hand for a state subsidy.

Fortunately, his position was soon eased by the great popular success of his latest production, Sergei Tretyakov's *Earth Rampant*, which had its premiere on 4 March 1923 and was performed forty-four times in the remaining eleven weeks of the season. The text was freely adapted by Tretyakov from a translation of Marcel Martinet's verse drama *La Nuit*. Originally published in 1921, the play concerns an abortive mutiny of troops engaged in an imperialist war. As with *The Dawn*, the aim of the adaptation was to transform the play's vague universality into a direct commentary on recent Soviet history. Tretyakov sought to strengthen the dialogue by giving it the laconicism of the agitatory placard and by schooling the actors in an appropriately aggressive style of declamation. The actions's relevance to historical events was underlined by familiar Civil War slogans projected onto screens above the stage during the performance; they also performed a formal function, replacing the long-discarded front curtain as a means of dividing the play up, and announcing the theme of each episode. Both in its form and objectives, Tretyakov's treatment closely resembled what Brecht was later to call 'Epic'.*

In *The Dawn* and *Mystery-Bouffe* both characters and events were synthesised through the medium of costumes and settings, but arbitrary aestheticism rather than universality was the overriding impression created by the abstract designs, and the topical relevance of the events depicted was obscured. In *Earth Rampant*, Meyerhold and his designer, Popova, sought to eliminate all risk of aesthetic blandishment by using purely utilitarian objects: cars, lorries, motor cycles, machine-guns, field telephones, a threshing machine, a field-kitchen – only that which was required by the dramatic events. The one exception was a stark, life-size wooden model of a gantry-crane which towered up into the flies, built only because a real crane proved too heavy for the stage floor to bear. The sole sources of light were huge front-of-house searchlights. The uniforms of the soldiers were authentic and the actors wore no make-up.

As in *Mystery-Bouffe*, the negative characters were depicted as grotesque archetypes, performing what Meyerhold still referred to as '*lazzi*', the traditional gags of the *commedia dell'arte*. Thus, when the 'Emperor' received news of the mutiny he squatted down on a chamber-pot emblazoned with the Imperial eagle and relieved himself to the accompaniment of a band playing 'God save the Tsar', after which an orderly removed the pot, holding his nose. As Meyerhold wrote soon afterwards, 'The actor-tribune acts not the situation itself, but what is concealed behind it and what it has to reveal for a specifically propagandist purpose.'

On this occasion the tedium of unalloyed virtue was completely overcome by the stirring evocation of civil-war heroism which struck to the

---

* Some years later, Brecht and Tretyakov became closely acquainted and Tretyakov was largely responsible for introducing Brecht to the Soviet public. In 1934 under the title *Epic Dramas* he published a translation of *St. Joan of the Stockyards*, *The Mother*, and *The Measures Taken*.

heart of many a spectator. For them, the receding throb of the lorry which had driven down the gangway of the auditorium and up on to the stage with the coffin of a martyred Red soldier seemed like the finest and the most fitting requiem for their own fallen comrades. Dedicated 'to the Red Army and the first Red Soldier of the R.S.F.S.R., Leon Trotsky', *Earth Rampant* was first performed at a special preview on 23 February 1923 to mark the Army's fifth anniversary. Ever since Meyerhold had returned from the Civil War, his theatre had shared a close relationship with the Red Army and had done much to foster the development of military drama groups. It was no empty gesture to dedicate *Earth Rampant* to the Army; at performances of the play regular collections were taken and in 1926 the money accumulated went to purchase a military aeroplane which entered service bearing the name 'Meyerhold'. On the occasion of his jubilee at the Bolshoi Theatre in 1923 Meyerhold was made an honorary soldier of the Moscow Garrison.

Meyerhold conceived *Earth Rampant* in the spirit of a mass spectacle, using the theatre aisles for the passage of vehicles and troops. Subsequently it was performed on a number of occasions in the open-air, being freely adapted for various settings. The most memorable performance was that given in honour of the Fifth Congress of the Comintern in Moscow in June 1924 when a cast of 1500, including infantry and horse cavalry took part and there was an audience of 25,000. For the occasion Tretyakov adapted the script to give it a victorious rather than tragic ending.

Meyerhold looked upon *Earth Rampant* as a production that it was necessary to stage; apart from Mayakovsky, no Soviet dramatist had yet written a revolutionary play of any quality, and after the experimental ventures of *The Magnanimous Cuckold* and *Tarelkin's Death* the Meyerhold Theatre (as it was now officially known) urgently needed to confirm its reputation with the mass audience as an exponent of revolutionary drama. His judgment was confirmed when *Earth Rampant* was enthusiastically received in a variety of venues during the theatre's summer tour of the Ukraine and Southern Russia.

In January 1924 Meyerhold staged his brilliant reinterpretation of Ostrovsky's most popular comedy, *The Forest*, dividing the original five acts into thirty-three episodes, shuffling them into new order, and inserting pantomime interludes for the sake of effective contrasts of mood and tempo. As with all Meyerhold's reinterpretations of the nineteenth-century classics after the Revolution, the aim was to rescue them from the deadening grip of academicism and to create what he called 'a Red folk theatre', enlivened by topical songs and clowning.[10] But with his next production, *D.E.*, presented six months later, he showed that his disregard for authors' rights was restricted by no means to the classics. This 'agit-sketch' was an amalgam by Mikhail Podgaetsky of two novels, *The D.E. Trust – The History of the Fall of Europe* by Ilya Ehrenburg and *The Tunnel* by Bernhard Kellermann, with additional material from Upton Sinclair and Pierre Hamp. Podgaetsky's scenario bore little resemblance to Ehrenburg's novel from which the bulk of the material was taken, and after numerous further alterations in the course of rehearsals the connection was attenuated still further. Only two years before Ehrenburg had proclaimed: '*Away with the author!* Theatre shouldn't be written in the study, but built on the stage.' Now he sprang to the defence of his novel, protesting 'I'm not some classic but a real, live person', and claimed to be working on a stage version of it himself. In an open letter Meyerhold, playing on Ehrenburg's doubtful cosmopolitan status, retorted scornfully:

> ... even if you had undertaken an adaptation of your novel,* *The History of the Fall of Europe*, you would have produced the kind of play that could be put on in any city of the Entente, whereas in my theatre, which serves and will continue to serve the cause of the Revolution, we need tendentious plays, plays with one aim only: to serve the cause of the Revolution.[11]

D.E. was even more fragmented in structure than Meyerhold's previous episodic productions. It took the form of a political revue in seventeen episodes, of which only two or three featured the same characters twice. There were no less than ninety-five roles divided between forty-five performers, amongst whom the champion quick-change artist was Erast Garin, who appeared as seven different inventors in a scene lasting fifteen minutes. Here is Alexander Fevralsky's synopsis of the bizarre plot:

> The international adventurer Jens Boot organises the 'D.E. Trust' (Trust for the Destruction of Europe), in which he is joined by three of America's most powerful capitalists. By various means the D.E. Trust succeeds in destroying the whole of Western Europe. A large proportion of the Western European proletariat manage to escape to the U.S.S.R., which joins with the Comintern to form a secret organisation under the cover-name of the 'U.S.S.R. Radium Trust' in order to build an undersea tunnel linking Leningrad to New York. The building of the tunnel provides employment for the European workers. The D.E. Trust is unable to follow up its triumph over Europe by over-coming the industrious zeal of the Soviet workers, and is obliged to support the recognition of the Soviet Union *de facto* and *de jure*. But it is too late: the American proletariat rises in revolt and is supported by the International Red Army, arriving unexpectedly in New York through the tunnel which the capitalists have never discovered. The social revolution prevails.

The production was remarkable for its settings, which were composed entirely of 'moving walls'. Devised by Meyerhold himself, these 'walls'

---

* In his memoirs Ehrenburg says that he had earlier refused Meyerhold's invitation to adapt the novel for the stage.

were a series of eight to ten dark red wooden screens, about 12 feet long and 9 feet high, which were moved on wheels by members of the cast concealed behind each one. With the addition of the simplest properties, they were deployed to represent now a lecture hall, now a Moscow street, now the French National Assembly, now a sports stadium, and so on. The action never faltered and in some scenes the walls played an active part, their motion emphasised by weaving spotlights. For example, Jens Boot escaping from the Soviet Union fled upstage to be confronted by two rapidly converging walls; managing to squeeze through the narrowing gap just before one crossed in front of the other, he seemed to have disappeared when they separated and moved on across the stage. In fact, he had simply concealed himself behind one wall and left the stage with it.

Once again Meyerhold employed projected captions, this time on three screens. As well as the title and the location of each episode, there were comments on characters, information relevant to the action, and quotations from the written works and speeches of Lenin, Trotsky and Zinoviev. The aim was to point the political significance of the events on stage and to relate them to as wide a context as possible.

The depravity of the Western world was portrayed in the customary grotesque style, whilst the vigour of the young Soviet state was expressed by marching and singing sailors borrowed from the Red Fleet and real Komsomols performing biomechanics, acrobatic dances, and playing football. Critics were quick to condemn this crude schematisation; not only were the scenes in 'foxtrotting Europe' far more energetic and diverting (helped greatly by the performance of the first jazz band to appear in Soviet Russia), but there was an obvious danger in representing a deadly political enemy as a collection of emasculated cretins, cowards and libertines. By all but his most devoted followers Meyerhold was accused of 'urbanism' and of 'infantile leftism' – Lenin's term for a naive conception of the social situation that was bound to foster disastrous complacency.[12]

Meyerhold defended himself fiercely: since writing *Mystery-Bouffe* Mayakovsky had contributed nothing to the theatre, and no other Soviet dramatist had yet emerged who could rival him in artistic skill or political acumen. There was an urgent need for far more sophisticated material than the schematised placard-drama that was currently being provided. The limited repertoire of the Meyerhold Theatre was now a cause for acute embarrassment, and several months of preparatory work, rehearsals and revisions were required before Meyerhold felt ready to reveal his next production to the public in January 1925. But Alexei Faiko's *Bubus the Teacher* was hardly the response the critics were expecting: yet another flimsy political farce depicting the exhausted last fling of the rulers of an imaginary capitalist country on the verge of revolution, it prompted the very schematisation of Western decadent types that Meyerhold had already exploited to its limits. The one exception was the character of Bubus himself, an intellectual idealist who vacillated ineffectually between two camps and found himself rejected by the revolution when it finally came. He was an individual embodying the conflict of class loyalties within himself, instead of displaying in two dimensions the attitudes of one particular side. In conception at least he represented a significant advance on earlier Soviet drama, a shift from crude agitation to more reasoned propaganda. But Bubus apart, Faiko's play was so insubstantial that it presented no intellectual challenge whatsoever to Meyerhold. Once more brushing aside the protests of a mere author, he adapted the text to suit his own ends and developed a whole new range of production tricks to invest it with heavy significance, slowing the lively farce tempo to the heavy rhythm of melodrama. Indeed, rhythm was restored to the pre-eminence it had enjoyed in his pre-revolutionary work. With only the occasional break, every movement was synchronised with a musical accompaniment, the text being spoken as a kind of recitative against a melody in counterpoint. As in *D.E.*, lascivious foxtrots and shimmies were danced to jazz accompaniment; but most of the music was taken from Liszt and Chopin and performed by the pianist Lev Arnshtam at a concert Bechstein perched high above the stage in a gilded alcove ringed with coloured lights. Meyerhold intended the effect to be similar to the piano accompaniment in the silent cinema; by revealing the source of the music to the spectator he hoped to counteract its stupefying effects and reinforce its ironical function.

In contrast to the aggressive angularity of recent productions, the setting, conceived by Meyerhold and excuted by Ilya Shlepyanov, consisted of a semicircle of suspended bamboo rods completely enclosing a stage area covered with a circular green carpet. The back wall was adorned with flashing neon signs and the whole picture framed by an ornate false proscenium arch. Properties were few, the most striking being a gilded fountain in the first act. The mellifluous tinkling of the bamboo curtain at the entrance of each character, the soft splash of the fountain, the rhythmical flashing of the neon all played their part in Meyerhold's complex orchestration.

The languid aristocrats moved in broad leisurely curves within the rounded confines of their fragile stockade, their footfalls silent on the green carpet. Faultlessly turned out, their fans, cloaks, top hats, walking-sticks and white gloves were the pretext for much elegant by-play. For the first time Meyerhold introduced a device that he called 'pre-acting', whereby the actor employed mime before he spoke his lines in order to convey his true state of mind. Justifying this technique he said:

Nowadays, when the theatre is once more being employed as a platform for agitation, an acting system in which special stress is laid on pre-acting is indispensable to the actor-tribune. The actor-tribune needs to convey to the spectator his attitude to the lines he is speaking and the situations he is enacting; he wants to force the spectator to respond in a particular way to the action that is unfolding before him ... The actor-tribune acts not the situation itself, but what is concealed behind it and what it has to reveal for a specifically propagandist purpose. When the actor-tribune lifts the mask of the character to reveal his true nature to the spectator he does not merely speak the lines furnished by the dramatist, he uncovers the roots from which the lines have sprung.[13]

The similarity to what Brecht later defined as '*gestus*' is unmistakable.* Unfortunately, this constant interpolation of mime emphasised rather than made good the vacuity of Faiko's text, and was seen by most critics as a regression to the self-indulgent aestheticism of Meyerhold's Petersburg period. Erast Garin recalls: 'The public's reception of *Bubus the Teacher* was reserved; they quickly grew tired, just as one grows tired in an unfamiliar museum. It was a spectacle overloaded with skill, a production for the appreciation of actors and directors.'

But despite all its shortcomings, *Bubus the Teacher* remained for Meyerhold and his company a valuable exercise in rhythmical discipline which told strongly in work soon to come. Less than three months after the relative failure of *Bubus* Meyerhold staged a production that won acclaim from all sides and marked a crucial advance in his production style. By the spring of 1925, the New Economic Policy was playing its part in the restoration of the Soviet economy by tolerating private enterprise; but the price to pay was chronic unemployment, a desperate housing shortage, a teeming underworld of petty crooks, fixers and parasites, and the 'internal emigrés' who regarded the Revolution as an aberration of limited duration. This alternative society was the target of *The Warrant* (or *The Mandate*), the first full-length play by the twenty-three-year-old Nikolai Erdman, which Meyerhold presented in April 1925. A satirical fantasy in the style of Gogol, *The Warrant* depicts a typical group of internal emigrés who still dream of the restoration of the monarchy, and preserve all the trappings and customs of the old order within the undignified confines of a communal flat in Moscow. In a series of hilariously involved peripeteia, Nadezhda Gulyachkina and her son Pavel seek to restore the family fortunes by arranging the marriage of Pavel's unprepossessing sister Varka to Valerian Smetanich, the son of prosperous bourgeois neighbours. As a dowry they offer Pavel's Party membership and the protection against the shocks of Communism that it will guarantee. Pavel's sole proof of his

* See pp. 173–174 below.

status is a warrant bearing his signature as chairman of the house committee, which, as it transpires, is forged by himself. The plan is foiled
when Valerian rejects Varka in favour of the Grand Duchess Anastasia,
the miraculously surviving heir to the Romanov dynasty – only to discover
that she is the Gulyachkins' cook Nastya Pupkina from Tula. A lodger
reveals all to the militia, but is sent packing: they have better things to do
than to arrest these pathetic remnants of the past.[14]

The emblematic portrayal of character, the 'social masks', which Meyerhold had employed in all his previous productions of the Soviet period,
was entirely unsuited to *The Warrant*. Erdman's characters did not divide
into the sharply contrasting social categories of *Earth Rampant, D.E.* or
Bubus; instead, they were all drawn from within the same narrow class, a
series of subtly inflected variations on the one theme. The secret of
Erdman's style lay in his ability to translate scrupulously noted details of
petty bourgeois speech and behaviour into the most extravagant and
arresting hyperbole without any sacrifice of authenticity. In effect, this
was the style that Meyerhold had defined as 'the grotesque' fourteen years
earlier in his essay *Balagan*, and which had so coloured his subsequent
work. *The Warrant* gave him full opportunity to draw on all those years
of accumulated experience and to apply it to a work of acute social
observation.

Inevitably mime played a vital role in the production, in particular,
sudden freezes that seemed to convey the characters' horrified subconscious awareness of their inescapable dilemma. Thus, says Rudnitsky:

> In Act One when Garin as Gulyachkin, in a kind of Khlestakovian ecstasy,
> surprised himself by blurting out the menacing and solemn words 'I am a Party
> man!', the fatal phrase made those around him and Gulyachkin himself freeze
> in horror. Ivan Ivanovich, the lodger, at whom the threat was addressed, shrank
> back and cowered to the floor. Gulyachkin's mama and sister stood with their
> mouths gaping wide. Gulyachkin himself, unhinged by his own heroism,
> remained motionless in an unnatural pose that suggested both pride and terror.
> And then immediately this entire 'sculptural group', this monumental photo-
> graph of the explosion that had rocked the petit bourgeois world, glided slowly
> and smoothly into the depths of the stage on the revolve.[15]

Meyerhold and his designer Shlepyanov devised a deep circular stage-
area with two large concentric revolves and a series of tall varnished
wooden screens which enclosed the action. Telling effects were achieved
with these simple mechanical means: a petrified group would silently
retreat, a gap would materialise in the seemingly impassable wall, and
they would be 'hurled from the stream of life onto the rubbish dump of
history'. The revolves were also used to bear on the properties, used
sparingly but effectively 'both as an instrument for acting and as a
symbolic generalisation of a way of life'. A domestic altar complete with

votive candles and horn-gramophone, a wrought-iron treadle sewing-machine, a piano decorated with paper flowers, a banquet table with epergne and candelabra: these were the objects the doomed 'nepmen' relied on to preserve their delusion of permanency.

But Meyerhold's production was more than a merciless jest at the expense of a helpless foe; there was little laughter at Pavel Gulyachkin's closing line 'What's the point of living, mama, if they don't even bother to arrest us?' It was a glimpse of the tragic aspect of the grotesque, which recalled Blok's bewildered Pierrot playing mournfully on his pipe at the end of *The Fairground Booth*. It was a significant change in mood from the derisive lampoons that had gone before. As the critic, Boris Alpers, wrote:

> Meyerhold's satirical theatre, merry and irreverent in mood and capable of malicious ridicule at the expense of those individuals who were receding into the past, suddenly paused for reflection, broke off its laughter. Its performances began to move one. In its voice there began to predominate the note of tragedy.[16]

The Warrant marked Meyerhold's effective rejection of placard-drama and his return to a theatre of disturbing complexity. Significantly, Stanislavsky, who had not even taken the trouble to see *The Forest*, was deeply impressed and commented on the last act: 'In this act Meyerhold has accomplished what I myself am dreaming of.'

The Warrant succeeded equally as entertainment and as propaganda, but although it ran for over 350 performances it only partially solved Meyerhold's repertoire problems. It was 1930 before Erdman delivered his next play, *The Suicide*, and then after two years of rewriting, rehearsals, and devious attempts to outflank the State Censorship Committee it was banned. Meanwhile, nearly twenty months elapsed after *The Warrant* before Meyerhold presented his masterpiece, *The Government Inspector*.[17] These two productions were the twin summits of his career, even though his theatre continued to function for a further eleven years until its liquidation in January 1938, two years before Meyerhold's execution in prison. In that time he achieved several more notable productions, in particular the premiere of Mayakovsky's *Bed Bug* in 1929, and his adaptations of *The Lady of the Camellias* by Dumas fils in 1934, and of Tchaikovsky's opera *The Queen of Spades* in Leningrad in 1935. But increasingly he was harried by censorship, and numerous promising projects never reached the stage for public performance. Between 1926 and 1933 he presented only six new Soviet plays and after that none at all. Mostly, he depended on revivals of his existing repertoire, and in the final week of his theatre's existence the repertoire consisted of five nineteenth-century works. For years, a new theatre designed to Meyerhold's specification was under construction in the centre of Moscow, but it remained uncompleted at his death. Like Gropius's 'Total Theatre' project for Piscator, it was amphitheatre in form and highly flexible. It would have been the logical conclusion to Meyerhold's thirty-year struggle to establish a new actor-audience relationship. Instead, it functions today as the Tchaikovsky Concert Hall.[18]

Shortly before his death in 1938 Stanislavsky said to his assistant, Yury Bakhrushin: 'Take care of Meyerhold; he is my sole heir in the theatre – here or anywhere else.' Since the official rehabilitation of Meyerhold in 1956 Soviet critics and memoirists have approached him with growing confidence, until today few would question Stanislavsky's appraisal, whilst some would claim that in actual theatrical achievement the master was far outstripped by the pupil. Within the past twenty years, Meyerhold's lessons have been re-absorbed to powerful effect by such Soviet directors as Lyubimov and Efros. Like him, their aim is to transform the performance of a play into an event that confronts and challenges its audience's safest assumptions. Thus, for all the conformism of most current Russian dramatic writing, their productions continue to generate a sense of risk and excitement that is seldom experienced in Western theatres.

10.   Piscator in Berlin

Unlike Meyerhold, Piscator brought little previous experience to the revolutionary theatre. Before completing his second year at Munich University, where he studied philosophy, art and theatre history, he was conscripted into the German army and spent two years in front-line service until the summer of 1917, when he was seconded to an army theatre unit. Prior to that his stage experience had been limited to the unpaid performance of small parts at the Bavarian Court Theatre. Politicized by his prolonged exposure to the war, Piscator came back to Berlin at the age of twenty-five and became involved with marxist members of the Berlin Dada movement. On 31 December 1918 he joined the newly-formed German Communist Party (KPD).

After a short spell with the Tribunal Theater in Königsberg, where he staged a number of Expressionist works and played Arkenholz in Strindberg's *The Ghost Sonata*, he returned to Berlin, and in October 1920 opened the Proletarisches Theater with Hermann Schüller, a Communist Youth leader. It was a group of mainly amateur actors, which toured working-class districts, performing mainly on improvised stages in beer-halls and workers' clubs. The repertoire consisted of short agitatory sketches and scripted plays which were extensively modified by the group in rehearsal in order to achieve maximum political clarity and relevance to the current situation in Germany. Thus the thesis of Lajos Barta's *Russia's Day*, performed as part of the opening triple bill, was summarised in the programme:

> The day of decision is upon us. Either active solidarity with Soviet Russia in the course of the coming months – or international Capital will succeed in annihilating the custodians of world revolution. Either socialism, or decline into barbarism.[1]

The style of performance was intentionally rudimentary, with robust workers ranged against emblematic figures representing world capital, the military high command, the church and the judiciary. Introducing the company in the magazine *Der Gegner*, Piscator wrote:

> The directors of the Proletarisches Theater must aim for simplicity of expression, lucidity of structure, and a clear effect on the feelings of a working-class

audience. Subordination of all artistic aims to the revolutionary goal: conscious emphasis on, and cultivation of, the idea of the class struggle.[2]

Although it frequently played to full houses, the Proletarisches Theater struggled to cover its costs, not least because the unemployed were admitted for a token charge or even free. Initially, the KPD remained unconvinced that art and propaganda could be reconciled, whilst Piscator himself felt that the plays at the company's disposal remained precisely that: '*plays*, fragments of our times, sections of a world picture, but never the whole, the totality, from the roots to the ultimate ramifications, never the red-hot, up-to-the-minute present, which leaped to overpower you from every line of the newspapers'.[3] Thus Piscator's political commitment impelled him to seek three qualities in his productions: totality, immediacy and authenticity. This search led him first to the revue form, and thence to the development of Epic theatre.

In March 1921 the police president of Berlin refused to renew the license of the Proletarisches Theater on the grounds that it was 'unartistic', and Piscator transferred his activities to the professional stage. But he remained in close enough contact with the KPD and with other communist artists to be commissioned by the Party in 1924 to organise a political revue as part of its Reichstag election campaign. His collaborators were a former journalist, Felix Gasbarra, and the composer, Edmund Meisel;* together they devised *The Red Revue* ('*Revue Roter Rummel*' or '*RRR*'), which was performed fifteen times in different parts of Berlin leading up to the elections on 7 December. Taking as its theme class injustice and the inevitable final triumph of communism in the Weimar Republic, the revue was a loose montage of sketches, employing music, song, dance, gymnastics, slide-projection, instant drawings by George Grosz, statistics and rhetoric, with actors representing Lenin, Karl Liebknecht and Rosa Luxemburg. The show was held together by the characters of a master butcher and an unemployed worker, who emerged arguing from the audience during the overture and came up onto the stage, where they remained throughout, like music-hall compères, to offer comments from the bourgeois and proletarian points of view. Once again, Piscator's aim was, as he put it, 'direct action in the theatre': '. . . I hoped to achieve propagandistic effects which would be more powerful than was possible with plays, where the ponderous structure and problems tempt you to psychologise and constantly erect barriers between the stage and the auditorium'.[4]

The Red Revue was a huge popular success, being seen by 'tens of thousands of proletarians, men and women' in a fortnight, according to

---

* In 1926 Meisel wrote the music for Eisenstein's film *Battleship Potemkin*, and later for *October*.

the estimate of the KPD newspaper, *Die Rote Fahne*. From a purely practical point of view, it was less effective, for the KPD vote fell by one million and one third of its seats in the Reichstag were lost. The Party was in no position financially to put the revue company on a permanent footing, but the example of *The Red Revue* led to the formation of groups all over Germany, and by the late 'twenties there were several hundred in existence, bearing such names as 'The Red Megaphone', 'The Red Rockets', 'The Drummers', and 'The Riveters'. Their style was often reminiscent of Meyerhold's early agitatory productions and the Soviet mass performances, but their development was independent: it was 1927 before the famous Russian agitprop collective, *Blue Blouse* first toured Germany, and 1930 before Meyerhold's theatre came. It was first and foremost Piscator's work that led to the theatre being recognised by the German revolutionary movement as a potent weapon of propaganda, and this was formally acknowledged in 1925 when the KPD began official sponsorship of workers' theatre groups.[5]

In July of that year the KPD commissioned a further revue from Piscator to celebrate its first party congress and to be staged for two performances at the 3,300-seat Grosses Schauspielhaus in Berlin. Called *Trotz Alledem!* (*In Spite of Everything*),* its form was sequential, tracing in twenty-four scenes events from the outbreak of war in 1914 up to the murder of Liebknecht and Luxemburg in 1919.[6] The high level of political consciousness that could be expected from an audience containing many congress delegates dictated extreme thematic precision, and in an attempt to reinforce the production's factual veracity, Piscator made constant use of recorded speeches and documentary film, often counterpointed with simultaneous action on the multi-level practicable structure designed by John Heartfield, the pioneer of photo-montage. Piscator describes the effect in Episode Four (set in August 1914):

> When the Social Democratic vote on War Loans (live) was followed by film showing the first dead, it not only made the political nature of the procedure clear, but also produced a shattering human effect, became art, in fact. What emerged was that the most effective political propaganda lay along the same lines as the highest artistic form.[7]

This juxtaposition of factual material and dramatic action was now to become a permanent feature of Piscator's work. It was a logical progression from both caricatured historical figures and projected factual captions, with the added advantage that it carried a far greater weight of authenticity. The theoretical basis of this practice was the concept of 'actuality', the aim being to imply a relationship between the stage action

---

* 'Trotz Alledem!' was the title of a proclamation issued by Karl Liebknecht after the failure of the Spartacist Rising in January 1919, shortly before his assassination.

and a wider socio-political reality. Thus, just as Meyerhold had inserted reports from the Civil War front into *The Dawn*, Piscator in Toller's *Hoppla, wir leben!* (*Hoppla, Such is Life:* 1927) changed the date of the imprisoned revolutionary's release nightly to the actual date of the performance; and in Credé's play about the inhumanity of the abortion laws §*218* (1929) he included reports from the current day's newspapers.

Party officials had voiced misgivings over Piscator's intention to represent real political figures in *Trotz Alledem!*, and afterwards the critic of *Die Rote Fahne* criticised their portrayal, finding Karl Liebknecht and Rosa Luxemburg not true to life, and the moderate SPD statesmen insufficiently harsh. Ironically, given Piscator's intentions, *Die Rote Fahne* suggested that perhaps the treatment was *too* documentary.[8] But nevertheless, critics of varying persuasions were agreed that the effect was both emotionally overwhelming and politically clarifying. The huge auditorium was packed for both performances and Piscator tried to extend the run to a fortnight, but the KPD was not prepared to take the financial risk, and the cast of over two hundred was disbanded.

By this time, Piscator had been working for three years in the Berlin professional theatre: with the writer, Max Rehfisch, he put on a number of productions at the Central-Theater, including works by Gorky, Tolstoy and Romain Rolland, then in the spring of 1924 he accepted an invitation to work at the Volksbühne.[9] This was Piscator's first opportunity to work on a properly equipped stage: built in 1914, the Volksbühne's Theater am Bülowplatz seated 1,800, and had a twenty-metre revolving stage, with cyclorama, hydraulically operated rake, and integral adjustable rostra. Here, on 26 May 1924, he presented *Fahnen* (*Flags*) by Alfons Paquet. The play is set in Chicago in 1886; its theme is the capitalist exploitation of immigrant workers and their struggle for an eight-hour working day. Drawn from documentary sources, the narrative centres around the provocation of a disturbance at a peaceful workers' meeting by the police, who have been bribed by the capitalist, Cyrus MacShure. The labour leaders are arrested and tried; one commits suicide in gaol and the remaining four are hanged. When it was published in 1923, *Fahnen* was subtitled 'A Dramatic Novel', but for the production this was changed (either by Paquet himself or by Piscator) to 'An Epic Drama', the formula on which Brecht was later to base his whole aesthetic. Commenting on this definition in 1963, Piscator said:

> Briefly, it was about the extension of the action and the clarification of the background of the action, that is to say it involved the continuation of the play beyond the dramatic framework. A didactic play [Lehrstück] was developed from the spectacle-play [Schaustück]. This automatically led to the use of techniques from areas which had never been seen in the theatre before.[10]

How was this achieved in the production? Using a composite revolving set of low cut-off walls, designed by Edward Suhr, Piscator moved the action rapidly through a narrative sequence of eighteen scenes and a prologue. In the 'Prologue on the Puppet Stage', a puppeteer introduced the principal characters in verse couplets whilst their original photographs were projected onto the backdrop and a ballad-singer commented in song. Throughout the action, slides were projected onto screens flanking the stage, showing posters, newspaper extracts, manifestos, and sometimes a title for the next scene in the manner of the silent cinema. Thus, the verdict of the trial was anticipated by the title 'Condemned to Death', and the judges' verdict undercut by 'The Police Threw the Bombs Themselves'. Then to emphasise further the theme of collusion, the court was cleared, the judges were disrobed by three attendants to reveal white tie and tails, in which they stepped straight into the next scene: the capitalist MacShure's celebration banquet already in progress. In the final scene a coffin bearing a Soviet star was lifted up by unseen extras concealed in the catafalque as an offstage chorus swore allegiance to the hammer and sickle and huge red flags fluttered down from the flies. Reviewing *Fahnen* in the Viennese *Arbeiterzeitung*, Leo Lania, a future collaborator of Piscator, wrote:

> The production had a direct and powerful impact, people forgot that the case was twenty [sic] years old and related it directly to present-day events; this 'general validity' was achieved only because the production stripped the subject of its particular historical associations and emphasized the social and economic background. So *Flags* was in a sense the first Marxist drama, and this production was the first attempt to make the forces of materialism tangible and comprehensible.[11]

Probably Lania had little detailed knowledge of what Meyerhold had achieved already in Moscow, but even so he is strictly correct in describing *Fahnen* as the first Marxist drama, to the extent that Piscator was concerned to establish the details of the socio-economic process, whereas Meyerhold worked invariably in terms of satire and dramatic hyperbole.

Following the success of *Fahnen*, Piscator was in great demand as a director, and over the next two years he was responsible for eleven productions, including the two political revues for the KPD already mentioned and six further plays for the Volksbühne, where he had been appointed as a staff director. The first play of his own choosing at the Volksbühne was *Sturmflut* (*Tidal Wave*), which had its premiere on 20 February 1926. Though written by Alfons Paquet, it had none of the factual basis of his earlier play, being much closer in style to the political fantasies that Meyerhold was staging in Moscow, such as *D.E.* and *Bubus the Teacher*. Piscator summarises the plot:

Contents: The revolution triumphs. But there is no money to carry it through. So Granka Umnitsch, the leader, sells St. Petersburg to an old Jew who resells it to England. Granka and his band take to the woods. At this point there is a lovers' quarrel between him and a Swedish woman who goes over to the opposition party, represented by Ssarin, a White Guardsman. Granka returns to St. Petersburg in secret, incites the proletariat and conquers the city back for the Revolution.[12]

In his preface to the published version of the play Paquet wrote 'It is not the history of a revolution. Not a description of Lenin's life. Not a picture of Soviet Russia. Not even a milieu-piece ... It was not a matter of copying reality, but of capturing the motive forces of our times in a few figures ... in images which would awaken in us the feelings that reality awoke.'[13]

Like Meyerhold, Piscator was experiencing difficulty in finding plays that were not only revolutionary in content but also satisfying artistically. Pressure of time had forced him to choose *Sturmflut*, and in the mere three and a half weeks available for rehearsals he reworked it extensively with the collaboration of his company and the ready aquiescence of Alfons Paquet. Only material factors had prevented Piscator from using film rather than slide projections in *Fahnen*, and now with the encouraging experience of *Trotz Alledem!* behind him, film was the medium that he chose to add a dimension of concrete reality to the fanciful intrigue of *Sturmflut*.* The permanent setting of steps and blocks was backed by a transparent screen with a black frame of variable aperture, onto which film was back-projected from four projectors upstage. The critic, Herbert Ihering, describes some of the effects achieved:

> Radio bulletins: Revolution in China – on the screen in the background Chinese mass-meeting; speech by Lloyd George – Lloyd George speaking on film ... Or at the beginning: the stage is the shore, the harbour, the square in Petersburg. The Film: ships, sea, a flood. Or at the end: fighting. Or in between: a motionless background which suddenly springs to life, contrasts or parallels with other revolutions, or an aeroplane, the stone canyons of the city, forest.[14]

Most critics (as well as Piscator himself) were of the opinion that no amount of additional documentary background could make good the lack of concreteness in Paquet's symbolic heroes, but there was general agreement that for the first time film had been seen to supplement theatre, not merely for the sake of stylistic trickery, but to genuine dramatic purpose.†

---

* John Willett has suggested that Piscator was encouraged further in his use of film by a pre-release viewing of *Battleship Potemkin* in January 1926.

† This was by no means the first use of film in the theatre. In his review of *Sturmflut*, Herbert Ihering recalls cinematic effects in a Berlin production of a French farce called *A Million* before the First World War.

Film now became for Piscator 'the theatre's fourth dimension'. 'In this way', he said in 1926, 'the photographic image conducts the story, becomes its motive force, a piece of living scenery'.[15] The 'motive force' was of course, a political one, as his production of Ehm Welk's *Gewitter über Gottland* (*Storm over Gottland*) in March 1927 demonstrated to controversial effect. The play is set at the end of the fourteenth century and, using the language and style of the medieval drama, deals with the conflict between the capitalist Hanseatic League and the proto-communist Vitalian Confederacy. By now, the cautious and predominantly Social Democratic management of the Volksbühne had become acutely embarrassed by Piscator's intransigent Marxism, and hoped with *Gewitter über Gottland* to placate conservative opinion by offering an historical spectacle whilst simultaneously meeting the radical demand for plays of political content. But Piscator would entertain no such compromise; seizing on Ehm Welk's prefatory comment 'The play takes place not only in 1400', he set about establishing continuity with the class struggle down the centuries. One of the Vitalian leaders was made up to resemble Lenin and his part rewritten in the sober, rational style of a modern revolutionary. Film was used much as it had been in *Sturmflut*, but in a specially shot prologue the Vitalian Brothers advanced steadily on the audience, their costumes changing in period to convey the inexorable progress of socialism. Further documentary footage emphasised parallels with Russia and China, and the performance concluded with a red star rising over the stage. Both the censor and the Volksbühne management insisted on the removal of sections of the film; a lengthy controversy ensued which split the membership of the Volksbühne and led directly to Piscator's resignation. Ehm Welk, whilst deploring what he regarded as the eventual artistic demolition of his play, publicly affirmed his support for Piscator's objective, and in a letter rebuking the Volksbühne management wrote '... if I am reluctant to place myself as a shield in front of the Piscator of *Storm*, I am much more reluctant to be used as a battering ram against him'.[16]

Piscator could afford to chance his arm with the Volksbühne over *Gewitter über Gottland*, for six months before it opened he had begun negotiations for the financial backing of a theatre of his own with a Berlin brewing magnate called Ludwig Katzenellenbogen. The original idea was for a completely new 2,000-seat theatre designed by the Bauhaus architect Walter Gropius. Called the Total-Theater, it was conceived to meet all Piscator's technical demands, with extensively variable performance areas and a series of seventeen slide or cine-projection booths, nine around the single-tiered auditorium, seven behind the cyclorama, and one in a turret that could be lowered from the roof.[17] For financial reasons the project was never realised, so Piscator was denied space for the mass audiences that might perhaps have covered the costs of the ambitious productions that he was now to stage. As an interim measure the 'Piscator-Bühne', as his company was called, was housed in the Theater am Nollendorfplatz, a well-equipped theatre of conventional design, but with seating for 1,100, located in the fashionable West End of Berlin, and normally given over to operetta and light entertainment.

The organisation of the Piscator-Bühne involved an embarrassing compromise with bourgeois society: not only did it depend on the munificence of a capitalist brewer, but its financial survival was bound to depend on the patronage of a fashionable audience willing to pay high prices for the best seats, the more so given that an arrangement was concluded with the Volksbühne to offer seats at only a nominal charge to a large proportion of its membership.[18] Piscator himself was realistic about the idealogical alliance that he was forced to conclude. In 1929, he wrote in his book *The Political Theatre*:

> This contradiction in the structure of the theater is nothing more or less than a contradiction in the times as a whole: it proves to be impossible to build up a proletarian theater within the framework of our current social structure. A proletarian theater in fact presupposes that the proletariat has the financial means to support such a theater, and this presupposes that the proletariat has managed to make itself into a dominant social and economic power. Until this happens our theater can be no more than a revolutionary theater which uses the means at its disposal for the ideological liberation of the proletariat and to promote the social upheaval which will free both the proletariat and its theater from these contradictions. The fact that we were under no illusions about the contradictory aspects of our situation, the fact that we felt that these contradictions did not absolve us from any responsibility but obliged us to work out our line of thought more clearly and sharply in the light of our years of experience – these were perhaps the only substantial entries on the credit side when we founded our theater.[19]

Whilst the resultant torsions failed to break the political resolve of Piscator and the writers who now comprised his 'dramaturgical collective', they took their financial toll, and within nine months the Piscator-Bühne was forced into liquidation. By that time, however, it had achieved four remarkable productions. The first of these was Ernst Toller's new play, *Hoppla, wir leben!*, which opened on 3 September 1927. Not only was Toller the leading dramatic exponent of the political aspect of German Expressionism, but he had been chairman of the central council of the short-lived Munich Soviet Republic in April 1919. Following its overthrow, he narrowly escaped execution but subsequently served five years in prison, receiving no remission of sentence. Subjectively, if not factually, *Hoppla* was an autobiographical play, and had a direct bearing on the political realities of the outwardly stable year of 1927. Piscator summarises the action:

The hero of Toller's play, Karl Thomas, was a postwar revolutionary who was condemned to death after the Revolution had been put down. In 1919, shortly before the hour at which he was to be executed – along with his friend Kilmann, who had also been condemned to death – he was pardoned. Karl Thomas goes out of his mind, is committed to a lunatic asylum and drops out of sight for eight years until 1927, when he returns to an entirely new world. His friend Kilmann has made his peace with the new regime and has been made a government minister; his former girlfriend has become a political agitator. When he reappears on the scene, she takes him in for a while but eventually turns him out onto the street. Karl Thomas becomes a waiter. In his desperation at the times, he conceives a plan to shoot Kilmann, who is now a reactionary. A right-wing radical student beats him to it, but Karl Thomas comes under suspicion and is arrested and put back in the lunatic asylum; he hangs himself at the moment at which his innocence is established ...[20]

In fact, Thomas's suicide was one of the numerous amendments that Toller, Piscator and his collective made to the script in order to sharpen its political focus. The main problem in Piscator's view was that Toller's hero saw the revolution in emotional terms, and so his final defeatist action (condemned in the production by other revolutionaries) was inserted in order to emphasise the subjectivity of his perspective. Piscator tried further to undercut Thomas's heroic posture by deliberately casting a solid proletarian actor instead of the 'little son of a bourgeois' that Toller specifies in the play's prologue.* Discussing the acting problems posed by *Hoppla*, Piscator writes:

> Each actor had to be quite conscious of the fact that he represented a particular social class. I remember that a great deal of time was spent at rehearsals discussing the political significance of each role with the actor concerned. Only when he had mastered the spirit of the part in this way could the actor create his role.[21]

The objectives defined here are very similar to what Meyerhold had in mind for his 'actor-tribune', and clearly anticipate the motivation behind what Brecht later defined as 'Epic acting'.† Again echoing Meyerhold, Piscator wrote in 1929: 'I see in the craft of the actor a science which belongs to the intellectual structure of the theatre, to its pedagogy,' and he described the style of acting developed in his productions as 'hard, unambiguous, unsentimental'.[22] When the first Piscator-Bühne opened in

---

*The actor in question was Alexander Granach. The director, Leopold Lindtberg, remembers his performance: 'His acting was fueled by passionate political involvement, erupting in sound and fury in his Expressionist phase, but no sharp, concentrated dialectic. He never ... succumbed to dogma ... needed no theories ... for he knew what it was like to work sixteen hours for a pittance, and had been in strikes when he was a baker's apprentice.'[22]

† See pp. 140-141 above and pp. 173-174 below.

1927, Piscator also established a Studio which yielded a number of small-scale productions and also offered courses in acting, with great emphasis on physical training. However, the Studio suffered the same fate as the parent company, and Piscator did not resume systematic actor training until he arrived in New York in 1939. Brecht, who joined Piscator's dramaturgical collective in 1927, comments somewhat caustically in *The Messingkauf Dialogues*:

> He was not so wholly uninterested in acting as his enemies said; none the less he was more so than he himself gave out. Possibly he failed to share their interests because they failed to share his. At any rate he established no new style for them, even though he was not bad at showing how a part should be acted, particularly small and sharply etched ones. He tolerated several different ways of acting on his stage at the same time: not really a sign of specially good taste. He found it easier to master great subjects critically by means of ingenious and spectacular scenic presentation than by the actors' art.[23]

Granach's performance as Karl Thomas notwithstanding, this last observation was certainly true of *Hoppla*, in which the technical achievements overshadowed everything else. Traugott Müller designed a structure made with three-inch gas piping, 36 feet wide, 26 feet high, 10 feet deep, and weighing over 4 tons. Piscator writes: 'Toller had managed to hint at a cross section of society in the choice and grouping of the settings. We had come up with a stage-set that would display this cross section and lend it precision: a multi-storied structure with many different acting areas above and beside one another, which would symbolise the social order.'[24] One segment after another was lit to represent prison cells, various ministerial offices, a series of hotel rooms, a radio station under the domed roof; a mass scene such as a polling station was played across the main stage area. Piscator had equipped the Theater am Nollendorfplatz for simultaneous film projection from four sources backstage, and for this production three thousand feet of film were shot in the two weeks before the premiere and edited together with archive footage from the past ten years. The film was still being spliced when the curtain went up.

Film was used to both documentary and emblematic effect. Thus the prologue, projected onto a screen lowered over the entire acting area, 'showed a close-up of a general's tunic covered with medals, cut to clips of infantry assaults, advancing tanks, shellfire, machine guns, wounded men, rows of crosses, an army in retreat, then cut back to a huge hand ripping the medals off the general's chest. Karl Thomas appeared intermittently among the soldiers in the film.'[25] Then the opening prison scene was played with front-projected film of a marching sentry on a gauze. The eight lost years of Thomas's incarceration were conveyed in a seven-minute montage of documentary footage showing the key historical events leading up to the election of Field Marshal von Hindenburg as President in 1925 and the stabilisation of the Weimar Republic. In the final act, Thomas and his revolutionary comrades, now back in prison, tapped messages to each other on their cell walls, and their text moved silently across a screen overhead until Thomas answered no more: 'flickering words from one person to another – the master-stroke of a stagecraft that presses ever forwards and sets ever new standards', as Monty Jacobs of the *Vossische Zeitung* put it.[26]

The critic of *Germania* wrote:

> The greatness of Piscator's achievement: he expanded the scope of our theatrical experience, time and space passed before our eyes in a telescopic vision, gripping scenes ... The resounding applause from the balcony may be directed primarily at the 'political aims' served by this theatre. But the deafening applause from the front orchestra was for the artistic boldness of the task the director has taken on, for his courageous and successful forays in new directions.[27]

This precisely sums up the dual appeal of the production, which ensured it a successful two-month run. It was followed in November by *Rasputin, the Romanovs, the War and the People that rose against them*, a free adaptation of a melodramatic thriller by Count Alexei Tolstoy and the historian, Peter Schegolev, originally performed in Leningrad in 1924. The prologue and three of the original ten scenes were scrapped, and eight new ones interpolated to juxtapose scenes at the Imperial court with military and political events, beginning with the major Russian defeats in Poland in 1915 and culminating in the October Revolution. Leo Lania, co-author with Felix Gasbarra of the new material, explained the objective in a programme note for the production:

> We are not concerned here with the figure of Rasputin the adventurer, nor with the Czarina's conspiracy, nor with the tragedy of the Romanovs. The idea is to create a piece of world history, where the spectator in the orchestra and balcony of this theatre is just as much the hero as the miraculous Russian monk.[28]

The desire to reflect the global scale of events dictated both the adaptation of the script and the form of the setting: just as the construction for *Hoppla* was designed to reflect the strata of society, so the '*Globus-Bühne*' for *Rasputin*, again designed by Traugott Müller, was a silver fabric covered revolving hemisphere intended to suggest the surface of the globe. Segments containing the numerous settings on two levels were disclosed by thick flap-like doors, film was projected onto its surfaces, and the entire top could be hoisted up to reveal a large screen at the rear for back projection. Downstage left of the globe there was a narrow 'calendar screen', the height of the proscenium opening, on which a running ribbon of dates and events was projected.

Using three projectors and some six thousand feet of film, acquired mainly from Soviet sources, Piscator achieved frequent strokes of brutal irony. For instance, a discussion on military tactics between Marshal Foch and Marshall Haig was accompanied by film of the futile slaughter on the Somme and captions such as 'Losses: half a million. Gains: 300 square kilometres'. Shots of mutilated Russian corpses were projected onto the rear screen during a scene in the Tsar's headquarters whilst the 'calendar screen' to the side showed a quotation from an actual letter to his wife: 'The life I am leading at the head of my armies is healthy and invigorating'. In the penultimate scene, as the Tsarina planned the arrest of revolutionaries in 1917, the screen above her head foreshadowed the murder of the imperial family at Yekaterinburg the following year. As Bernhard Diebold of the *Frankfurter Zeitung* wrote:

> The Tsarina is still defiant – but the film knows better. 'Time' only exists for the Tsarina – we are above time. The individual speakers are aware only of their own situation, or the situation of those nearest them. The film projected on the gauze knows the general situation, the collective situation. It is fate, the voice of wisdom. It knows everything.[29]

Some critics noted the danger of the momentous historical events on film dwarfing the performances of the live actors, and to judge from the recollection of Tilla Durieux, who played the Tsarina Alexandra, the actors themselves were likely to experience this:

> I was in my boudoir with my lady-in-waiting. We were not yet fully aware of the danger, and conversed gaily. Suddenly, on the film next to the segment of the open stage on which I stood, I saw the Red Army troops on the march. I was so shaken up that I forgot my lines and couldn't go on. It was hard to understand, and then I wondered how terrifying the impression must have been to the audience at that moment.[30]

With *Rasputin*, Piscator felt he had at last made it impossible for the public to judge his art in isolation from his politics. This view was certainly shared by the right-wing press; Friedrich Hussong, political correspondent of the *Lokal Anzeiger*, wrote:

> ... this public has not yet understood what it is all about, or that their necks are at stake, not to speak of their diamond tie-pins and pearl necklaces, silver evening capes and gold shoes, and all the other things they need to have a night out together like this. They haven't grasped it, though the Nollendorf Soviet pressed into their hands the first number of its official bulletin with the unequivocal title, *Political Theatre*, whose every contribution is a declaration of war on all those people who spend good money on seats at the Nollendorf-theater, because it's the thing to do at the moment.[31]

The production gained an added notoriety when both the ex-Kaiser Wilhelm II and an ex-financial adviser to Tsar Nicholas, Dmitri Rubinstein, sued Piscator for defamation in his portrayal of them on stage. Both characters had to be deleted, but Piscator made the most of the loss by substituting a reading of the court's injunction for the Kaiser's lines.

Rasputin was followed in January 1928 by the Piscator-Bühne's greatest popular success, a free dramatic adaptation in twenty-five scenes of Jaroslav Hašek's novel, *The Good Soldier Schwejk*. The script was the work of Felix Gasbarra, Piscator himself, and Brecht, who had already contributed to *Rasputin*. For once, Piscator was heavily indebted to the performance of an individual actor, the celabrated Viennese comedian, Max Pallenberg, whose portrayal of Schwejk dominated the production. In fact, he had been engaged for the part before the start of the season and the whole play was built round him. Piscator devised two electrically powered conveyor belts, located upstage and downstage parallel to the setting line and backed by white flats. The background to Schwejk's progress from Budweis to the Eastern Front was conveyed both by naturalistic film and by a sequence of savage animated cartoons drawn by George Grosz. The conveyor belts served to bring the actors and their properties onto the stage, and made it possible for them to simulate movement on the spot. Grosz also designed a series of life-size cut out figures to represent the characters who played no active part in the action, or in Piscator's words, 'the ossified types which populated the political and social life of prewar Austria'.[32]

Schwejk played to packed houses and might well have proved the means of Piscator's financial salvation, but Pallenberg was committed to leave for a South American tour in April, and in any case the theatre was committed to offering its subscribers four further productions in the season. After a series of mishaps only one further major work was staged, Leo Lania's 'comedy of economics', *Konjunktur (Boom)* in April 1928. On this occasion, the play was devised from scratch in close collaboration with the director and the dramaturgical collective, which facilitated the integration of subject matter and means of production that Piscator had previously been obliged to impose on pre-existent texts. The plot of *Konjunktur* concerned the repercussions of an oil-strike in Albania: starting with a bare stage to represent virgin territory, the action gradually generated a forest of oil derricks and other equipment, in front of which the pages of the newspapers representing the rival French and Italian interests were projected onto a gauze in order to convey the contradictions in world politics that were exposed by the economic conflict. The reports were precisely synchronised with the action onstage; at the end when the Albanian revolution came to a climax, and the oil-wells were sabotaged, the newspapers too burst into flames. The problem was that the plot in its final version hinged on surprise reversals better suited to operetta, and the cuts that political logic dictated were impeded by the need to preserve the leading role played by Tilla Durieux, shortly to become the wife of

Ludwig Katzenellenbogen, the company's benefactor. *Konjunktur* failed with the public, and in June 1928, a month after its four-week run had ended, Piscator was bankrupt.

The next year passed with only one commercial production from Piscator, but, as John Willett points out, it was a time of increasing activity for German left-wing theatre.[33] There were now several hundred workers' theatre groups, and in Autumn 1929 Maxim Vallentin's 'Red Megaphone' toured the Soviet Union; late in 1928 members of the Piscator Studio, re-formed themselves into the Gruppe Junger Schauspieler ('Group of Young Actors') and were responsible for a series of interesting productions, culminating in Brecht's *The Mother* in 1932; finally the Volksbühne, having presented Brecht's *Man Equals Man* in January 1928, confirmed its leftward shift a year later by appointing Karlheinz Martin as its Intendant. By the summer of 1929 Piscator had secured fresh backing and returned to the Theater am Nollendorfplatz to open the second Piscator-Bühne. The inaugural production was Walter Mehring's *The Merchant of Berlin*, the saga of an immigrant Jew's financial rise and fall in the inflation year of 1923. Technically, it outdid even *Hoppla* and *Rasputin*: not only was there film projection onto four screens and a front gauze, but the setting by Moholy-Nagy utilised a revolve, two conveyor belts, and three gantries that could be raised and lowered from the flies. Though the machinery helped to create overwhelming images of the big city, it was noisy and slow in operation. What is more, the action was schematic and laboured, and the performance ran from 7.30 to nearly midnight. Worst of all, the production offended all sections of opinion, being seen variously as anti-capitalist, anti-German, and anti-semitic.

With *The Merchant of Berlin* losing money with each performance, the theatre's licensee first banned the red flag from the production and then even removed the title of Piscator-Bühne from the building. After a run of less than six weeks, Piscator was again broke and without a company.

Almost immediately, however, a group of his young actors formed themselves into a 'Piscator-Collective', with Piscator himself engaged on an equal basis as a director. In ten days they rehearsed §*218* by Carl Credé, a doctor who had been gaoled for offences against, paragraph 218, the section of the German criminal code dealing with abortion. In simple naturalistic style, the play showed the effects of a law that drove the poor to seek back-street abortions. On this occasion Piscator used no more than a simple two-room setting, with the interpolation of occasional still projections. The relevance of the action to life outside the theatre was established by planting the actors due to play the parts of a lawyer, a magistrate, a doctor, a clergyman, and an industrialist in the audience, where they expressed their views on abortion before entering the play on stage. The ending was rewritten to include a fight among the characters, at which point the magistrate would initiate a debate among the audience, concluding in a vote on the abortion laws. Beginning in Mannheim in November 1929, the production toured thirty German cities, and whenever possible, local legal and medical figures were invited to speak in the debate. In April 1930, the Collective returned to Berlin and gave a further fifty performances of §218 at the Wallner Theater, a decrepit auditorium in the unfashionable East End. The production was revived in the autumn, and after a further tour returned to the Wallner Theater.

Piscator's involvement of the audience was no idle ploy: it would have involved itself without his invitation – as regular attempts at disruption by both the Catholic Centre Party and the Nazis demonstrated. With unemployment reaching 4.4 million, it was a time of renewed political polarisation; in the elections of September 1930 the Nazis polled six million votes to gain ninety-five seats in the Reichstag and became the second biggest party ahead of the KPD with seventy-seven seats. Hence, Piscator's reversion to an overt agit-prop style was a logical response to the political situation. During the election campaign, Piscator presented a dramatic adaptation of Theodor Plivier's novel about mutiny in the German Navy, *The Kaiser's Coolies*. Based on fact, it encouraged Piscator once again to introduce film sequences and employ Traugott Müller to design a complex cross-section of a battleship as the setting. The music was written by Edmund Meisel, the composer of a powerful score for the German premiere of *Battleship Potemkin*, but *The Kaiser's Coolies* failed to match the revolutionary pathos of Eisenstein's masterpiece and it is remembered only for being one of a whole string of revolutionary naval plays that were staged in Berlin in 1930.

In January 1931 Piscator reverted to his simpler agitprop manner for the production of *Tai Yang erwacht* (*Tai Yang Awakes*) by the leading communist playwright, Friedrich Wolf. Against the background of the Shanghai textile-workers' revolt of the 1920's, the play, like Brecht's *The Mother* (1932), traces a woman worker's progress to revolutionary consciousness. At Piscator's suggestion, Wolf reworked his naturalistic narrative into an expository didactic form in order to make clear the parallels with the current situation in Germany. The designer, John Heartfield, transformed the theatre into a Chinese meeting hall with posters and banners, those held by the actors being reversible to provide a screen for the projection of documentary film. Bamboo bridges linked the auditorium to the stage, and once again Piscator planted actors amongst the spectators. For the prologue, the cast entered through the auditorium, and changed and made-up while discussing the relative situations in China and Germany. At the end one of them dressed again in his everyday clothes, stepped forward and terminated the action with the lines 'So run the battle-fronts through China today. And the same battle-lines divide Germany. Right or Left – You must commit yourselves!' Again it was no mere theatrical gesture: by February 1931 there were nearly five million registered unemployed, and in the course of the year the membership of the Nazi Party rose to 800,000, plus over 300,000 para-military 'Brown Shirts' of the SA available for demonstrations, marches, and street fighting with the Communist Roter Frontkämpferbund.

Piscator's next intended production was an adaptation by Felix Gasbarra of Theodore Dreiser's *An American Tragedy*, but a few days after the premiere of *Tai Yang erwacht* the tax authorities renewed their demands for the unpaid arrears from the second Piscator-Bühne, and for a few days Piscator was imprisoned in Charlottenburg Gaol. Shortly after his release, Piscator abruptly left the Collective and went to Moscow, where he made a film of Anna Seghers' novel *The Revolt of the Fishermen*, which took until 1934 to complete. By then, the time had long passed when he could have returned to Berlin. In January of the previous year Hitler had become Chancellor and in July all parties except the Nazis had been suppressed. Brecht, on the first stage of his sixteen-year exile, had settled in Denmark, and the Jewish Max Reinhardt had fled to Austria.

Piscator was not to return to Berlin until 1955. At the beginning of 1936 the offensive against formalism in the arts was launched in earnest in the Soviet Union, leading to the closure of theatres and the imprisonment or execution of many individual artists. In October, while in Paris on a visit, Piscator received a telegram warning him not to return. After more than two years in France, during which time he was able to direct nothing, Piscator left with his wife in December 1938 for America, where they remained for the next thirteen years. During this time Piscator managed nine productions and ran the Dramatic Workshop. Returning to West Germany in 1951, he worked freelance in numerous theatres until 1962, when he was appointed artistic director of the Freie Volksbühne in West Berlin. Among other productions there he directed the world premieres of Rolf Hochhuth's *The Representative*, Heinar Kipphardt's *In the Case of J. Robert Oppenheimer*, Peter Weiss's *The Investigation*, and Hans Hellmut Kirst's *The Officers' Revolt*, all controversial documentary dramas in the tradition that he himself had done so much in the 1920's to create. He died on 30 March 1966.

Throughout his early years in Berlin, from the opening of the Proletarisches Theater in 1920 until his departure for the Soviet Union in 1931, Piscator was working within the context of an acutely polarised society – even during the years of so-called 'stabilisation'. Despite his constant struggle for economic survival, he never ceased in challenging his public to confront the social problems surrounding them, and the furore caused by production after production is proof of his effectiveness.

13. *Man equals Man* (Brecht, Berliner Staatstheater, 1931)

14. *The Mother* (Brecht, Komödienhaus Berlin, 1932)

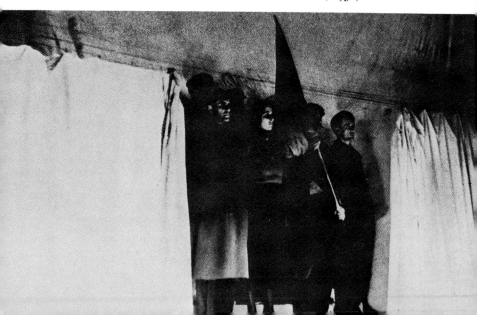

15. *The Cenci* (Artaud, Folies Wagram Paris, 1935)

16. *Apocalypsis cum Figuris* (Grotowski, Laboratory Theatre, Wrocław, 1975)

It is significant that, for all the boldness of his production methods, it was invariably the issues raised by his work that provoked controversy. Above and beyond all his technical innovations, Piscator's greatest achievement was a Marxist achievement: he demonstrated how theatre can create a dialectical relationship with its audience in order to accelerate the transformation of society. Piscator remained unshaken in his commitment; in March 1966, a few days before his death, reflecting on Germany's recovery since 1945, he said:

> After the war a great number of new theatres were built. The awareness of the Western cultural tradition and the duty to be representative had to be taken into account. Yet behind glass and concrete, in the wonderful new buildings and on wide stages the theatre seems to have gone back to its original, elementary character: to play. Only now and then does it penetrate further, into the spiritual realm, beyond a mere interpretation of a work, to gain a far wider significance, to represent the spirit of a nation. The theatre as the home of the nation's conscience, the stage as the moral institution of the century; this should be the image of the theatre twenty years after . . .[34]

11. Brecht's Formative Years

More than one critic has observed that whereas Piscator, the director, has made his most lasting impression in the field of dramatic writing, the lessons of Brecht, Germany's greatest modern playwright, have been most deeply absorbed by directors, designers and actors. Partly, this is explained by the fact that the past fifty years have seen a merging of the roles of dramatist and director, with Brecht the ultimate example of the two in one; but equally it is because both men, in their striving for a theatre that would reflect society in its totality, needed to master all the resources at the stage's command. In the years from 1922, when his first play reached the stage, up to his death in 1956 Brecht usually took some active part in any production of his play that was within reach. Of them, some twenty can be ascribed to him personally as director, usually working in collaboration with others.

Towards the end of 1921 Brecht, at the age of twenty-three, was gaining recognition as a dramatist: his first play *Baal* was due shortly to appear in print and his second, *Drums in the Night*, had been accepted for performance by the Munich avant-garde theatre, Die Kammerspiele. But with the publication of *Baal* deferred for fear of censorship and the production of *Drums in the Night* slow to materialise, Brecht decided to force his luck by abandoning his university studies in Munich and moving to Berlin. By the time he returned to his home-town of Augsburg the following Easter he had little to show for his initiative: no Berlin management had made a firm commitment to stage any of his plays, and his first venture as a director, Arnolt Bronnen's expressionist drama *Vatermord* (*Patricide*) for the Junge Bühne, had ended abruptly when two of the leading performers left a rehearsal in protest at Brecht's caustic comments.[1]

However, Brecht left Berlin with many invaluable contacts established and the first draft of a third play, *In the Jungle*, completed. Back in Munich it was accepted by the Residenztheater, and then on 29 September 1922 *Drums in the Night* was finally presented by Otto Falkenberg at the Kammerspiele. Brecht had persuaded Herbert Ihering, drama critic of the *Berliner Börsen-Courier*, to attend and a few days later he wrote:

'The twenty-four year-old writer Bert Brecht has transformed the literary face of Germany overnight. With Bert Brecht a new tone, a new melody, a new vision have come into being. ... No dramatist since Wedekind has afforded such a soul-shattering experience.' [2] A month later, Brecht was awarded the Kleist Prize as that year's outstanding new dramatist, Ihering being the judge. As a result, other productions of *Drums in the Night* soon followed, including one at the Deutsches Theater in Berlin, again by Falkenberg. Then in May 1923 *In the Jungle* (later retitled *In the Jungle of Cities*) was staged by Erich Engel at the Residenztheater, with designs by Brecht's boyhood friend and close collaborator, Caspar Neher. Much as the critics admired the acting, they could make little of this most enigmatic of Brecht's plays, their task being made even more difficult by attempts to disrupt the performances by members of the newly-formed Nazi Party. After six nights it had to be taken off, and the theatre's dramaturg was dismissed.

By now, though, Brecht was well established, having been appointed to the dramaturgical and directing staff of the Kammerspiele immediately following the premiere of *Drums in the Night*. He was not slow to make his presence felt; as Arnolt Bronnen recalls, 'Even before he had been performed anywhere, he was the terror of the mediocre stage director, the absolute horror of the manager. He dictated the casting from the first to the twenty-second role; he fought with a never tiring tenacity for the actor and the actress whom he had built into his scenes.' [3]

Originally, it was intended that Brecht's first production for the Kammerspiele should be a Shakespeare, probably *Macbeth*. However, he argued that a lesser known work would be a safer choice for his debut, and proposed Marlowe's tragedy *Edward the Second*. It was agreed that Brecht would adapt it in collaboration with his friend and mentor, the successful writer Lion Feuchtwanger, who also worked as a dramaturg for the company and had a good command of English. Apart from the possible appeal of the play's homosexual theme (which had already figured in *Baal* and *In the Jungle*), Brecht was attracted by its loose chronicle form with rapidly shifting scenes and discontinuity of mood and action. Thirty years later he recalled: 'We wanted to make possible a production which would break with the Shakespearian tradition common to German theatres: that lumpy monumental style beloved of middle-class philistines.' [4]

The adaptation took the greater part of 1923 to complete and finally contained no more than one-sixth of Marlowe's original lines. Entitled *The Life of Edward the Second of England*, the new version was altogether swifter moving and sacrificed much of Marlowe's sensuous rhetoric for the sake of a harsher mode of expression and jerky, irregular speech rhythms. It also introduced a number of dramaturgical devices that were

later to become familiar features of Brecht's style, notably the interpolated
sardonic street ballad or '*Moritat*', and titles announcing the date, location
and content of the scene to come.[5]

Brecht's work as adaptor by no means ended when rehearsals began in
January 1924. Bernhard Reich, the Kammerspiele's artistic director at the
time, writes:

> The rehearsals directed by Brecht took a curious course. Brecht as director
> liked one of the actors: ergo he must be shown off to better advantage. Brecht
> as dramatist took a piece of paper from his pocket and wrote new lines for the
> actor. Director Brecht discovered that the intentions of the author could not be
> implemented stagewise. Next morning Dramatist Brecht brought altered and
> more suitable lines. The final rehearsal drew ever nearer, and Brecht grew ever
> more active, handing to the actors over the footlights whole rolls of new lines.
> If one of them protested, Brecht looked at him with such unconcealed honest
> amazement that he took the manuscript and got down to the job of learning the
> new text.[6]

Edward the Second took eight weeks to rehearse, the longest period in the
company's history, partly due to the delays caused by Brecht's rewriting
of the text, but equally because of the demands for precision and clarity
that he made of his actors. He insisted on making the story of the play
plain in order that the audience should understand precisely what the
characters were doing and what was happening to them. 'Pedantically' –
says Reich – 'he exposed at the rehearsals the plot of the drama, the basic
events of each single scene, the chain of events.' Henceforth, nothing in
the theatre was more important for Brecht than the story (*Die Fabel*), and
to ensure its clarity every physical action was made as concrete as possible.
Hence, when rehearsing the scene in *Edward the Second* where Baldock
surrenders his friend Edward to enemy soldiers (Scene 10) by handing
him a handkerchief, Brecht objected to the haste and the insignificance of
the gesture, and explained:

> Baldock is a traitor . . . You must demonstrate the behaviour of a traitor. Baldock
> goes about the betrayal with friendly outstretched arms, tenderly and submis-
> sively handing [Edward] the cloth with broad, projecting gestures . . . The
> public should note the behaviour of a traitor and thereby pay attention![7]

Similarly, he insisted that the hanging of Gaveston be carried out with
the same attention to detail – 'professionally', as he put it:

> Brecht stopped the actors and told them to do it properly, to tie the noose and
> make it fast to the cross-beam. Shrugging their shoulders, the actors did their
> best to follow the director's unexpected instructions. Brecht stopped them
> again and, refusing to give way, insisted relentlessly that they repeat the
> hanging, but do it like experts. The audience had to get pleasure from seeing
> them put the noose round the fellow's neck.[8]

As models of this demonstrative style of acting Brecht held up the players in the popular fairground booths, and invited the celebrated clown Karl Valentin to sit in on rehearsals. It was Valentin who supplied the solution to the portrayal of the soldiers in the long battle scene. 'What's the truth about these soldiers? What *about* them?' – asked Brecht, at his wits' end. 'They're pale, they're scared, that's what!' – replied Valentin. 'They're tired,' added Brecht, and it was straightway decided to make up the soldiers' faces thickly with white chalk. Brecht regarded this as the point at which the production's style was determined, and in latter years quoted it as the moment when the idea of Epic theatre first came into his head.[9]

To some degree this precision of style was dictated by the small stage of the Kammerspiele and the proximity of the audience. Brecht and Caspar Neher made a virtue of the enforced simplicity in the production's decor: 'Brecht primitivised the settings: a room was a room, and a king's chair was a chair, but the rooms and the chairs were kept in the style of the old German masters in their simple, merely suggested style. The costumes of the king and the barons were made of coarse dyed material: the spear-carriers wore sacks.'[10] The collaboration between Brecht and Neher, though interrupted by exile between 1933 and 1947, formed the basis for Brecht's work in the theatre. Neher's remarkable approach precisely suited Brecht's perception of man's behaviour, his social relationships and his environment; his design sketches did much to concretise Brecht's imagery. As Brecht wrote in 1951:

> His sets are significant statements about reality. He takes a bold sweep, never letting inessential detail or decoration distract from the statement, which is an artistic and intellectual one. At the same time everything has beauty, and the essential detail is most lovingly carried out. ... And there is no building of his, no yard or workshop or garden, that does not also bear the fingerprints, as it were, of the people who built it or who lived there. He makes visible the manual skills and knowledge of the builders and the ways of living of the inhabitants. In his designs our friend always starts with 'the people themselves' and 'what is happening to or through them'. He provides no 'decor', frames or backgrounds, but constructs the space for 'people' to experience something in. ... He is a great painter. But above all he is an ingenious story-teller. He knows better than anyone that what does not further the narrative harms it.[11]

In insisting on concreteness and narrative clarity in *Edward the Second* Brecht and his collaborators were reacting on the one hand against the operatic monumentality with which the classics were habitually staged in the German theatre, and on the other against the idealised abstractions of Expressionism. Erwin Faber describes the style as 'naturalistic'; but far from meaning the creation of a lifelike illusion, he has in mind the emphasising of significant detail, of cause and effect, as typified by the examples quoted of the betrayal of Edward and the execution of Gaveston. In this sense, Brecht was never other than 'naturalistic', both aesthetically and philosophically.

Thus *Edward the Second* was of enormous importance in Brecht's development, containing many of the seeds of what was his particular conception of Epic theatre. The premiere took place on 18 March 1924, just over two months before *Fahnen*, Piscator's first major production in Berlin. Hence, although Brecht learnt much from Piscator subsequently, he owed little to him at this point.

Despite the fact that the future film star, Oskar Homolka, who played Mortimer, was incoherent from drink by the end of the first performance, the production was warmly received and by a few critics at least it was recognised as a significant advance in staging technique. Whereas Julius Bab objected to the sensation of 'the fair-barker Brecht ... with his invisible pointer' standing on the sidelines, Ihering saluted his capacity to respond to the public of 'the streets, the sports arenas, the six-day cycle races, the boxing matches', and to treat history as 'a medium for human communication, a ballad or a broadsheet (*Moritat*)'.[12] Looking back in 1948, Ihering wrote:

> Brecht substituted for the concept of greatness that of *distance*. ... He did not reduce the human being. Nor did he anatomize him. He 'removed' him. ... This production in Munich was the turning point of the classical theatre.[13]

Ihering was not being merely wise after the event; two years before he staged *Edward the Second* Brecht had written in his diary:

> There is one common artistic error which I hope I've avoided in *Baal* and *Jungle*, that of trying to carry people away. Instinctively I've kept my distance and ensured that the stage realisation of my (poetical and philosophical) effects remains within bounds. The spectator's 'splendid isolation' is left intact, it is not *sua res quae agitur*, he is not fobbed off with an invitation to feel sympathetically, to fuse with the hero and cut a meaningful and indestructible figure while watching himself in two simultaneous versions. There is a higher type of interest to be got from making comparisons, from whatever is different, amazing, impossible to take in as a whole.[14]

In September 1924 Brecht moved to Berlin to become a dramaturg at Reinhardt's Deutsches Theater, though he did little there but observe productions and draw his pay. By December both *In the Jungle* and *Edward the Second* had been given their premieres in the capital, and Brecht was working on his next play, *Man equals Man*, which took the best part of a year to complete in the first of its several drafts.

Despite the promise he had shown with *Edward the Second* Brecht had to wait nearly two years for another opportunity to direct. The play was a considerably shortened version of *Baal*, retitled *Life Story of the Man*

Baal, purged of its expressionistic timelessness and set in the period 1904–1912 against a background of developing technology. Baal was now a garage mechanic-turned-poet from Augsburg instead of the 'simple clerk' of the original version.

Introduced by Brecht himself singing the 'Hymn of Baal the Great', the production, described as 'a dramatic biography', was given an 'epic' framework of 'factual' scene titles, announcing date, location and event, all designed to confer documentary authenticity on the action. With Oskar Homolka as Baal, the production was given a single Sunday matinee in February 1926 at the Deutsches Theater under the auspices of the 'Junge Bühne'. The performance provoked the now predictable scenes in the auditorium and was covered extensively by the Berlin critics. It was a clear sign of the times that Johannes Harnisch of the right-wing paper *Der Montag* saw the play as proof of the degeneracy of German culture and called on the Prussian authorities to put a stop to the theatre being used as an 'institution for public pollution'.[15]

Brecht, however, saw little prospect in exploiting the established theatre as it then functioned. A few days before the premiere of *Baal* he published an article in the *Berliner Börsen-Courier* entitled 'More Good Sport', in which he wrote:

> There is no theatre today that could invite one or two of those persons who are alleged to find fun in writing plays to one of its performances and expect them to feel an urge to write a play for it. They can see at a glance that there is no possible way of getting any *fun* out of this. No wind will go into anyone's sails here. There is no 'sport'. . . . A play is simply unrecognizable once it has passed through this sausage machine. If we come along and say that both we and the public had imagined things differently – that we are in favour, for instance, of elegance, lightness, dryness, objectivity – then the theatre replies innocently: Those passions which you have singled out, my dear sir, do not beat beneath any dinner jacket's manly chest.[16]

Brecht was constantly in search of ways to overcome the numbing effect of theatrical convention. In December 1926 he persuaded the director of his one-act comedy *The Wedding* (later retitled *A Respectable Wedding*) in Frankfurt am Main to stage it in a boxing ring. The following summer he collaborated for the first time with the composer Kurt Weill to produce a work for the Baden-Baden chamber music festival called *Mahagonny*. Subtitled as a 'Songspiel', it was a dramatised setting of six poems from Brecht's recently published collection *Devotions for the Home* (*Hauspostille*). Described in a programme note as 'a short epic play which simply draws conclusions from the irresistible decline of our existing social classes', *Mahagonny* was performed, once again in a boxing ring, in front of projections of drawings by Caspar Neher. Weill's music – said Brecht – 'precisely because it behaved in a purely emotional way and eschewed none of the usual narcotic stimuli . . . played its part in exposing the bourgeois ideologies'.[17]

By now Brecht had been engaged for several months in a systematic study of Marxism. His collaborator Elisabeth Hauptmann says that this was prompted by the need to elucidate the workings of the stock exchange whilst working on a play called *Joe P. Fleischhacker from Chicago*. The play was never completed, but Brecht's enquiries led him to the realisation that the only dramatic means adequate for the elucidation of the complex workings of capitalist society was the Epic theatre, which he now formulated as 'acting from memory (quoting gestures and attitudes)'.[18] The inference of this is that the actors tell a story with foreknowledge of its outcome, and use the characters to 'illustrate' the narrative, rather than 'live' their roles. As we have seen, Brecht had gone a long way towards realising this style intuitively in his work on *Edward the Second*, but at that time it had no political underpinning. By 1927, he had had the chance to observe Piscator's work and to explore the prospects revealed by such productions as *Revue Roter Rummel*, *Trotz Alledem!*, and *Sturmflut*. In autumn 1927 Brecht joined Piscator's dramaturgical collective and worked on adaptations of *Rasputin* and *Schwejk* as well as the rewriting of Lania's *Konjunktur*. Thus, for nearly a year he was in a position to assimilate Piscator's methods at close quarters.

The extent of Piscator's influence on the development of Brecht's Epic theatre has been discussed by a number of critics in recent years, and numerous references in Brecht's own writings acknowledge the extent of his debt to Piscator.[19] However, there remain fundamental differences between the two men that help to explain why none of Piscator's plans for staging Brecht's work ever materialised,[20] and why they never actually got round to collaborating in the 1950's when they were both back in Germany. Piscator summarised their differences in a note in his diary in 1955:

> B.'s starting point is episodic succession
> P.'s is political fatality
> B.   demonstrates it in miniature
> P.   on the big scale. I wanted to comprehend fate as a *whole*, showing how it is made by men and then spreads beyond them. (Hence the machinery, film etc.)[21]

Also, having once written to Brecht, 'I believe for my part, that no writer came closer to the conception I had of the theatre than you',[22] Piscator later commented in an interview:

> Brecht is my brother, but our views of totality differ. Brecht unveils significant details of human life while I attempt to give a conspectus of political matters as a whole. In a sense you can say that his Mother Courage is a timeless figure.

I'd have tried to portray her more historically by showing the Thirty Years' War.[23]

Readily as Brecht acknowledged Piscator as his forerunner in the field of political theatre, and deeply as he respected his credentials as a Communist, he was not convinced that the mechanisation of the stage carried out by the Piscatorbühne was the right means for the revolutionising of the theatre. In essence, he argued, it remained anti-revolutionary, because it was passive and reproductive. All Piscator's technological innovations 'merely created an active atmosphere', whilst failing to show individual characters in the process of change. What was needed, he said, were new principles of dramatic construction and a new approach to acting. In his view, Piscator was relatively little interested in the actor, and hence stood no chance of fundamentally changing the nature of the communication between performer and spectator.[24] Piscator was only too aware of the need to develop a more 'scientific', politically conscious attitude towards acting, but he was never able to tackle this problem systematically.* On the other hand, he was as anxious as Brecht to achieve a new, active relationship with the audience, as his efforts with §218 and *Tai Yang erwacht* demonstrate.† Nevertheless, Brecht owed a vast debt to Piscator which only recently has been fully acknowledged; around 1940 Brecht wrote in *The Messingkauf Dialogues*: 'Above all, the theatre's conversion to politics was Piscator's achievement, without which the Augsburger's [his own] would hardly be conceivable.'[25]

Piscator had announced the premiere of *Joe P. Fleischhacker* (now titled *Wheat*) for the 1927/28 season at the Theater am Nollendorfplatz, but in spring 1928 *The Threepenny Opera*, Brecht and Weill's free adaptation of John Gay's *Beggar's Opera*, was commissioned for the reopening of the disused Theater am Schiffbauerdamm. Lotte Lenya, Weill's wife and the play's original Jenny, has described the hectic and acrimonious months that culminated in the totally unanticipated triumph of the first night on 31 August 1928.[26] The production ran for over a year to become by far the most celebrated work in the German repertoire of the 1920's. It made an international reputation for Brecht and Weill, not to mention the director, Erich Engel, Caspar Neher, again Brecht's designer, and a number of the cast, most notably Lotte Lenya. How far the fashionable public who flocked to *The Threepenny Opera* recognised it as an oblique attack on the political corruption of Weimar Germany is questionable: Ernst Josef Aufricht, the fortunate impresario who commissioned it, called it 'a literary operetta with flashes of social criticism', whilst the Communist Party organ *Die Rote Fahne* commented: 'Not a trace of

* See p. 154 above.
† See pp. 158–160 above.

modern social or political satire, but all in all, a lively and entertaining hotch-potch.'[27]

However, what nobody doubted was the theatrical significance of the production, on which Brecht, Weill, Engel and Neher worked closely together. Both in terms of the music's function and of the staging, it represented a significant advance in the direction of what Brecht was later to term '*Verfremdung*', the 'alienation' or 'distancing' of the audience from the action that Brecht had sought in his early years in Munich. Although in terms of dramatic structure *The Threepenny Opera* is far closer to being 'well-made' than anything else Brecht ever wrote, he and Weill conceived the songs as a means of interrupting and commenting on the narrative. In 1931 Brecht wrote in his 'Notes to *The Threepenny Opera*':

> Nothing is more revolting than when the actor pretends not to notice that he has left the level of plain speech and started to sing. The three levels – plain speech, heightened speech and singing – must always remain distinct, and in no case should heightened speech represent an intensification of plain speech, or singing of heightened speech. In no case therefore should singing take place where words are prevented by excess of feeling. The actor must not only sing but show a man singing ... As for the melody, he must not follow it blindly: there is a kind of speaking-against-the-music which can have strong effects, the results of a stubborn, incorruptible sobriety which is independent of music and rhythm.[28]

The separation of the music from all the other elements of the play was emphasised by the production:

> ... the small orchestra was installed visibly on stage. For the singing of the *songs* a special change of lighting was arranged; the orchestra was lit up; the titles of the various numbers were projected on the screens at the back, for instance 'Song concerning the Insufficiency of Human Endeavour' or 'A short song allows Miss Polly Peachum to confess to her Horrified Parents that she is wedded to the Murderer Macheath'; and the actors changed their positions before the number began.[29]

As regards the setting, Siegfried Melchinger writes: 'Neher erected a giant circus calliope [steam organ] at the back of the stage and illuminated it for the moritat. He painted the [projected] scene titles on blotting paper in a child's scrawl, and threw in a cannibal's head whose derivation from Klee could be overlooked only by the innocent. Pieces of scenery were rolled on stage, raised from below, or lowered from above.'[30] In fact, there were two screens upstage flanking the steam organ and a white half-curtain downstage on a visible steel wire, eight-foot high so that the audience could glimpse something of the preparations for the scene to come. The scene titles in child's scrawl were projected on to the front curtain, which then parted to disclose the action, whilst the upstage screens were used to display a synopsis of the events in the scene to come (*'Die Fabel'*, or story) and the titles and texts of songs as they were sung. Both the white half-curtain and the screens now became regular features of Brecht's production style.

The debt to Piscator did not escape the critics, but, as Brecht pointed out some years later, there was an important difference:

> In Piscator's productions or in *The Threepenny Opera* the educative elements were so to speak *built in*: they were not an organic consequence of the whole, but stood in contradiction to it. . . . [*The Threepenny Opera*] *has a double nature. Instruction and entertainment conflict openly. With Piscator it was the actor and the machinery that openly conflicted.* [my italics, E.B.][31]

The success of *The Threepenny Opera* placed Brecht financially in a position to pursue his studies in Marxism more intensively and systematically. As a consequence he came into closer contact with workers, labour leaders and Communist Party members. Like Piscator, Brecht recognised that the rapidly growing power of the extreme Right called for a form of drama that was politically useful. This need was brought home to him forcefully on May Day 1929 when he saw the police open fire on a prohibited workers' demonstration, killing twenty-five and severely wounding thirty-six. In contrast to Piscator and his Collective, whose touring production of Credé's pro-abortion play §*218* in November 1929 was a highly effective reversion to the agit-prop style, Brecht responded by developing the *Lehrstück* or learning play, 'meant' – as he said – 'not so much for the spectator as for those who were engaged in the performance . . . art for the producer, not art for the consumer'.[32] This was not to say that his learning plays were written regardless of audience requirements, but their analytical style was intended to provoke the debate of specific issues raised by Communism rather than mobilise the audience to action, which was more the aim of Piscator and the workers' theatre movement at large.

Altogether, Brecht completed seven *Lehrstücke*, four of which he staged himself between 1929 and 1930. They took the form of concert performances with orchestra, singers, performers, and sometimes the director, sharing the same platform. The action was further clarified by the use of placards and projected titles. Mostly, these plays were devised for performance by school children, but *The Measures Taken* (*Die Massnahme*) was performed in December 1930 at the Grosses Schauspielhaus with a chorus of four hundred of the Greater Berlin Workers' Choir and Brecht's leading actors, Helene Weigel (his wife since 1929), Alexander Granach, Ernst Busch, plus a tenor from the Berlin State Opera, as the four soloist-performers. The score was by Hanns Eisler, a noted Communist composer with whom Brecht was collaborating for the first time. It was the beginning of a long partnership; as John Willett says, Eisler was ideally suited to the style that Brecht was now developing:

He had none of the faintly cheap nostalgia that haunts much of the work of Weill: he is an even more skilled (and in many ways highbrow) composer, who used his gifts like Brecht himself to make the meaning simple and clear. Like Brecht he used ecclesiastical (the Lutheran chorale) and popular models (folk-song, popular ballads and jazz), and made of them something in no way imitative or spiced-up but recognizably his own.[33]

Many of the Party comrades who saw *The Measures Taken* disliked the play, and *Die Linkskurve*, the organ of the Proletarian-Revolutionary Writers League, took him to task for his evident lack of revolutionary experience:

> One feels that he does not draw his knowledge from practice, that he is merely deducing from theory. ... The unreal analysis of the premises leads to a false synthesis of their political and artistic consequences. All this mirrors an abstract attitude towards the manifold and complicated store of knowledge, derived from experience, which the Party possesses.[34]

Brecht was to answer his critics resoundingly a year later with his adaptation of Gorky's novel *The Mother*. But meanwhile he continued to pursue the parable form, set in exotic never-never lands of his own imagining, which confronted his audience on an aesthetic rather than an ideological plane. *Happy End*, his unlikely fantasy of gangsters and the Salvation Army set in 'modern Chicago', was a fiasco when he staged it as a follow-up to *The Threepenny Opera* at the Theater am Schiffbauerdamm in August 1929, and he immediately disowned it. However, *The Rise and Fall of the City of Mahagonny*, also written in collaboration with Kurt Weill and with the no less bizarre setting of a Wild West boom-town, was a wild success if judged by the offence it caused at its premiere in Leipzig and at subsequent performances in other provincial opera houses. Mindful of the innocent enjoyment that *The Threepenny Opera* had afforded Aufricht's patrons in Berlin, Brecht was determined to allow no escape from the implications of *Mahagonny*. Thus, at the play's climax when the hero is condemned to the electric chair for the capital crime of running short of money, the projected inscription reads (in Auden and Kallman's translation):

> Execution of Jimmy Gallaher. Many of you, perhaps, will be shocked at what you are about to see. But, Ladies and Gentlemen, ask yourselves this question: 'Would I have paid Jimmy Gallaher's debts?' Would you? Are you sure?

Brecht regarded *Mahagonny* as a programmatic statement of his notion of Epic theatre, now refined in the light of his early experience of the *Lehrstück*. In a lengthy series of notes appended to the published text he attempted to demonstrate how the opera could be developed from 'the means of pleasure into an object of instruction' by dismantling all the components of Wagner's *Gesamtkunstwerk* ('integrated work of art'):

> Once the content becomes, technically speaking, an independent component, to which text, music and setting 'adopt attitudes'; once illusion is sacrificed to free discussion, and once the spectator, instead of being enabled to have an experience, is forced as it were to cast his vote; then a change has been launched which goes far beyond formal matters and begins for the first time to affect the theatre's social function.[35]

But Left critics remained sceptical towards Brecht's emphasis on theatrical form as the primary means of alerting the audience. After the Leipzig premiere, Kurt Tucholsky wrote in *Die Weltbühne*:

> Life is not like that, not even in the Klondike of yesteryear, certainly not in the America of today; and the relevance of it all to the Germany of 1930 is very thin. This is stylized Bavaria. . . .[36]

In February 1931 Brecht launched his most violent assault on what he termed 'the culinary theatre' (because it catered to the audience's sensual gratification) when the Berlin Staatstheater incautiously allowed him to direct a much revised version of his earlier play *Man equals Man*. Consistent with the work's thesis that human personality can be dismantled and reassembled like a motor-car, the production adopted a radically different approach to the portrayal of character. The vague location of 'Kilkoa Barracks' in India under the British Raj (in 1925 with Queen Victoria on the throne) was rendered by Brecht and Neher in their familiar style with fragmented setting, projected titles (plus a huge caricature of the soldier Galy Gay) and exposed half-curtain – only as much as was necessary to tell the story. It was the depiction of the British Army that was startlingly different; the visiting Soviet dramatist Sergei Tretyakov wrote: 'Across the stage strode giant soldiers, holding on to a rope* so as not to fall from the stilts concealed in their trousers. They were hung about with rifles and wore tunics smeared with lime, blood and excrement.'[37] In fact, only two of the soldiers were on stilts, the third being massively padded, whilst Helene Weigel as the canteen proprietress Begbick, the young Peter Lorre as Galy Gay, and the rest were normal size.

What particularly puzzled and exasperated the audience and critics was Lorre's manner of delivery: in order to convey the conflicts and contradictions in the character of Galy Gay, Brecht made him speak in a broken and disjointed manner, heavily stressing some phrases and withholding others. As Brecht explained to his critics soon after the performance,[38] the aim was to bring out the underlying meaning or *'gestus'* of each fragment of Galy Gay's behaviour. This concept of *'gestus'* was to become a cardinal feature of Brecht's theatre practice; in John Willett's

---

* Probably the wire for the half-curtain.

definition 'It is at once gesture and gist, attitude and point: one aspect of the relation between two people, studied singly, cut to essentials and physically or verbally expressed. It excludes the psychological, the sub-conscious, the metaphysical unless they can be conveyed in concrete terms.'[39]

This is closely akin to the style of acting already developed by Meyerhold out of his training system of 'Biomechanics';* but although Meyerhold's company had performed in Berlin in 1930 there is no particular reason for presuming a direct influence on Brecht, the idea of *gestus* being a logical extension of his earlier work. Willett draws attention to its close affinity with Behaviourism, the doctrine that psychological theories should be based on outwardly observable data of human actions without reference to the products of introspection. It is here that the obvious link with Meyerhold can be traced, Behaviourism being one of the acknowledged sources of Biomechanics.

The failure of *Man equals Man*, which ran for only six performances, was not necessarily due to its daunting formal innovations; much as it had been revised, it remained a work from Brecht's early years, laden with bizarre absurdities that did little to advance the central, important, argument concerning personality. But this should not detract from the production's importance for Brecht: for the first time he had applied the principle of Epic theatre systematically to the elements of acting. He was not to use the actual term '*Verfremdung*' to describe this technique until 1935 when he visited Moscow,[40] but with *Man equals Man* the technique was developed in all but name and ready for refinement in his post-war productions.

Later in 1931 Brecht embarked on two projects that were a total contrast to *Man equals Man* in the concreteness of their style and subject matter. The first was the script (written with Ernst Ottwalt) for the film *Kuhle Wampe*, a semi-documentary account of Berlin working-class life, directed by Slatan Dudow and released in May 1932. The second was his play *The Mother*, describing the growth to revolutionary consciousness and activism of a working-class woman in the context of events in Russia between 1905 and 1917. Loosely derived from Gorky's novel, completed in 1906, the play was written in collaboration with Slatan Dudow, Günther Weisenborn, and Hanns Eisler.

The Mother was the most fully developed of Brecht's *Lehrstücke*; its aim, he said, 'was to teach certain forms of political struggle'; addressed mainly to women, it was 'a demonstration of illegal revolutionary struggle'. Such a demonstration could not have been more timely: by 1932 there were six million unemployed in Germany and in the July elections the Nazis were by far the largest party in the Reichstag with 230 seats against the KPD's

* See p. 135 f. above.

89; with no overall majority, further elections were held in November at which the Nazis lost 34 seats and the KPD gained eleven.

Originally the dramatisation of *The Mother* had been commissioned by the Volksbühne, but cancelled when Brecht's involvement was discovered, as he was no longer considered politically acceptable there. Instead, it was taken over by the 'Group of Young Actors', a company born of the Piscator Studio, which since 1928 had staged a sequence of challenging left-wing plays. The twenty-seven-strong cast for *The Mother* included such notable professional actors as Helen Weigel (then thirty-one) as Pelagea Vlasova, and Ernst Busch as Pavel Vlasov, but the majority were young amateurs. Under the auspices of the Junge Volksbühne, it was given its premiere at the Komödienhaus am Schiffbauerdamm on 17 January 1932 to mark the thirteenth anniversary of Rosa Luxemburg's murder. On the five preceding days the production had been previewed at the Wallner Theater before invited audiences of trade unionists and extensively modified in the light of their comments. Whilst Emil Burri was named as the director, it was a collective undertaking closely involving Brecht, Hanns Eisler and Caspar Neher.[41]

The run of *The Mother* in the centre of Berlin was due largely to the unlikely backing of Aufricht, the impresario for *The Threepenny Opera*, but after thirty or so performances the production was taken out to halls in the working-class district of Moabit. Caspar Neher's setting was designed with this in mind: a simple booth was created from white material stretched on metal frames with a half-curtain in front; the furniture was minimal and purely functional, with locations indicated by small suspended placards; behind the acting area a single screen was suspended for the projection of quotations (mostly from Lenin) and occasional photographs, which remained throughout the scenes 'to show the great movement of ideas in which the events were taking place'.[42] Once again, there were obvious similarities to Piscator's recent work (*Tai Yang erwacht* having been staged twelve months earlier), not to mention the workers' theatre groups. As Brecht wrote:

> The production showed some features of the agit-prop theatre of those days: the pointed, sketch-like situations, the songs and choruses directed at the audience, the threadlike dramaturgy, loosely linking scenes and songs. But although both play and production owed much to the agit-prop theatre they none the less remained distinct from it. Whereas the agit-prop theatre's task was to stimulate immediate action (e.g. a strike against a wage-cut) and was liable to be overtaken by changes in the political situation, *The Mother* was meant to go further and teach the tactics of the class war. Moreover play and production showed real people together with a process of development, a genuine story running through the play, such as the agit-prop theatre normally lacks.[43]

Thus, the style of *The Mother* combined the cool, expository delivery and the direct address to the audience of the earlier *Lehrstücke* with three-dimensional characters who were seen to develop through the episodic sequence of the action. At the same time, care was taken to make the characters universal 'types' who could be seen as directly relevant to the audience's own experience; hence, no attempt was made to 'russify' them, and their clothes merely conveyed their social positions. Similarly, the typical was emphasised in the use of simple groupings: 'No more "casual", "like-like", "unforced" grouping' – said Brecht – 'the stage no longer reflects the "natural" disorder of things. The opposite of natural disorder is aimed at: natural order. This order is determined from a social-historical point of view.' [44] The actor, he added, needed 'to make himself observed standing between the spectator and the event'. One example of this was the opening scene in which Vlasova shows the audience her incapacity to feed her son properly and the consequent growing gulf between them:

> In the first scene the actress stood in a particular characteristic attitude in the centre of the stage, and spoke the sentences as if they were in the third person; and so she not only refrained from pretending in fact to be or to claim to be Vlasova (the Mother), and in fact to be speaking those sentences, but actually prevented the spectator from transferring himself to a particular room, as habit and indifference might demand, and imagining himself to be the invisible eye-witness and eavesdropper of a unique intimate occasion. Instead what she did was openly to introduce the spectator to the person whom he would be watching acting and being acted upon for some hours. [45]

Another was Scene Five, the 'Report on 1st May 1905' in which a worker Smilgin is shot down by the police when leading a demonstration:

> The May Day demonstration was spoken as if the participants were before a police-court, but at the end the actor playing Smilgin indicated his collapse by going down on his knees; the actress playing the Mother then stooped during her final words and picked up the flag that had slipped from his hands. [46]

Eisler's music played a crucial part in the production. There were ten songs, scored for chorus, soloists and a band comprising trumpet, trombone, piano and drums (seated this time in front of the stage). As Brecht says, the style, designed to induce in the spectator a critical attitude, was careful to keep 'well clear of the general drug-traffic conducted by bourgeois show business':

> Eisler's music can by no means be called simple. Qua music it is relatively complicated, and I cannot think of any that is more serious. In a remarkable manner it makes possible a certain simplification of the toughest political problems, whose solution is a life and death matter for the working class. In the short piece which counters the accusation that Communism leads to chaos the

friendly and explanatory gest* of the music wins a hearing, as it were, for the voice of reason. The piece 'In Praise of Learning', which links the problem of learning with that of the working class's accession to power, is infected by the music with a heroic yet naturally cheerful gest. Similarly the final chorus 'In Praise of Dialectics', which might easily give the effect of a purely emotional song of triumph, has been kept in the realm of the rational by the music. (It is a frequently recurring mistake to suppose that this – epic – kind of production simply does without all emotional effects: actually, emotions are only clarified in it, steering clear of subconscious origins and carrying nobody away.)[47]

Repeated attempts were made by the authorities to obstruct the production. Originally, it was planned to project documentary film of the October Revolution after Vlasova's closing lines, but this was banned by the censor. Later, when the production was taken to Moabit, the police first used fire regulations as a pretext to stop it, and then argued that 'there was no demand for the performance' – despite the fact that the hall had only recently been used for theatrical purposes and was now sold out for *The Mother*. The performance went ahead regardless, without setting, props and costumes – whereupon the police declared even the use of the curtain illegal. Finally, the performers sat in a semi-circle on stage and recited their lines. As Herbert Ihering reported in the *Börsen Courier* of 29 February, 'Even in this abbreviated and limited form, the question of the need for the performance was answered by the audience in the affirmative'.[48] By their intervention, the police had unwittingly lent a whole new dimension of *Verfremdung* to the performance, thereby endorsing Brecht's argument that characters can be more effectively 'demonstrated' than impersonated.

Brecht remarked on the contrasting reactions to the production:

... Since the audience for some of the performances was almost entirely bourgeois, while that for others (the bulk) was purely working-class, we were able to get an exact idea of the difference between their respective reactions. It was very wide. Where the workers reacted immediately to the subtlest twists in the dialogue and fell in with the most complicated assumptions without fuss, the bourgeois audience found the course of the story hard to follow and quite missed its essence. The worker – it was the working-class women who reacted with particular liveliness – was not at all put off by the extreme dryness and compression with which the various situations were sketched, but at once concentrated on the essential, on how the characters behaved in them. His reaction was in fact a political one from the first. The West-ender sat with so bored and stupid a smile as to seem positively comic; he missed the emotional embroidery and embellishment he was used to ...[49]

On this occasion Brecht was successful in winning the approval of the Left, though some critics still had reservations about his interpretation of events in Russia. *Die Rote Fahne* announced:

---

* or 'gestus' (see pp. 173–174 above).

This is a new Bert Brecht. He has escaped from the desert of bourgeois theatre business; he is fighting for the revolutionary working class. As yet he has not torn off all the shackles that bind him to his past. But he will. He must – soon.[50]

In little more than a year Brecht was forced to tear off those shackles in the most literal sense. On 30 January 1933 Hitler became Chancellor; on 27 February the Nazis engineered the burning of the Reichstag building, and within twenty-four hours the Communist Party was declared an illegal organisation. That day Brecht, who was in hospital recuperating from an operation, escaped to Prague with his wife Helene Weigel and their son Stefan. *The Mother* proved to be the last production of Brecht to be staged in Berlin for seventeen years.

Brecht's exile took him through Scandinavia, the Soviet Union, America and finally Switzerland. Throughout this entire period his only large-scale productions were the celebrated *Life of Galileo* with Charles Laughton in Los Angeles in 1947,[51] and his adaptation of *Antigone* the following year in Switzerland. However, this period of exile saw the writing of virtually all his major plays, a number of important theoretical works, and numerous poems. By the time he returned with Helene Weigel to Berlin in October 1948, he had a clear view of the kind of theatre he wanted to establish, thanks mainly to the experience he had gained before 1933. Not that he saw his method as finalised: as numerous accounts testify, each production continued to be a learning process, with Brecht seeming (or affecting) to know less about the script than anyone, and with suggestions welcome from any quarter, artistic or otherwise.[52] When the Berliner Ensemble was founded at the Deutsches Theater in 1949* rehearsals were open to all comers and Brecht placed absolute reliance on audience reaction, mercilessly cutting and rewriting his own scripts to avoid boredom or obscurity. 'The word of the writer' – he argued – 'is only as sacred as it is true.' With massive support from the state (75% of the company's total budget in 1959),[53] the Ensemble could afford to devote as much as a year to preparation and rehearsal of each new production, the great proportion of this time being taken up with clarifying the narrative and making the action concrete and true, 'cleaning the stage' – as Carl Weber says – 'of the "sweet lies" which keep man from recognising the world as it is'.[54]

With the Swiss production of *Antigone* in 1948 Brecht initiated the practice of documenting his work in so-called 'model books', a number of which have since been published. He emphasised that the model was intended only as a starting point, one of many possible solutions to the play: 'They are intended' – he said – 'not to render thought unnecessary but to provoke it: not as a substitute for artistic creation but as its stimulus'.[55] Unfortunately, since his death in 1956 this caution has not

* It moved to the Theater am Schiffbauerdamm in 1954.

prevented a great deal of dull and imitative 'Brechtian' orthodoxy by directors totally unaware of the fun ('*Spass*') that Brecht never ceased to demand of himself, his designers, his musicians and his actors, and incapable of applying his simple maxim: 'the proof of the pudding is in the eating'.

12. Artaud's Theatre of Cruelty

In February 1925 Antonin Artaud addressed an open letter to the Director of the Comédie Française which began:

> Sir,
> You have infested the news long enough. Your brothel is too greedy. It is time the representatives of a dead art stopped deafening us. Tragedy does not need a Rolls Royce nor prostitutes jewellery. Enough comings and goings in your state brothel. We look above tragedy, the cornerstone of your poisonous old shed, and your Molière is a twat. But it's not only a question of tragedy; we deny your alimentary organism the right to perform any play, past future, or present ...[1]

The previous October, Artaud had allied himself with the Surrealist movement, whose aim it was to overthrow all existing systems, social, political, religious, philosophical and aesthetic, and to achieve total liberation of the mind through 'the future fusion of these two states – outwardly so contradictory – dream and reality, into a sort of absolute reality, a *surreality*'.

Viewed from this vantage point, there was no part of the French theatre that could evade the charges levelled by Artaud at the Comédie Française. Ever since the first 'drames surréalistes',* Apollinaire's *The Breasts of Tiresias* and Cocteau and Satie's ballet *Parade*, were given their first performances in 1917,[2] sporadic attempts had been made to revive the spirit of Jarry and undermine the composure of the French stage, but nothing had approached the radical transformation that the Surrealists now sought.

In 1926, Artaud wrote in the introductory brochure of the Alfred Jarry Theatre:

> The illusion we are seeking to create has no bearing on the greater or lesser degree of verisimilitude of the action, but on the power of communication and reality of this action. By this very act, each show becomes a sort of event. The audience must feel a scene in their lives is being acted out in front of them, a truly vital scene. In a word, we ask our audiences to join with us, inwardly,

---

* The term was coined by Apollinaire in his programme note for the first performance of *Parade*.

deeply. Discussion is not in our line. With each production we put on, we are in deadly earnest. ... Audiences must be thoroughly convinced we can make them cry out.[3]

The direct experience of the theatre that Artaud was speaking from was somewhat limited. He was given his first opportunity as an actor at the age of twenty-four in 1921 when Lugné-Poe gave him a part at the Théâtre de l'Œuvre. Subsequently, he played a large number of small roles, mostly with Charles Dullin and Georges Pitoëff. Interestingly, they included First Mystic in Pitoëff's production of Blok's *The Fairground Booth* in 1923, and the Prompter in his 1924 revival of Pirandello's *Six Characters in Search of an Author*, both of them plays that were the sort of event that Artaud later hoped to stage at the Alfred Jarry Theatre. In the cinema Artaud was rather more successful, appearing in over twenty films between 1922 and 1935, notably Abel Gance's legendary *Napoleon* (as Marat) and Dreyer's *The Passion of Joan of Arc* (as the young monk, Massieu).

The Alfred Jarry Theatre was founded at the end of 1926 by Artaud and the two writers, Robert Aron and Roger Vitrac. It was conceived as a society for the presentation of occasional performances, of which there were a total of eight between 1927 and 1929 in three different theatres, usually with only one rehearsal on stage beforehand.

The first programme, which was given two performances in June 1927, comprised three works, one each by Artaud, Aron (under the alias 'Max Robur'), and Vitrac. Artaud's contribution was called *Acid Stomach, or The Mad Mother*, the text of which is lost but which Artaud described as 'a lyrical piece, a comic exposition of the clash between theatre and the cinema' and which, according to one critic 'showed a young man in almost complete darkness, moving a chair forward then back, uttering mysterious phrases as he did so. He died, then a Queen passed by, who died in turn, and other characters, who also died.' Of *Gigogne* by 'Max Robur' about all we know is that it was 'written and produced with the deliberate aim of needling people'. Vitrac's play in five tableaux, *The Secrets of Love*, was described by Artaud as 'An ironic play, physically staging the misgivings, dual isolation, eroticism and criminal thoughts lurking in the minds of lovers. A *real dream* brought into being for the first time on stage.'[4] The action concentrates on obliterating the distinctions between illusion and reality, both within the play and between performance and audience. The performance took place in a series of complex multiple settings on the stage, in a box suspended above it, and also involved various 'spectators' in the audience, one of whom was killed by the last of the evening's many shots. The several dozen characters included Lloyd George, Mussolini, the Author, the Theatre Manager, and various ghosts, children and dogs. According to one critic, Roger Vitrac summarised the objective as 'producing a certain state of tension in the audience. The moment the audience think they understand, show them the opposite.' In other words, it was the old familiar strategy of the grotesque, long since initiated by Wedekind, Blok, Apollinaire, and of course by Alfred Jarry himself.

Although the two performances were well attended, the fashionable audiences seem to have reacted with no more than polite indulgence, and critics compared the event unfavourably with the *Ubu* scandal of thirty years earlier. Six months later, Artaud and his allies launched a further assault with a programme consisting of the first Paris screening of Pudovkin's film *Mother*, shown because it had been banned by the censor, together with 'an original Act by a "well-known" author, put on with the author's permission on the principle that any published work is public property'. This item proved to be Act Three of Claudel's *Partage de midi*, acted crudely and followed by a denunciation from the stage by Artaud of Claudel, who was the French Ambassador to the United States, as a 'filthy traitor'.

In June 1928 Artaud staged the first French production of *A Dream Play*, a work in which Strindberg, writing in 1901 with no awareness of Freud, had employed remarkable concrete imagery to convey the workings of the unconscious mind. There could be no more logical choice for Artaud; in 1927, he had written in one of his manifestos 'What we would like to see sparkle and triumph on stage is whatever is a part of the mystery and magnetic fascination of dreams, the dark layers of consciousness, all that obsesses us within our minds.'[5]

The cast assembled for *A Dream Play* was unusually strong, but of necessity Artaud's production was a simple affair which made little attempt to achieve the complex tableaux prescribed in the text; instead it relied on the actors, their costumes, carefully selected props, and non-realistic lighting effects. Both performances were dominated by scandals that had nothing to do with the play itself. The opening night on 2 June 1928 was attended by a glittering society gathering, including the Swedish and Danish ambassadors, and many representatives of the international press. From the start the performance was heckled by a group of thirty Surrealists who had occupied seats in the stalls to protest at the liaison that the renegades Artaud and Aron had formed with Swedish capitalism. Artaud came on to protest that he had agreed to stage Strindberg with Swedish financial assistance only because Strindberg himself had been ostracised by Swedish society. But the Surrealists remained sceptical and threatened to break up the second performance a week later; Artaud and Aron resorted to police protection, with the result that André Breton and several others were arrested when they attempted to enter the theatre. The Alfred Jarry Theatre stood condemned of treason in the Surrealists' eyes, and shortly afterwards Robert Aron withdrew from the company.

Artaud's enthusiasm for Strindberg was unimpaired; subsequently he devised a production plan for *The Ghost Sonata* which, though unrealised, remains a highly original reading of the play. According to Artaud, *The Ghost Sonata* '... shows nothing but what is known, although hidden and out of the way. In this play the real and unreal merge, as they do in the mind of someone falling asleep, or someone waking up under a false illusion. We have lived and dreamed everything the play reveals, but we have forgotten it.' In his projected production Artaud envisaged a blurring of the divisions between the real and the imaginary, with 'voices changing tone arbitrarily, overlapping one another, sudden stiffening of attitudes and gestures, lighting changed, decomposed, unusual importance suddenly given to a small detail, characters *morally* fading away, leaving the noises and music dominant, and being replaced by inert doubles, in the form of dummies, for example, which suddenly take their place'.[6]

The final production of the Alfred Jarry Theatre was Vitrac's 'middle-class play in three acts' *Victor or Power to the Children*, which was performed on 24 and 29 December 1928 and 5 January 1929. *Victor* again is, in the broader and more significant sense, a dream play, to the extent that it renders concrete hidden states of mind. There is in its style a distinct resemblance to Jarry, though the setting is ostensibly realistic. The action takes place at the home of the Paumelle family between 8 pm and midnight on 12 September 1909, and concerns the Paumelles and their friends the Magneaux. The occasion is the ninth birthday of Victor Paumelle, a hyper-intelligent child, who in the course of the play increases in height from six feet to six feet, seven inches. In league with the Magneaux' six-year-old daughter Esther, Victor with masterly cunning exposes the marital scandals and secret obsessions of the puppet-like adults. Monsieur Magneau is driven to hang himself from the flagpole on the balcony, Victor dies at the exact second of his anniversary, and finally the adulterous Charles Paumelle and Emilie Magneau shoot themselves – at which point Lili the maid enters with the final curtain line 'Mais, c'est un drame!' There is, in addition, the mysterious and lovely visitor, Ida Mortemart, who suffers from a chronic inability to control her repeated loud farts. After one horrified actress had withdrawn from the part, Artaud explained to her successor that this malady signified the intrusion of the sordid side of matter into the realm of spiritual beauty.

Most critics reacted by adopting their customary patronising stance towards Artaud, though some objected to the aspersions cast in the play on the army, French patriotism, and the hallowed institution of the family. Almost the only significant detail of the actual production that was noted was the device of suspending empty picture frames downstage, placing the audience in the position of voyeurs spying on the scandalous goings-on in the Paumelle menage.

As before, Artaud's frontal assault on bourgeois sensibilities was comfortably ridden by the public, and he and Vitrac finally parted company. Artaud continued to seek financial backing for various projects, including an updated version of *Ubu*, Büchner's *Woyzeck*, Seneca's *Thyestes*, and Tourneur's *The Revenger's Tragedy*, but he was unsuccessful and the Alfred Jarry Theatre ceased to exist.

Over the next six years Artaud did virtually no work in the theatre, and scraped a living from occasional small parts in films, from lectures, and from writing. The majority of essays and letters that make up *The Theatre and its Double*, published in 1938, date from this period. He began to expound his idea of a 'Theatre of Cruelty' as early as 1932. In 'The Theatre of Cruelty (First Manifesto)' he writes:

> Theatre will never be itself again ... unless it provides the audience with truthful distillations of dreams where its taste for crime, its erotic obsession, its savageness, its fantasies, its utopian sense of life and objects, even its cannibalism, gush out, not in an illusory make-believe, but on an inner level.[7]

His notion of cruelty, then, concerns the need to confront man with the dangers inherent in his own nature, which can never change. It is in this sense that he contends 'We are not free, and the sky can still fall on our heads. And above all else, theatre is made to teach us this.'[8] But Artaud sees this as grounds neither for passive resignation nor for attempted rationalisation, but rather for defiance and celebration:

> ... impelling us to see ourselves as we are, making the masks fall and divulging our world's lies, aimlessness, meanness, and even two-facedness, the theatre shakes off stifling material dullness which even overcomes the senses' clearest testimony, and collectively reveals their dark powers and hidden strength to men, urging them to take a nobler, more heroic stand in the face of destiny than they would have assumed without it.[9]

For this reason Artaud rejected both the measure and nobility of Sophocles and the introspective 'psychology' of Shakespeare in favour of the sense of cosmic vertigo conveyed by the Roman dramatist, Seneca, and the tragedies of blood of Ford, Tourneur, and Webster. He was prepared to risk their remoteness of age and custom for the sake of their timeless elemental power, which he proposed to invoke by means of a total theatrical experience.

In the field of theatrical innovation, Artaud acknowledged the achievements of the Russian and German theatres. He had doubtless heard of the mass spectacles staged in Moscow and Petrograd in the early twenties, and he would have had a chance to see the work of Meyerhold and Tairov, both of whose companies had visited Paris. As for Reinhardt and Piscator, Artaud knew of their work from a visit to Berlin in 1932. But perhaps most influential of all was his experience at the Paris Colonial Exhibition in 1931 of the Balinese dance-drama, which he discusses in detail in *The Theatre and its Double*; above all, he was impressed by its independence from merely verbal language:

> In the Balinese theatre productions the mind certainly gets the impression that concepts clashed with gestures first, establishing themselves among a whole ferment of sight and sound imagery, thoughts as it were in a pure state. To sum it up more distinctly, something like a musical condition must have existed to produce this staging, where everything that is imagined by the mind is only an excuse, a virtuality whose double produced this intense scenic poetry, this many-hued spatial language.[10]

As Grotowski has pointed out, the 'language' of the Balinese theatre was probably far more specific and concrete in meaning for the Balinese themselves than Artaud chose to believe,[11] but this should not detract from the impulse that it afforded him. The following year, in a letter elaborating his idea of a 'theatre of cruelty', he wrote to Jean Paulhan:

> I have added another language to speech and am attempting to restore its ancient magic effectiveness, its spellbinding effectiveness, integral with speech, and whose mysterious potential is now forgotten. When I say I will not put on written plays, I mean I will not act plays based on writing or words; rather, in the shows I intend to put on, the predominant part will be physical and could not be determined or written in normal word language. Even the written or spoken parts will be performed in a different way.[12]

Inevitably, this led Artaud to assume the function both of author and director, or, as he put it in a letter to André Gide, 'creator or investor of a theatrical reality which is absolute and self-sufficient'.[13] He had arrived at the same point as Craig and Piscator, or as Meyerhold in 1926 who styled himself 'production author' in order to express the extent of his reworking of *The Government Inspector*.

It took Artaud until 1935 to secure the backing for his long-projected Theatre of Cruelty. His eventual aim was to stage his scenario *The Conquest of Mexico*, which depicted the defeat of Montezuma by Cortez and the subsequent massacre of the Spanish forces. Artaud was attracted to this episode because, as he said, 'It revives Europe's deep-rooted self-conceit in a burning, inexorably bloody manner, allowing us to debunk its own concept of supremacy.' As Ronald Hayman has noted, in one respect Artaud's conception was strikingly close to Brecht's formulation of Epic Theatre:

> [*The Conquest of Mexico*] will stage events rather than men. Men will appear in their proper place with their emotions and psychology interpreted as the emergence of certain powers in the light of the events and historical destiny in which they played their role.[14]

The Conquest of Mexico was deferred in favour of Artaud's version of *The Cenci*, which it was hoped would serve as an introduction to some of the ideas behind the Theatre of Cruelty, and would also help to raise money for the far more complex and visionary Mexico project.

At first glance, Artaud's choice of Shelley's verse tragedy *The Cenci* as the basis for his own play may seem surprising, given that Shelley derives his effects so much more from poetic imagery and rhetoric than from direct action. But what appealed so strongly to Artaud was the theme, which he was able to document further by drawing on Stendhal's fuller account of the actual events, which had been published in 1837 in his *Chroniques Italiennes*. In a letter to André Gide Artaud wrote 'The dialogue of this tragedy is, I dare to say, of extreme violence. And there *isn't anything* that won't be attacked among the antique notions of Society, Order, Justice, Religion, Family and Country.'[15] Briefly, *The Cenci* is based on the true story of Count Francesco Cenci, born in Rome in 1527, who devoted himself to a life of blasphemy, crime and debauchery and used his vast fortune to purchase regular absolution from the Pope. At the play's opening, he is in his seventy-second year and celebrating the violent deaths of two of his hated sons who had tried unsuccessfully to secure his execution for proven sodomy. Infatuated with his sixteen-year-old daughter Beatrice, he rapes her; she in turn conspires with her step-mother Lucretia, her brother Giacomo, and Orsino, a priest in love with her, to bribe two assassins to murder him, which they do by impaling him through the eye. The crime is revealed by betrayal, and Beatrice and Lucretia are first tortured and finally executed. Shelley's version was completed in 1819, but not performed until 1886 when the Shelley Society gave it a private matinee performance.[16]

In one important respect, Shelley was faithful to the tradition of Revenge Tragedy which so commended itself to Artaud. In his Preface, Shelley writes:

> There must ... be nothing attempted to make the exhibition subservient to what is vulgarly termed a moral purpose. The highest moral purpose aimed at in the highest species of drama is the teaching the human heart, through its sympathies and antipathies, the knowledge of itself; in proportion to the possession of which knowledge, every human being is wise, just, sincere, tolerant and kind. If dogmas can do more, it is well: but a drama is no fit place for the enforcement of them.[17]

On the other hand, his formal conception was fundamentally different from Artaud's:

> The person who would treat such a subject must increase the ideal, and diminish the actual horror of the events, so that the pleasure which arises from the poetry which exists in these tempestuous sufferings and crimes may mitigate the pain of the contemplation, of the moral deformity from which they spring.[18]

Artaud wrote: 'Shelley embellished nature with his style and language, which is like a summer night bombarded by meteors. But I prefer the starkness of nature.' Yet, interestingly, he remained faithful to Shelley in showing neither the rape of Beatrice nor the murder of Cenci. Elsewhere, though, he greatly compressed the text by replacing verbal imagery and description with concrete stage action. For instance, in dealing with the first abortive attempt on Cenci's life on a lonely road on the Apennines, Shelley has Beatrice describe the chosen spot in twenty-three lines of vivid detail (Act III, Scene One). Then, in the following scene, the failure of the assassination attempt is summarily reported on ('He passed by the spot appointed for the deed an hour too soon'). Artaud, by contrast, first briefly sets the scene:

> But I remember that two miles from the castle a path comes to a kind of chasm – deep down, a black torrent of water frothing and eddying ceaselessly through rocky caverns – and at that point a bridge spans the chasm.

And then depicts the attempt as follows:

> *(Dusk. The scene follows the last one without interruption. A fearful storm breaks out. Several claps of thunder explode at close intervals. Immediately,* ORSINO *can be seen entering, followed by his two assassins. They are struggling against a violent wind.* ORSINO *posts his assassins.)*

> ORSINO. Yes, you understand well enough. We ourselves are the hurricane, so scream your lungs out if you wish.
> GIACOMO. Do you think they know how to go about it? Just tell them to strike their man down, don't confuse them by telling them to match their silent throats with the screech of the hurricane.

> *(Three thunderclaps reverberate. Several armour-clad men appear, moving extra-ordinarily slowly, like the figures on the face of the great clock of Strasbourg cathedral. Repeated peals of thunder.)*

> ORSINO. Calm yourself. Everything is all right. Each of the two knows the part he has to play.
> GIACOMO. My fear is that they may overplay their parts and be no longer capable of doing anything real.

> *(The jerky tramping of feet can be heard again.* LUCRETIA, BERNARDO, BEATRICE *appear, walking at the same statue-like pace, and very far behind them, bringing up the rear, is Count* CENCI. *The storm rages with increasing fury, and, mingled with the wind, one can hear voices repeating the name* 'CENCI', *first in a single prolonged, high-pitched tone, then like the pendulum of a clock.)*
> Cenci, Cenci, Cenci, Cenci.

> *(At moments all the names blend together at one point in the sky, like countless birds whose individual flights have converged together. Then the voices grow louder and pass by like a flight of birds very close at hand.)*

CENCI *(facing the voices, shouts into the storm).*
    WHAT, THEN!

(Immediately, the outlines of the assassins can be seen surging forth, spinning like tops and meeting and passing each other in the illumination of a flash of lightning. At the same time, the roar of two pistol shots is heard. Night has fallen, the lightning flashes cease. Everything vanishes.)

GIACOMO. What, failed?
ORSINO. FAILED!

(Curtain.)[19]

Consistent with his idea that *The Cenci* was an archetypal tragedy motivated by elemental forces common to all men, Artaud based his interpretation of the play on 'that general gravitation that moves plants and beings like plants and which we also find in a static form in the volcanic eruptions of the earth'. Thus:

> If Orsino traces circles like a bird of prey around groups he is animating, characters whom he affects individually; if Camillo and Orsino turn and move around Giacomo in an atmosphere of a cave, in a subterranean light, like the hypnotist of carnivals around a client he wants to petrify; if Beatrice moves the automated assassins like pieces on a chessboard, if she swaddles them like living mummies, if they both laugh unanimously like organisms in tune; if the veiled guards turn in a circle and change places like the hours; if they return to their places in succession with the rhythm of a pendulum: here is this secret gravitation whose subtlety few saw.[20]

Artaud based his entire approach to the production on the principle of engulfing the audience with a massive accumulation of effects, so that its response would be sensual and involuntary rather than detached and intellectual. Sound was a vital element in his design, and was worked out in great detail between him and the conductor, Roger Désormière. Loudspeakers were placed at the four corners of the auditorium (perhaps the earliest attempt at stereophonic sound in the theatre), and a range of recorded effects bombarded the audience: tolling bells, screeching machines, echoing footsteps, an oscillating metronome, thunder and lightning, whispering voices in counterpoint, deafening fanfares, ringing anvils, the electronic notes of an Ondes Martenot. Thus, Artaud's direction for the opening of the banquet scene reads 'The bells of Rome can be heard in full peal, but muffled, following the dizzy rhythm of the banquet. Voices are raised, taking on the deep or high-pitched, almost crystal-clear note of the bells. From time to time, a thick heavy sound spreads out then dissolves, as though stopped by some obstacle which makes it rebound in sharp ridges.'[21]

The sound effects were frequently synchronised with abrupt lighting changes, sometimes blinding in their intensity. The settings, designed by Balthus, 'were like a design as for some grandiose phantoms, like a ruin which one dreams'. The critic Pierre-Jean Jouve wrote:

> The tragedy is inseparable from its *space* ... The setting is practicable, essentially architectural – it reminds you of one of Piranesi's gigantic palace-prisons, but with a certain discordance conveyed by the clash of colours and the ruptures in form, which together produce the kind of dissonant sonority which we expect nowadays.
>
> One could write a great deal about the secret symbols which are active just below the surface of the visible reality – just as they are in Balthus' paintings. Thus the scaffolding like a giant ladder and the round column against the sky which elevate the Cenci palace to a terrifying height, yet still retain their meaning; the red curtains hanging like 'iron tatters' or clots of congealed blood, the arches broken off in space. Against this imposing background the costumes stand out in brilliant and vivid contrast, but without their 'living' matter ever subduing the dead matter of the stones, stairs, pediments, porticos, wheels and ropes.[22]

The only theatre that Artaud was able to hire for *The Cenci* was the Folies-Wagram, whose vast tasteless auditorium with surrounding promenade was designed for music hall rather than tragic drama. The production opened on 6 May 1935 before the familiar society audience, and ran for a total of seventeen performances. Artaud had been careful to ensure extensive advance publicity, but the production was received by most critics with a mixture of condescension and puzzlement.[23] Those who did not object to the audio-visual battering they received, tended to be scathing about the acting. As Beatrice, Artaud had cast Lady Ilya Abdy, a society beauty of Russian extraction, who had acting ambitions and had helped to raise the financial backing. Whilst she was admired for her physical portrayal, she was ridiculed for her Russian accent and inaudible delivery. Artaud himself played Count Cenci, and was generally regarded as far too frenzied and melodramatic. Yet for all the blasé detachment of the critics' notices, they still convey a certain sense of unease together with a grudging recognition of Artaud's daring and originality.

The production left Artaud in financial ruin, artistically discredited, and exhausted by the immense burden of writing, acting, direction and promotion. As Martin Esslin says, the failure of *The Cenci* was not merely the end to Artaud's ambitions as a working director but the end to his prolonged struggle to maintain an existence within conventional society.[24] Soon, he was to embark on disastrous journeys to Mexico and Ireland, which culminated in his loss of sanity and his confinement in a series of mental institutions, where he lived out a life ravaged by delusions, drug abuse and finally cancer. He died in 1948 at the age of fifty-one without ever returning to the stage. Without doubt, the full impact of *The Cenci* was inhibited greatly by its confinement within a conventional proscenium-arch stage. Artaud's *Conquest of Mexico* project shows his awareness of the importance of theatre space, and of the need to break the bounds of the stage so that 'just as there are to be no empty spatial areas, there must be no let up, no vacuum in the audience's mind or sensitivity'.[25] Artaud was by no means alone in this conviction: Reinhardt, Piscator and the architect Gropius in Germany, and Meyerhold and Okhlopkov in the Soviet Union had been working along similar lines. However, nobody had envisaged the total emotional involvement of the spectator that Artaud demanded. It is in this that the full meaning of his theatre of cruelty is to be found, and to which directors in the modern theatre from the Théâtre du Soleil to the Bread and Puppet, from the Living Theatre to the Grand Magic Circus, from Brook to Grotowski have all aspired and found their inspiration in Artaud's visionary writings.

13. Grotowski's Laboratory Theatre*

In 1959 Jerzy Grotowski, in collaboration with the writer Ludwik Flaszen, established a small, experimental theatre company in the provincial town of Opole, sixty miles from Auschwitz, in Poland. At that time a young theatre director of twenty-six, Grotowski had received a conventional theatrical training at the Cracow Advanced Acting School. In addition, during his student years he had travelled widely, studying ancient and classical theatre techniques, and as part of his training had spent one year at the State Institute of Theatre Art in Moscow. He was fascinated by the forms of Oriental and Asian theatre he had witnessed in his travels, and, not surprisingly, was greatly influenced by Stanislavsky – to whom he has referred as 'my spiritual father'.

Grotowski's co-founder in the establishment of what was initially named the Theatre of Thirteen Rows was Ludwik Flaszen. Literary and dramatic critic, and author, his official position was that of literary adviser to the theatre – but the role he actually played was far more crucial in the development of the theoretical concepts that motivated the theatrical experiments. Grotowski sees Flaszen's role – which he likens to that of a 'devil's advocate' – as absolutely essential in a research-orientated theatrical establishment. Flaszen has said himself of his work: 'For example, when I analyzed Grotowski's work for him, I tried to find all that had become merely a shell, the reasoned, or the artificial. I analyzed what could be rejected. When I felt my analysis was helpless, I knew I was dealing with something alive . . .'[1]

According to Grotowski, the membership of the group they directed was quite fluid during the first two to three years. Of the half-dozen or so actors who formed the company in 1959, three were still working with Grotowski more than twenty years later. In time, they were joined by four other actors, and this central core of nine (including Grotowski and Flaszen) has remained, at the time of writing, virtually unchanged in all their years of collective research. Whilst the theatre received, as a matter

*By Jennifer Kumiega.

of course, a grant from the municipality, it must be borne in mind that this was a very small subsidy indeed. The Polish writer Jan Kott has pointed out that Poland was probably the only country at that time to allow itself the luxury of a 'theatre-laboratory', and yet so poor that its actors had to starve.

In the first three years, from 1959 to 1962, there were at least ten premieres at the Theatre of Thirteen Rows. These were a series of disparately experimental productions, presented on a regular basis both in Opole and on tour in Poland. It was not until after the first contact between Grotowski and the contemporary theatrical world outside Poland (in Finland in 1962 and at the International Theatre Institute Congress in Warsaw in 1963) that a significant cohesion of direction became perceptible in the group's activities. Less time was being devoted to the preparation and presentation of a repertoire, as the gradually stabilising company began to turn their attention more forcefully to research and experiment. By 1962 the number of premieres had been reduced to two (Słowacki's *Kordian* and Wyspiański's *Akropolis*), with only *Dr. Faustus*, based on Marlowe's text, appearing in the following year.

On 1 January 1965 this change of emphasis was officially recognised when the company was transferred to Wrocław (its present base), re-named itself the Laboratory Theatre, and had conferred upon it the status of 'Institute of Actor's Research'. Now no longer bound by the premise that the first duty of a theatre is to produce plays, Grotowski realised his concept of an organisation dedicated primarily to research. Shortly after this move the company presented *The Constant Prince*, the first major new production since 1963. Based on the adaptation of Calderon's text by Julius Słowacki, the production has been seen as the summit of the Laboratory Theatre acting method, and the synthesis of all that Grotowski attempted to achieve in his years of research.

It was to be another three years, filled with international tours and intense preparation, before *Apocalypsis Cum Figuris*, the Laboratory Theatre's final collective theatrical production, was shown in 1968. It was realised then, in retrospect, that *The Constant Prince* had marked the end of one stage of work for the Laboratory Theatre, a period of slow, assiduous experimentation into the actor's craft, centred on the theatrical processes of the actor in the given limited structure of a production.

In the early years, the Laboratory Theatre's reception in its own country was disappointing. But the key-word to Grotowski's approach was asceticism, and in the colourful atmosphere that followed the easing of the post-war period of enforced 'socialist realism', Poland was in no mood for such a philosophy. Not so the western world: to some, Grotowski's appearance was barely less than messianic. Theatre was in some spheres faltering under the weight of accumulated technical refinements.

Facing the straightforward commercial competition of cinema and television, directors had begun to make a necessity of what had once been luxury. To the conventional aids of lighting and sound were added the accumulated resources of technological invention, and only the most acute were able to keep the art of the actor alive in the fairground spectacle. Grotowski called this trend 'artistic kleptomania . . . conglomerates without backbone or integrity', and recognising the inevitability of the decline of the domain of theatre, he sought through his work and research to give renewed vitality to an age-old truth: that the core of theatre is the communion between actor and spectator. By eliminating a dependence on what is superfluous to this core (lighting, sound, make-up, decor, props), he arrived at the concept of the 'poor theatre'.

What Grotowski and his team were primarily concerned with, then, were 'detailed investigations of the actor–audience relationship . . . (considering) the personal and scenic technique of the actor as the core of theatre art'.[2] The preoccupation with the technique and motivation of the actor was of course germane to the work of Stanislavsky. Grotowski acknowledges him as his first master, and has absorbed from him some basic principles: daily work and training, a quasi-scientific attitude to research, a respect for the value of detail, and, perhaps most importantly, the ethical value of theatre. Their conclusions differ because Grotowski has gone so much further in questioning the requirements of theatre, both ethically and technically. Eventually, the questioning had end results that Stanislavsky could never have envisaged or possibly desired – for the answers partly directed Grotowski towards a total re-evaluation of the relevance of theatre, and ultimately a personal rejection of its strict confines.

But this is a conclusion that has been reached only after an uncompromising and painstaking investigation of every feasible area of study involving the actor, his body and his craft. Yet Grotowski specifically emphasises that the intention has never been to train an actor in a collection of skills. Elements are employed or jettisoned strictly in accordance with their usefulness in eliminating from the actor's psyche all that blocks his path towards the transgression of self, which Grotowski considers necessary for the act of communion, the 'total act' of theatre.

In pursuit of this goal Grotowski has set out, besides a succession of inimitable productions, a well-charted route along which an actor may with confidence proceed towards excellence in his craft. He abhors any reference to Grotowski 'methods', strongly resisting any attempt to categorise and 'package' the results of the theatre's research into a method to be merchandised alongside those of Stanislavsky or Brecht. He in fact rejects the very concept of 'method', seeing any fixed framework externally adopted by a developing actor – and therefore not emanating from his personal organic research and needs – to be ultimately stultifying. And it probably *is* accurate to say that there exists no one technique, exercise or method that has any absolute value for the Laboratory Theatre team and was a permanent feature of their training – just as there is little, in fact, in the way of technique or method that is in any sense *unique* to the Laboratory Theatre, an objective result of their research that may be passed on. All techniques of actor-training have been available in the past to any theatre researcher.

Nevertheless, a record of the techniques of actor-training used in the Laboratory Theatre between 1959 and 1966 are included in *Towards a Poor Theatre*,[3] and much may be learnt of how this work was qualified in terms of ethic and motive by studying Grotowski's theatrical writings. Whatever Grotowski's view of the matter, the world sees its debt to him as centering on his work with the actor and his body, and in the practical area at least the body has always been the pivotal point of the majority of the Laboratory Theatre work. Grotowski sees the actor's body as an instrument that must be capable of more than the spectator's. The body must be able to achieve those physical extremes that usually only occur in conditions of emotional excess or trance. It is to this end that he has drawn on the techniques of the European and Eastern masters.

But Grotowski issues a caution about the attitude with which one confronts any training process – it can never, according to him, be a voluntary, active attitude, which is the result of intellectual control; it is rather what he calls a 'non-active process' or 'via negativa'. This is the guiding principle of all the physical training. In terms of the exercises, rather than advocating a positive, methodical acquisition of physical skills, it demands an emphasis on the elimination of the muscular blockage that inhibits free, creative reaction. 'The result is freedom from the time-lapse between inner impulse and outer reaction in such a way that the impulse is already an outer reaction.'[4] This is an empirically verifiable proposition, and a familiar precept in the training of a gymnast.

As a principle, it also has an ethical application, and this is the key to what elevates the craft of the Laboratory Theatre actor to a transcendent art. Grotowski states categorically that the process is 'not voluntary. The requisite state of mind is a passive readiness to realise an active role, a state in which one does not *want to do that* but rather *resigns from not doing it*.'[5] Grotowski also refers to this as 'internal passivity'. It is not a comfortable concept for the western mind, which tends to prefer positive, intellect-guided action; but clarification may be aided by reference to the Taoist principle of *wu-wei*, which translates literally as 'non-action', remarkably close to Grotowski's 'non-active principle'. In elaboration, Chuang-Tzu has said: 'Non-action does not mean doing nothing and keeping silent. Let everything be allowed to do what it naturally does, so that its nature will be satisfied.'[6]

But this is a spiritual and personal process, and in their daily training it was to the physical and empirical that the actors of the Laboratory Theatre gave their attention. Grotowski constantly underlines the need for concretisation of the process, to avoid a retreat into the amorphous. This is achieved, as with Stanislavsky, by attention to minute detail. Using the metaphor of a river, Grotowski says: 'Between the two shores of my precision, I allow the river, which comes out of the authenticity of my experience, to advance, slowly or rapidly.'[7] The daily work of the actors at the Laboratory Theatre, then, concentrated on artifice: 'There is no contradiction between inner technique and artifice (articulation of a role by signs). We believe that a personal process that is not supported and expressed by a formal articulation and disciplined structuring of the role is not a release and will collapse in shapelessness.'[8]

But it must be emphasised that these processes at the Laboratory Theatre were always in service of Grotowski's central definition of theatre as 'what takes place between spectator and actor'. Admittedly, he was not able to educate the former systematically. Hence his preoccupation with the 'personal and scenic technique of the actor', which he elevated to the level of 'secular holiness': 'One must give oneself totally, in one's deepest intimacy, in confidence, as when one gives oneself in love. Here lies the key. Self-penetration, trance, excess, the formal discipline itself . . .'[9]

At the same time Grotowski has never been content to renounce fully an investigation into the psychic presence of the audience, and the possibilities inherent not only for the internal processes of the actor, and the 'unities' of the production, but also in terms of the postulated reactions of the spectators themselves. 'The performance engages a sort of psychic conflict with the spectator. It is a challenge and an excess.'[10] This investigation found shape in Grotowski's constant exploration of spatial concepts and relationships in performance. For each production, he claimed 'the essential concern is finding the proper spectator/actor relationship for each type of performance and embodying the decision in physical arrangements'.[11]

The fact that he called his designer an 'architect' may give some insight into his approach. He proceeded from a use of the conventional end-stage (with brief forays into the spectator area), to an attempt in *Forefather's Eve* (based on Mickiewicz, 1961) at both total spatial integration of actors and spectators and a partial elimination of the intellectual division between the two, by designating the latter as 'participants' and assigning them 'roles'. This form of active involvement was not repeated, and thereafter the audience were relegated to the passive role of 'spectator-witness'. Gradually they were forced into a more alienated position, as Grotowski began to concentrate more fully on the role of the actor. In *Kordian* (based on Słowacki, 1962), set in a psychiatric ward, the audience became ambivalently patients together with the hero; in the production of Marlowe's *Dr. Faustus* (1963), they were guests invited to Faustus's Last Supper at which he served up episodes from his life. And in the penultimate play from the Laboratory Theatre, *The Constant Prince* (1965), the audience were made to watch the drama of persecution from elevated positions surrounding a wooden enclosure with the guilty curiosity of voyeurs.

But in the final production, *Apocalypsis Cum Figuris*, Grotowski at last dispensed with these charades. Actors and audience, without pretence and on equal footing (as far as this is possible within theatrical convention), together entered the playing-area, a large empty room: the ones to give and present, the others to receive and witness. It was the furthest Grotowski could proceed in his obsessive manipulation of that elusive actor/spectator relationship while still remaining within the bounds of theatre.

As Director of the Laboratory Theatre and its actors, Grotowski has from the beginning assumed a role far more complex than any conventional director. The depth of his commitment is perhaps unique, and is certainly one of the significant reasons for the group having stayed so long together. In describing it, Grotowski does not spare the emotionally reticent: 'This is not instruction of a pupil but utter opening to another person, in which the phenomenon of "shared or double birth" becomes possible. The actor is reborn – not only as an actor but as a man – and with him I am reborn.'[12] The fruits of this commitment were seen and acknowledged in the production of *The Constant Prince*, in which the actor Ryszard Cieślak achieved as nearly as is possible Grotowski's definition of 'the total act'.*

But although theatrically brilliant, *The Constant Prince* had highlighted aspects of a question on which Grotowski was gradually concentrating his critical faculties: to what extent can theatrical activity successfully eliminate the manipulative elements in the director/actor/audience relationships and still remain theatre? Grotowski was acutely aware that there remained, integral to the spiritual closeness of the unique actor-director relationship that he enjoyed with his company, elements of the conventional, manipulative alliance. Flaszen: 'Working with Grotowski, I understand several things: for example, how, when starting with manipulation (an idea indispensable to theatre) one reaches a point where it all falls away and what remains is something else. The usual professional rela-

* Recalling Artaud's aspiration: 'Actors should be like martyrs burnt alive, still signalling to us from their stakes.'[13]

tionship between master and disciple falls away. What remains can be witnessed by no-one. It happened, for example, in Grotowski's work with Cieślak on *The Constant Prince*.'[14]

Years of silence and private work followed *The Constant Prince* before the presentation in 1968 of *Apocalypsis Cum Figuris*. Although pushed to the furthest extremes, it was still theatre – undeniably so. And yet in the years of work, and in the realisation of the production itself, it would appear that Grotowski answered his own questions, and reached his own pragmatic conclusions. *Apocalypsis Cum Figuris* remained within the Laboratory Theatre repertoire for twelve years for most of that time the only theatrical presentation – and the last theatrical act that Grotowski himself was to accomplish.

Apocalypsis took several years to prepare. As a play it contained no intrinsic life of its own – there was no original dramatic text to which the actors were able to respond creatively as with the previous productions of the Laboratory Theatre. In place of a dramatic text, the actors responded to a network of interwoven myths, historical events, literary fable and everyday occurrences, which formed in their totality a multi-level parable of the human race. But without the actors who performed it, it would have ceased to exist – for on one level it was drawn uniquely from the life-experiences of the actors involved, and the levels on which it operated were so completely interdependent that destruction of any single level would have resulted in the collapse of the whole. For most of the period of its creation there was no script as such: action was improvised, and speech as well where it was absolutely essential. Not until the action was crystallised were the actors asked to make a personal and individual search through literature for the texts to which they and their creation responded. The text as it eventually stood contained mingled passages from Dostoyevsky, T. S. Eliot, The Bible and Simone Weil.

An objective, definitive interpretation of *Apocalypsis* is simply not possible. From the myriad conscious responses one simply seeks to extract the most obvious, or the least personal. On one level it was a parable of the Second Coming, but with neither a total sense of acceptance nor denial. A Christ-figure was certainly evoked, and the final words spoken to him in darkness were 'Go and come no more'. But when the lights came on and the room was discovered empty, it did not necessarily mean that he had gone – or even that he had been. The room had simply been returned to the state it was in when the first spectator entered.

So what *had* been witnessed? A group of ordinary people, in everyday clothes. Roles were assigned, amidst mirth, and assumed, rejected, fought against. But each role, once assumed, possessed that person who was trapped within it, drained by the excesses with which he fulfilled or denied it. There was a Simon Peter, calculating, intellectual, mouthing the twentieth-century revolt of Dostoyevsky's Grand Inquisitor. A John, who, animal-like, was consumed by the excesses of the body. A Mary Magdalene who, procured by John, became the bride of the Son of God and made an irrevocable, carnal reality of his humanity. Judas and Lazarus, mocking, trivial, often aloof, parodied the episodes from the sidelines. And there was the Simpleton – his name in Polish means 'The Dark One' and holds associations of a touched innocence, the medieval idiot unknowingly holding powers of light and dark. He was drawn, an unwilling victim, into the group's games and elected to be their Saviour. Desperate for their love and acceptance, he was gradually consumed by the power of his own role, and struggled helplessly towards the final extinction. His agonies produced in his tormentors pleasure, rage, pity and final acceptance.

For a period towards the end of the action the room was plunged into darkness. The actors were scattered around the playing-area, exhausted by their games. Then the room was gradually filled with flickering light as Simon Peter re-entered, carrying candles. From this point the action moved swiftly, following more nearly the gospel sequence of events. The actors were finally acquiescent in their roles. The Last Supper, the Betrayal, Golgotha, and at last the Crucifixion. At the very end only Simon Peter was left to confront the Simpleton with his academic arguments. To these the Simpleton had no logical response, and the second and final crucifixion at Simon Peter's hands was a cold, intellectual verification of the earlier emotional one. The Simpleton, in a state of agonised delirium, floundered on the floor. From his lips there came his final response – a Latin hymn, a prayer in the ritual language of organised religion. It deepened and soared to envelop the darkening room, as Simon Peter stealthily circled towards him, extinguishing the candles one by one. The final image before total darkness was that of a helpless moth, pinned to the floor, but yearning towards the last rays of light.

In attempting any interpretation of *Apocalypsis*, the thought constantly returns that as an art form it was possibly closer to poetry than anything else. There was a poetry of body complementing poetry of sound, in which the reverberations of each action or word were inexhaustible. Associations were condensed into rich metaphors or naked imagery, and a response from actor or audience did not necessarily operate on the conscious level. It was this that gave the performances their unique life and energy, for despite initial impressions that the performance was a series of random actions and responses, operating on each occasion on an improvisational level, the score for each actor and each movement was in fact a rigidly constructed framework into which renewed life was to be breathed. How did this operate? It was a spiritual process. Grotowski states: 'the tropistic* tension between the inner process and the form strengthens both. The form is like a baited trap, to which the spiritual process responds spontaneously and against which it struggles.'¹⁵ It was the discipline of a commitment to the validity of each action – a demanding process. A hand nightly performed a single action. As an actor, kneeling, sang an ancient Polish hymn, his hand caressed his own naked chest. As an action it was rigidly orchestrated, but if it were to have been performed without the discipline of response demanded by Grotowski, and achieved through laboured training, it would have lost the density of its own possibilities, and disappeared into a two-dimensional tableau.

In contrast to the richness of action and possible interpretation, there was one particular aspect in which Grotowski had pushed his theory of a 'poor theatre' to the extreme. In *Apocalypsis*, the scenic space was created entirely by the actions of the actors and the constantly shifting relative positions of actor/actor/spectator. When at one point the persecuted Simpleton encircled the tight-knit group of the other actors, who were placed in the centre of the room in a mobile tableau of invitation, rejection, provocation, he fluttered anxiously around them, softly whistling. But he was not only excluded from their group consciousness – he was also trapped between their active rejection and the passive refusal of the surrounding witnesses to intervene. By their own awareness of the roles they had accepted for the duration of an hour, and their inability to cast off these roles, all present forced the cycle of events nightly to its pre-ordained conclusions. Just as there was no previously constructed scenic arrangement, so it would seem that for this production there was no specified policy regarding the role of the spectators. They were witnesses, yes, but it was not possible to seek security in that fact. To maintain that position, unassailed, throughout *Apocalypsis Cum Figuris* was to maintain that position in regard to life. As the Simpleton, nearing the end of the torment, raised himself slowly to his knees from where he had been slumped on the ground in exhaustion, and turned in bewilderment to search with blind, unseeing, all-knowing gaze the minds and faces of those spectators sitting only inches from him, it was they who chose their position and response, as did the other spectators all around the room who witnessed this silent conversation.

But doubtless they would say that the choice was unfairly balanced, since the weight of convention is on the side of the *status quo*. Were they doomed to sit as silent witnesses? One obvious answer was to lift the weight of convention – in this case theatrical convention. And that is what

---

* I understand this word in terms of Grotowski's Taoistic acceptance of the essential polarity of inner process and form. Being polar opposites there exists a dynamic link between the two, and in their interplay is found the constant striving for both unity and supremacy that gives life. [J. K.]

Grotowski finally chose to do: 'We noted that when we eliminate certain blocks and obstacles what remains is what is most elementary and most simple – what exists between human beings when they have a certain confidence between each other, and when they look for an understanding that goes beyond the understanding of words ... Precisely at that point one does not perform any more ... One day we found it necessary to eliminate the notion of theatre (an actor in front of a spectator) and what remained was a notion of meeting – not a daily meeting and not a meeting that took place by chance ...'[16]

In place of theatrical activity, the energies of the group were, during the 1970's, directed towards the exploration of a form of collective activity which has been termed both 'paratheatre' and 'active culture'. Formally, these terms relate to an activity that has its roots in drama, but specifically does not result in a theatrical presentation before an audience. The terms 'spectators' and 'actors' lose their divisive significance, and both the action and the creation become the collective responsibility. It may be said that, in the many years of their exploration, the members of the Laboratory Theatre exhausted for themselves the possibilities of conventional theatrical form. They finally decided to abandon the framework in an attempt to explore more fully the furthest implications of what they had been moving towards in theatre. The search remains the same – the terrain is unfamiliar.

Afterword

Most of the directors discussed in this book are acknowledged today as major forces in the development of the modern theatre and are identified with the various 'traditions' that they inaugurated. Such is the fate of all artists: to be classified by posterity into schools, movements and influences. Thus their significance is validated in retrospect, and such events as the undoubted shambles of *Ubu the King*'s first night or Meyerhold's improbable interpretation of *Hedda Gabler* emerge as crucial turning-points in the history of the theatre. It is perhaps inevitable that a book such as this will reinforce this view, but it should not be allowed to obscure the fact that in their day these events were regarded as only marginally interesting by the theatrical establishment. The classic case is Stanislavsky. Looking at the two imposing buildings occupied by the Art Theatre in Moscow today and considering the importance of Stanislavsky's System in actor training throughout the Western world, it is hard to imagine that for years he suffered virtual isolation within his own company for the sake of the principles he felt driven to pursue. Similarly, with the Berliner Ensemble housed today in the Theater am Schiffbauerdamm on the renamed Bertolt-Brecht Platz, one needs to remind oneself that in 1930 *The Measures Taken* was dismembered by Party critics and two months later Brecht's 'crucial' production of *Man equals Man* folded after six performances.

Who was 'right' and who was 'wrong' is not the point at issue – and in any case it would be impossible to adjudicate, given the fragmentary nature of the surviving evidence. What *is* important is that not only with Stanislavsky in 1910 and Brecht in 1930, but in numerous other instances described in these pages, there was a significant distance between what the performance presented and what the audience anticipated. There are the obvious cases of this: Jarry's calculated violation of the laws of representation, Brecht's disrupting of the action with songs, Piscator's juxtaposition of the medieval and the modern. But equally, the creation of illusion by the Meininger, Antoine, and the Moscow Art Theatre was no less challenging to an audience inured to artificial convention. It is a fallacy automatically to equate naturalistic illusion with the passive acceptance of life 'as it is', and to regard Epic theatre as the sure means of activating the spectator's political responses. There is a world of difference between a projected slogan in a workers' hall in Berlin in 1932 and in the Olivier Theatre in 1981, and between *The Cherry Orchard* as a disturbing vision of a collapsing society in 1904 and as a nostalgic genre picture fifty years later. For successful innovation inevitably becomes convention. Any play-text, any method of staging, is significant insofar as it is conceived in response to, or in the face of, its audience's preconceptions; it is as possible to make *Troilus and Cressida*, *Spring Awakening* or *The Mother* familiar and reassuring as it is to make *The Government Inspector*, *A Midsummer Night's Dream*, or *Uncle Vanya* strange and disturbing.

Jean Mounet-Sully once said, 'Chaque texte n'est qu'un prétexte'. And Meyerhold claimed, 'the art of the director is the art not of an executant, but of an author –so long as you have earned the right'. He might have added that it is a right that must be earned afresh every time; for reputation alone does not confer it, only the constant striving to present the audience with a view of life relevant to their time and place. That is what in their various ways the directors in this book achieved, and it is the single lesson they can offer those who come after them.

Notes

One. The Meiningen Theatre

1. The principal source of information on the Meiningen Theatre is Max Grube, *The Story of the Meininger* (trans. A. M. Koller, University of Miami, 1963). Referred to below as 'Grube'.
2. See Muriel St. Clair Byrne, 'Charles Kean and the Meininger Myth', *Theatre Research*, Vol. VI, No. 3; 'What We Said about the Meiningers in 1881', *Essays and Studies*, XVIII (1965).
3. See *Essays and Studies*, XVIII, pp. 62 ff.
4. André Antoine, *Memories of the Théâtre Libre* (trans. M. Carlson, University of Miami, 1964), pp. 84–85.
5. Constantin Stanislavski, *My Life in Art* (trans. J. J. Robins, London, 1924 and 1980), pp. 197–201.
6. Grube, pp. 33–34.
7. Quoted in Marvin Carlson, *The German Stage in the Nineteenth Century* (Metuchen, N. J., 1972), pp. 172–173.
8. See Grube, p. 54.
9. Quoted in Marvin Carlson, 'Meininger Crowd Scenes and the Théâtre Libre', *Educational Theatre Journal*, Vol. 13, p. 246.
10. *Essays and Studies*, cit., p. 51.
11. Antoine, op. cit., pp. 81–82.
12. *Theatre Research*, cit., pp. 141 ff.
13. See J. C. Trewin, *Benson and the Bensonians* (London, 1960), p. 30.
14. See John Osborne, *The Naturalist Drama in Germany* (Manchester University Press, 1971), Chapter 2.
15. Lee Simonson, *The Stage is Set* (New York, 1932). pp. 272–273.
16. Grube, p. 41.
17. John Osborne, 'From Political to Cultural Despotism: the Nature of the Saxe-Meiningen Aesthetic', *Theatre Quarterly*, Vol. 5, No. 17, p. 46.
18. Ibid., p. 48.
19. *Educational Theatre Journal*, Vol. 13, p. 246.
20. Grube, p. 107.
21. Osborne, op. cit., p. 50.
22. See Ann Marie Koller, 'Ibsen and the Meininger', *Educational Theatre Journal*, Vol. 17, pp. 101–102.
23. See Michael Meyer, *Henrik Ibsen: Volume 2* (London, 1971), p. 220.
24. See Muriel St. Clair Byrne, op. cit.
25. Quoted in Marvin Carlson, *The German Stage in the Nineteenth Century*, cit., p. 179.

Two. Antoine and the Théâtre Libre

1. *Oeuvres complètes de Eugène Scribe* (Paris, 1874), Vol. I, p. xxiv.
2. John A. Henderson, *The First Avant-Garde (1887–1894)* (London, 1971), p. 19.
3. Quoted in Cole, T. & Chinoy, H. K. (eds.), *Actors on Acting* (New York, 1949), p. 207.
4. I am quoting here and elsewhere in this chapter from *Le Naturalisme au théâtre* (Paris, 1881), a collection of critical articles written by Zola over the previous five years. For extracts in English translation see Eric Bentley (ed.), *The Theory of the Modern Stage* (London, 1968), and Cole, T. & Chinoy, H. K. (eds.), *Playwrights on Playwriting* (London, 1960).
5. See Lawson Carter, *Zola and the Theatre* (Yale University Press, 1963).
6. Ibid., pp. 98–99.
7. Quoted in André Antoine, *Memories of the Théâtre Libre*, cit., p. 47 (referred to below as '*Memories*').
8. *Memories*, p. 10.
9. For a detailed account of Antoine's career up to 1890 see Francis Pruner, *Les Luttes d'Antoine – Au Théâtre Libre*, Tome I (Paris, 1964).
10. Samuel Waxman, *Antoine and the Théâtre Libre* (Harvard University Press, 1926), p. 82.
11. *Memories*, p. 64.
12. Pruner, op. cit., p. 161.
13. *Memories*, p. 73.
14. *Memories*, p. 84.
15. Quoted in John Stokes, *Resistible Theatres* (London, 1972), p. 122.
16. See Pruner, op. cit., pp. 270–271.
17. Stokes, op. cit., p. 122.
18. Ibid., p. 120.
19. See *Memories*, p. 103.
20. See Pruner, op. cit., pp. 311 ff.
21. *Memories*, p. 138.
22. George Moore, *Impressions and Opinions* (London, 1891), pp. 220–221.
23. '*Die Gespenster* in Paris' in *Freie Bühne*, 1890, No. 18, pp. 499–501.
24. *Memories*, p. 216.
25. Quoted in Stokes, op. cit., p. 121.

Three. The Symbolist Theatre

1. *Memories*, p. 171.
2. *The Heritage of Symbolism* (London, 1943), p. 2.
3. Quoted in Jacques Robichez, *Le Symbolisme au théâtre: Lugné-Poe et les débuts de l'Œuvre* (Paris, 1957), p. 15 (referred to below as 'Robichez').
4. Robichez, p. 21.
5. Marcel Raymond, *From Baudelaire to Surrealism* (London, 1970), p. 12.
6. For a brief introduction to Baudelaire and Symbolism see Charles Chadwick, *Symbolism* (London, 1971).
7. For a translation of this essay see Roland N. Stromberg (ed.), *Realism, Naturalism, and Symbolism – Modes of Thought and Expression in Europe, 1848–1914* (London and Melbourne, 1968).
8. For accounts of Appia see Walther R. Volbach, *Adolphe Appia: Prophet of the Modern Theatre* (Wesleyan University Press, 1968); Lee Simonson, *The Stage is Set*, cit., pp. 351–377.
9. Quoted in Robichez, p. 83.
10. Quoted in John Henderson, op. cit., p. 134.
11. See Henderson, op cit., Chapter VIII.

12. For a discussion of *The Cenci* see Chapter Twelve.
13. See František Deák, 'Symbolist Staging at the Théâtre d'Art', *The Drama Review*, Vol. 20, No. 3 (T71), pp. 117-135 (includes the scripts of *The Girl with Severed Hands* and *Song of Songs*).
14. See Denis Bablet, *Esthétique Générale du Décor de Théâtre de 1870 à 1914* (Paris, 1965), p. 148.
15. For an account of the relationship between symbolist painters and the theatre see Robert Goldwater, *Symbolism* (London, 1979).
16. See F. Deák, op. cit.
17. See Robichez, pp. 254-255.
18. Ibid, p. 157.
19. Ibid, p. 156.
20. Ibid, p. 169.
21. For an account of the Théâtre de l'Œuvre's London season, see John Stokes, op. cit., pp. 168-172.
22. Robichez, p. 193.
23. Some are reproduced in A. Lugné-Poe, *Ibsen* (Paris, 1936).
24. Robichez, pp. 247-248.
25. Translation from Maurice Valency, *The Flower and the Castle* (New York, 1963), p. 380.
26. Robichez, p. 251.
27. Ibid., pp. 246-247.
28. See Lugné-Poe, op. cit., p. 80; Michael Meyer, *Henrik Ibsen: Volume 3* (London, 1971), pp. 239-240.
29. Meyer, op. cit., p. 236.
30. Stokes, op. cit., p. 168.

Four. Alfred Jarry

1. For a vivid account of Jarry's life and work see Roger Shattuck, *The Banquet Years* (London, 1955).
2. Maurice Nadeau, *The History of Surrealism* (trans. R. Howard, London, 1968), p. 73.
3. Roger Shattuck & Simon Watson Taylor, *Selected Works of Alfred Jarry* (London, 1965), p. 83.
4. Ibid., pp. 67-68.
5. See A. Lugné-Poe, *Acrobaties* (Paris, 1931), p. 175.
6. The fullest account of the first performance of *Ubu Roi* is in Noel Arnaud, *Alfred Jarry d'Ubu roi au Docteur Faustroll* (Paris, 1974).
7. For the full text of Jarry's address see *Selected Works of Alfred Jarry*, cit., pp. 76-78.
8. Quoted in Roger Shattuck, *The Banquet Years*, cit., p. 161.
9. See Noel Arnaud, op. cit., pp. 312 ff.
10. Quoted in R. Shattuck, op. cit., p. 163.
11. See p. 53 above.
12. Included in *Selected Works of Alfred Jarry*, cit.
13. *Acrobaties*, cit., p. 183.
14. For accounts of the grotesque see Wolfgang Kayser, *The Grotesque in Art and Literature* (New York, 1966); Philip Thomson, *The Grotesque* (London, 1972).

Five. Stanislavsky and Chekhov

1. For a detailed account of this meeting see Constantin Stanislavski, *My Life in Art* (London, 1948 and 1980), pp. 294-299.
2. Stanislavsky, K. S., *Sobranie sochinenii* (Moscow, 1954-1961), Vol. V, pp. 174-175.

3. See Ronald Hingley, *A New Life of Chekhov* (Oxford University Press, 1976), pp. 220 ff.
4. Maurice Valency, *The Breaking String* (Oxford University Press, 1966), p. 169.
5. Letter to Suvorin, 4 May 1889.
6. Published as S. D. Balukhaty, ed. (trans. D. Magarshack), *The Seagull Produced by Stanislavsky* (London, 1952).
7. See E. Braun (ed.), *Meyerhold on Theatre* (London, 1969), p. 30.
8. Ibid., p. 26.
9. Letter dated 9 May 1899.
10. Letter dated 23 October 1899.
11. Quoted in A. P. Chekhov, *Polnoe sobranie sochinenii i pisem* (Moscow, 1978), pp. 396-397.
12. Letter dated 30 September 1899.
13. Quoted in *Sobrannye sochineniya v 12 tomakh*, Vol. 9 (Moscow, 1956), pp. 487-488.
14. Letters quoted in Valency, op. cit., p. 208; R. Hingley, op. cit., p. 272.
15. Quoted in D. Magarshack, *Stanislavsky - A Life* (London, 1950), p. 221.
16. Quoted in M. N. Stroeva, 'The Three Sisters in the Production of the Moscow Art Theatre' in R. L. Jackson (ed.), *Chekhov - A Collection of Critical Essays* (Englewood Cliffs, N.J., 1967), p. 123.
17. Ibid., p. 130.
18. Ibid., p. 127.
19. Ibid., p. 129.
20. Quoted in M. N. Pozharskaya, *Russkoe teatralno-dekoratsionnoe iskusstvo ...* (Moscow, 1970), p. 124.
21. Letter dated 24 September 1901.
22. See R. Hingley (ed. and trans.), *The Oxford Chekhov*, Vol. 3 (Oxford University Press, 1964), pp. 325-329.
23. Quoted in M. N. Stroeva, *Rezhisserskie iskaniya Stanislavskogo 1898-1917* (Moscow, 1973), p. 126.
24. Letter dated 19 November 1903 in C. Stanislavski (ed. and trans. E. R. Hapgood), *Stanislavski's Legacy*, New York, 1958, London, 1981, pp. 125-126.
25. Loc. cit.
26. *My Life in Art*, cit., p. 420.
27. Quoted in M. N. Stroeva, op. cit., p. 121.
28. See *My Life in Art*, cit., Chapter XLVIII.

Six. Edward Gordon Craig

1. See Hugh Hunt, Kenneth Richards, John Russell Taylor, *The Revels History of Drama in English, Vol. VII - 1880 to the Present Day* (London, 1978).
2. An account of Godwin's career is contained in J. Stokes, *Resistible Theatres*, cit.
3. See Edward Craig, *Gordon Craig: The Story of his Life* (London, 1968), p. 57 (cited below as 'Edward Craig').
4. Ibid., p. 115.
5. Quoted in Denis Bablet, *The Theatre of Edward Gordon Craig* (London, 1966 and 1981), pp. 39-40 (cited below as 'Bablet').
6. Edward Craig, pp. 117-118.
7. See Edward Craig, 'Gordon Craig and Hubert von Herkomer' in *Theatre Research-Recherches Théâtrales*, Vol. X, No. 1 (1969), pp. 7-16. For an account of Herkomer's work see J. Stokes, op. cit., 71-110.
8. Quoted in Bablet, p. 43.
9. Ibid., p. 45.
10. Ibid., p. 174.

11. Edward Craig, p. 136.
12. Arthur Symons, 'A New Art of the Stage', reprinted in Eric Bentley (ed.), *The Theory of the Modern Stage* (London, 1968), p. 139.
13. Edward Gordon Craig, *Index to the Story of My Days* (London, 1957; Cambridge, 1981), p. 235.
14. Bablet, p. 49.
15. A. Symons, op. cit., p. 140.
16. Edward Craig, p. 152.
17. Edith Craig was later to become an important director in her own right. For an account of her career see Julie Holledge, *Innocent Flowers* (London, 1981).
18. Quoted in Michael Meyer, *Henrik Ibsen – The Making of a Dramatist 1828-1864* (London, 1967), p. 170.
19. Edward Craig, p. 172.
20. Ibid., p. 173.
21. E. G. Craig, *On the Art of the Theatre* (London, 1911 and 1962), p. 138 (*The Art of the Theatre* was reprinted in this later work).
22. Quoted from Craig's complete programme note in Bablet, pp. 87-88.
23. Isadora Duncan, *My Life* (London, 1928 and 1968), p. 219.
24. Except where indicated, the account here is based on the authoritative documentation of the production by Laurence Senellick in *Theatre Quarterly*, Vol. VI, No. 22 (Summer, 1976), pp. 56-122 (cited below as 'Senellick').
25. Quoted by Senellick, p. 62.
26. Laurence Senellick explores this conception in detail in 'Moscow and Monodrama', *Theatre Research International*, Vol. VI, No. 2, pp. 109-124.
27. Senellick, p. 74.
28. Ibid., p. 87.
29. Edward Craig, p. 261.
30. For an account of Craig's Screens see Bablet, Chapter VII.
31. Senellick, pp. 108, 116.
32. Edward Craig, p. 271.
33. C. Stanislavski, *My Life in Art*, cit., p. 524.
34. Senellick, p. 105.
35. Reprinted in *On the Art of the Theatre*, cit.
36. See J. Olf, 'The Man/Marionette Debate in Modern Theatre', *Educational Theatre Journal*, Vol. XXVI, No. 4, pp. 488-494.

Seven. Max Reinhardt in Germany and Austria

1. Gottfried Reinhardt, *The Genius: A Memoir of Max Reinhardt* (New York, 1979), p. 132 (referred to below as '*The Genius*').
2. Russian sources state that *Enemies* was given its world premiere at 'Reinhardt's theatre' on 16 February 1907, but no German work on Reinhardt mentions this.
3. Quoted in M. Esslin, 'Max Reinhardt – High Priest of Theatricality', *The Drama Review*, Vol. 21, No. 2 (T74), p. 9, reprinted in M. Esslin, *Mediations* (London, 1981).
4. Loc. cit.
5. Ibid., p. 7.
6. Quoted in G. E. Wellwarth and A. G. Brooks (ed.), *Max Reinhardt 1873-1973 (A Centennial Festschrift)* (New York, 1973), p. 1.
7. W. R. Fuerst and S. J. Hume, *Twentieth-Century Stage Decoration* (New York, 1929 and 1967), Vol. I, pp. 16-17.
8. Quoted in *The Genius*, p. 354.
9. See S. Jacobsohn, *Max Reinhardt* (Berlin, 1910), pp. 46-51, 93-97.

10. Ibid., pp. 29–30.
11. F. E. Washburn-Freund in O. M. Sayler (ed.), *Max Reinhardt and his Theatre* (New York, 1924), pp. 52–53.
12. See Elisabeth Bond, Introduction to Frank Wedekind, *Spring Awakening*, trans. Edward Bond (London, 1980).
13. Ibid., p. xx.
14. H. Fetting (ed.) *Max Reinhardt-Schriften* (Berlin, 1974), pp. 92, 394.
15. Quoted in M. Esslin, op. cit., pp. 9–10.
16. *The Genius*, pp. 363–364.
17. Esslin, op. cit., p. 20.
18. Quoted in Felix Felton, 'Max Reinhardt in England' in *Theatre Research – Recherches Théâtrales*, Vol. V, No. 3, 1963, p. 139.
19. See especially *The Genius*, pp. 38–42, 341–343, and Oliver Sayler, op. cit., pp. 249–322 (for Reinhardt's production book).
20. Quoted in John Willett, *The New Sobriety: Art and Politics in the Weimar Period 1917–1933* (London, 1978), p. 57.
21. For a detailed account of the Grosses Schauspielhaus see W. Volbach, 'Memoirs of Max Reinhardt's Theatres 1920–1922' in *Theatre Survey*, Vol. XIII, No. 1a, Fall 1972.
22. *The Genius*, p. 347.
23. Quoted in H. Braulich, *Max Reinhardt – Theater zwischen Traum und Wirklichkeit* (Berlin, 1969), p. 173.
24. M. Esslin, op. cit., p. 14.
25. Ibid., p. 20.
26. H. Fetting, op. cit., p. 228.

Eight. Meyerhold: The First Five Years

1. For an account of Russian Symbolism see James West, *Russian Symbolism* (London, 1970).
2. Edward Braun (ed. and trans.), *Meyerhold on Theatre* (London, 1969), p. 43 (referred to below as 'Meyerhold').
3. Ibid., p. 44.
4. Ibid., p. 54.
5. Loc. cit.
6. Ibid., p. 56.
7. Konstantin L. Rudnitsky, *Rezhisser Meierkhold* (Moscow, 1969), p. 62 (referred to below as 'Rudnitsky').
8. *My Life in Art*, cit., p. 437 (the translation here is from the original Russian).
9. *Die Schaubühne der Zukunft* (Berlin, undated but published 1904–1905).
10. All quotations of Fuchs are taken from *Die Schaubühne der Zukunft*.
11. For further details of Kawakami's European tours see Leonard C. Pronko, *Theater East and West* (University of California Press, 1967), pp. 120–123.
12. For an account of the Munich Künstlertheater see W. R. Fuerst and S. J. Hume, *Twentieth-Century Stage Decoration*, cit., Vol. I, pp. 45–48.
13. V. E. Meierkhold, *Statyi, pisma, rechi, besedy* (Moscow, 1969), Vol. I, p. 244 (referred to below as '*Statyi*').
14. Meyerhold, p. 68.
15. Aleksandr P. Matskin, *Portrety i nablyudenia* (Moscow, 1973), p. 201.
16. *Statyi I*, p. 245.
17. Yevgeny Znosko-Borovsky, *Russky teatr nachala XX veka* (Prague, 1925), pp. 281–282.
18. *Zolotoe runo*, Moscow, 1907, No. 7–9, p. 150.

19. The following contain translations of *Balaganchik*: Sir Cecil Kisch, *Alexander Blok: Prophet of Revolution* (London, 1960); F. D. Reeve, *An Anthology of Russian Plays*, Vol. II (New York, 1963).
20. M. A. Valentei and others (ed.), *Vstrechi s Meierkholdom* (Moscow, 1967), p. 41 (referred to below as '*Vstrechi*').
21. *Teatre i muzyka*, Moscow, 1923, No. 1-2, pp. 427-428.
22. Letter to Alexander Gippius, 20 January 1907.
23. *The Banquet Years*, cit., p. 30.
24. Meyerhold, pp. 137-139.
25. A. Matskin, op. cit. 209.
26. For an account of Meyerhold's production of *Tristan and Isolde* see Edward Braun, *The Theatre of Meyerhold* (London, 1979), pp. 91-99.
27. See Meyerhold, pp. 23-64.
28. Jay Leyda, *Kino* (London, 1960), p. 82.
29. Quoted in Nikolai D. Volkov, *Meierkhold* (Moscow-Leningrad, 1929), Vol. I, pp. 345-346.

Nine. Meyerhold. Theatre as Propaganda
1. Rudnitsky, p. 203.
2. For an account of the 1918 production of *Mystery-Bouffe* see *The Theatre of Meyerhold*, pp. 148-152.
3. Meyerhold, p. 173.
4. See František Deák, 'Russian Mass Spectacles', *The Drama Review*, Vol. 19, No. 2 (T-66), pp. 7-22.
5. Meyerhold, p. 170.
6. *Pravda*, Moscow, 10 November 1920, p. 2.
7. For further accounts of Meyerhold's system of Biomechanics see *The Theatre of Meyerhold*, pp. 163-168; Mel Gordon, 'Meyerhold's Biomechanics', *The Drama Review*, Vol. 18, No. 3 (T-63), pp. 73-88.
8. *Teatr*, Moscow, 24 October 1913, p. 6.
9. These productions are discussed in detail in *The Theatre of Meyerhold*, pp. 169-179; Alma H. Law, '*Le Cocu Magnifique* de Crommelynck', *Les Voies de la Création Théâtrale*, No. 7, pp. 13-43; Nick Worrall, 'Meyerhold and Eisenstein' (on *Tarelkin's Death*) in David Bradby, Louis James and Bernard Sharratt (eds.), *Performance and politics in popular drama* (Cambridge, 1980), pp. 173-187; Nick Worrall, 'Meyerhold's *The Magnificent Cuckold*', *The Drama Review*, Vol. 17, No. 1 (T-57), pp. 14-34.
10. See *The Theatre of Meyerhold*, pp. 193-201.
11. *Novy zritel*, Moscow, 1924, No. 18, pp. 16-17.
12. See also Llewellyn H. Hedgbeth, 'Meyerhold's *D. E.*', *The Drama Review*, Vol. 19, No. 2 (T-66), pp. 23-36.
13. Meyerhold, p. 206.
14. For a translation see Nikolai Erdman, *The Warrant* (Ann Arbor, Mich., 1975).
15. Rudnitsky, p. 340.
16. Boris Alpers, *Teatr sotsialnoy maski* (Moscow-Leningrad, 1931), p. 48.
17. For detailed accounts of *The Government Inspector* see *The Theatre of Meyerhold*, pp. 207-223; Nick Worrall, 'Meyerhold Directs Gogol's *Government Inspector*', *Theatre Quarterly*, Vol. II, No. 7, pp. 75-95.
18. For a description of this project see 'A Theater for Meyerhold', *Theatre Quarterly*, Vol. II, No. 7, pp. 69-73.

Ten. Piscator in Berlin

1. Erwin Piscator, *The Political Theatre* (ed. and trans. Hugh Rorrison, London, 1980), p. 44. Referred to below as 'Piscator'.
2. Piscator, p. 45.
3. Ibid., p. 48.
4. Ibid., pp. 81-82.
5. For an account of workers' theatre in Germany see Cecil W. Davies, 'Working Class Theatre in the Weimar Republic 1919-33', *Theatre Quarterly*, Vol. X, No. 38, pp. 68-96, No. 39, pp. 81-96.
6. For the scenario of *Trotz Alledem!* see Piscator, pp. 86-89.
7. Ibid., p. 97.
8. See review reprinted in Günther Rühle (ed.), *Theater für die Republik* (Frankfurt am Main, 1967), pp. 646-649.
9. For an account of the Volksbühne see Cecil W. Davies, *Theatre for the People: The story of the Volksbühne* (Manchester, 1977).
10. Piscator, p. 75.
11. Ibid., p. 74.
12. Ibid., p. 107.
13. Quoted by Piscator, loc. cit.
14. G. Rühle, op. cit., p. 693.
15. Quoted in John Willett, *The Theatre of Erwin Piscator* (London, 1978), p. 60. Referred to below as 'Willett'.
16. Piscator, p. 152.
17. For further details of this project see Willett, pp. 116-118; Piscator, pp. 180-183.
18. See Willett, pp. 67-71.
19. Piscator, p. 173.
20. Ibid., p. 208.
21. Ibid., p. 214.
22. Ibid., pp. 121-122.
23. Bertolt Brecht, *The Messingkauf Dialogues* (trans. John Willett, London, 1965), p. 67. Brecht's view is contested by Piscator's last stage designer, Hans Ulrich Schmückle (see *Erwin Piscator - Political Theatre 1920-1966*, Arts Council exhibition catalogue compiled by Ludwig Hoffmann, London, 1971, pp. 38-40).
24. Piscator, p. 210. For a detailed account by Hugh Rorrison of Piscator's production of *Hoppla* see *Theatre Quarterly*, Vol. X, No. 37, pp. 30-41.
25. Piscator, p. 202.
26. G. Rühle, op. cit., p. 794.
27. Piscator, p. 219.
28. Ibid., p. 230.
29. Ibid., p. 239.
30. Quoted in Maria Ley-Piscator, *The Piscator Experiment* (New York, 1967), p. 85.
31. Piscator, p. 227.
32. Ibid., p. 264.
33. See John Willett, *The New Sobriety: Art and Politics in the Weimar Period 1917-1933* (London, 1978), p. 189.
34. Quoted in *Erwin Piscator - Political Theatre 1920-1966* (catalogue), cit., p. 67.

Eleven. Brecht's Formative Years

1. For an account of the incident by Arnolt Bronnen see Hubert Witt (ed.). *Brecht As They Knew Him* (London, 1975), pp. 32-34.
2. Reprinted in Monika Wyss (ed.), *Brecht in der Kritik* (Munich, 1977), pp. 5-6.

3. Quoted in Klaus Völker, *Brecht Chronicle* (New York, 1975), p. 35.
4. 'On looking through my first plays (iv)' in *Bertolt Brecht Collected Plays*, Vol. I, ed. J. Willett and R. Manheim (London, 1970), p. 454.
5. Brecht and Feuchtwanger also made fundamental changes in the action and characterisation. For a discussion by Eric Bentley of their version see Bertolt Brecht, *Edward II - A Chronicle Play* (trans. Eric Bentley, New York, 1966), pp. vii-xxviii.
6. *Brecht As They Knew Him*, p. 40.
7. W. Stuart McDowell, 'Actors on Brecht: The Munich Years' in *The Drama Review*, Vol. 20, No. 3 (T 71), p. 113.
8. Bernhard Reich, quoted in Klaus Völker, *Brecht: A Biography* (London, 1979), p. 72.
9. 'Conversations with Brecht' in Walter Benjamin, *Understanding Brecht* (London, 1973), p. 115. The incident is also mentioned by Brecht in *The Messingkauf Dialogues* (London, 1965), pp. 69-70.
10. *Brecht As They Knew Him*, pp. 41-42.
11. John Willett (ed. & trans.), *Brecht on Theatre* (London, 1964), pp. 231-232.
12. Reprinted in Günther Rühle (ed.), *Theater für die Republik* cit., pp. 509-10.
13. Quoted in Frederic Ewen, *Bertolt Brecht* (London, 1970), p. 130.
14. Diary entry for 10 February 1922 in *Bertolt Brecht Diaries 1920-1922* (trans. John Willett, London, 1979), p. 159.
15. G. Rühle, op. cit., pp. 689-90.
16. *Brecht on Theatre*, pp. 7-8.
17. Quoted in K. Völker, *Brecht: A Biography*, cit., p. 126.
18. See Elisabeth Hauptmann, 'Notes on Brecht's Work' in *Brecht As They Knew Him*, pp. 52-53. For a discussion of Brecht's conception of Epic Theatre see John Willett, *The Theatre of Bertolt Brecht* (London 1959), 167ff.
19. Among others see F. Ewen, op cit., pp. 148 ff; Christopher Innes, *Erwin Piscator's Political Theatre* (Cambridge, 1972), pp. 189-200; John Willett, *The Theatre of Erwin Piscator*, cit. (numerous references: see Index). For Brecht's comments on Piscator see *Brecht on Theatre*, in particular, pp. 77 ff, 130 ff.
20. Except *Mother Courage*, staged in Kassel in 1960, after Brecht's death.
21. Quoted in John Willett, *The Theatre of Erwin Piscator*, cit., p. 187.
22. Quoted in C. Innes, op. cit., p. 200.
23. Quoted in *The Theatre of Erwin Piscator*, cit., p. 188.
24. See K. Völker, *Brecht: A Biography*, cit., pp. 115-116.
25. *The Messingkauf Dialogues*, cit., p. 69.
26. See *Brecht As They Knew Him*, pp. 54-62.
27. Quoted in *Brecht: A Biography*, cit., p. 131 and M. Wyss, op. cit., p. 83.
28. *Brecht on Theatre*, p. 44-45.
29. Ibid., p. 85.
30. 'Neher and Brecht' in *The Drama Review*, Vol. 12, No. 2 (T-38), p. 140.
31. Lecture delivered by Brecht in 1939, *Brecht on Theatre*, p. 132.
32. Ibid., p. 80.
33. John Willett, *The Theatre of Bertolt Brecht* (London, 1959), p. 138.
34. Quoted in Martin Esslin, *Brecht: A Choice of Evils* (London, 1959; 3rd edition, 1981), p. 139.
35. *Brecht on Theatre*, p. 39.
36. Quoted in Martin Esslin, op. cit., p. 45.
37. Quoted in *Brecht As They Knew Him*, p. 72.
38. See *Brecht on Theatre*, pp. 53-56.
39. *The Theatre of Bertolt Brecht*, cit., p. 175.
40. On the origins of the term '*Verfremdung*' see *Brecht on Theatre*, pp. 91-99; Katherine

Eaton, '*Brecht's Contacts With the Theatre of Meyerhold*', *Comparative Drama*, Vol. 11, No. 1 (Spring, 1977), pp. 12–13.

41. The production is fully documented in Werner Hecht (ed.), *Materialen zu Bertolt Brechts 'Die Mutter'* (Frankfurt am Main, 1973) and Friedrich W. Knellessen, *Agitation auf der Bühne* (Emsdetten, 1970), pp. 192–201.
42. Brecht, 'Notes to *Die Mutter*', *Brecht on Theatre*, p. 58.
43. Ibid., pp. 61–62.
44. Ibid., p. 58.
45. Loc. cit.
46. Ibid., p. 59.
47. Ibid., p. 88.
48. See Herbert Ihering, *Von Reinhardt bis Brecht* (Hamburg, 1967), pp. 358–359.
49. *Brecht on Theatre*, p. 62.
50. *Die Rote Fahne*, 19 January 1932. Quoted in M. Esslin, op. cit., p. 142.
51. Admirably documented in James K. Lyon, *Bertolt Brecht in America* (Princeton, 1980).
52. See especially Carl Weber, 'Brecht as Director' in *The Drama Review*, Vol. 12, No. 1 (T-37), pp. 101–107.
53. See Michael Mellinger, 'Goodbye to East Berlin' in *Encore*, Vol. 7, No. 5 (September–October, 1960), pp. 11–18.
54. The notes to Brecht's *Collected Works*, edited by John Willett and Ralph Manheim contain extensive material relating to the work of the Berliner Ensemble. See also Part Four of Willett's *Brecht on Theatre*, and *Theaterarbeit* (ed. Brecht and others, Dresden, 1952), a large illustrated volume covering the Ensemble's work 1949–1951. Jan Needle and Peter Thomson's *Brecht* (Oxford, 1981) contains a chapter on Brecht's 1949 production of *Mother Courage*.
55. *Brecht on Theatre*, p. 216.

Twelve. Artaud's Theatre of Cruelty

1. Antonin Artaud, *Collected Works* (trans. Victor Corti, London, 1968–1974), Vol. 3, p. 102. Referred to below as '*Artaud 1–4*'.
2. For accounts of these productions see A. H. Melzer, 'The Premiere of Apollinaire's *The Breasts of Tiresias* in Paris', *Theatre Quarterly*, Vol. VII, No. 27, pp. 3–13; Francis Steegmuller, *Cocteau: A Biography* (London, 1970), pp. 160–197 (on *Parade*).
3. *Artaud 2*, pp. 18–19.
4. The details of this opening programme are taken from Artaud 2. For a translation of *The Secrets of Love* see M. Benedikt and G. E. Wellwarth, *Modern French Plays* (London, 1965).
5. *Artaud 2*, p. 23.
6. For the complete production plan see *Artaud 2*, pp. 97–105.
7. *Artaud 4*, p. 70.
8. Ibid., p. 60
9. Ibid., p. 20.
10. Ibid., p. 46.
11. Jerzy Grotowski, *Towards a Poor Theatre* (London, 1969), p. 121.
12. *Artaud 4*, p. 85.
13. Quoted in Ronald Hayman, *Artaud and After* (Oxford, 1977), p. 83.
14. *Artaud 4*, p. 97. For the complete published text of Artaud's scenario see Mary Caroline Richards (trans.), *The Theatre and its Double* (New York, 1958), pp. 126–132.
15. *The Drama Review*, Vol. 16, No. 2 (T-54), p. 91. This issue contains a comprehensive documentation of Artaud's production.

16. For a full account of this and subsquent performances see Stuart Curran, *Shelley's Cenci – Scorpions Ringed with Fire* (Princeton University Press, 1970).
17. Percy Bysshe Shelley, *The Cenci* (ed. Roland A. Duerkson, Indianapolis and New York, 1970), p. 7.
18. Loc. cit.
19. Antonin Artaud, *The Cenci* (London, 1969), Act III, Sc. 2.
20. *The Drama Review*, cit., p. 144.
21. *The Cenci*, cit., pp. 21–22.
22. Quoted in Alain Virmaux, *Antonin Artaud et le théâtre* (Paris, 1970), p. 308.
23. See *The Drama Review*, cit., pp. 127–141.
24. Martin Esslin, *Artaud* (London, 1976), p. 42.
25. *Artaud 4*, p. 97.

Thirteen. Grotowski's Laboratory Theatre
1. 'Conversations with Flaszen', *Educational Theatre Journal*, October, 1978, p. 304.
2. Jerzy Grotowski, *Towards a Poor Theatre* (London, 1969), p. 15. Referred to below as *'Poor Theatre'*.
3. *Towards a Poor Theatre* was published originally in Denmark in 1968.
4. *Poor Theatre*, p. 16.
5. Ibid., p. 17.
6. Joseph Needham, *Science and Civilization in China*, Vol. II, Cambridge, 1956, pp. 68–69.
7. J. Grotowski, 'External Order, Internal Intimacy', *The Drama Review*, Vol. 14, No. 1 (T-45), p. 174.
8. *Poor Theatre*, p. 17.
9. Ibid., p. 38.
10. Ibid., p. 47.
11. Ibid., p. 20.
12. Ibid., p. 25.
13. *Artaud 4*, p. 6.
14. 'Conversations with Flaszen', cit., p. 303.
15. *Poor Theatre*, p. 17.
16. Richard Mennen, 'Grotowski's Paratheatrical Projects', *The Drama Review*, Vol. 19, No. 4 (T-68).

Index

(Works are given under authors' names. Names are not indexed if mentioned only in passing.)